ROBERT IVERMEE

Hooghly

The Global History of a River

HURST & COMPANY, LONDON

First published in the United Kingdom in 2020 by
C. Hurst & Co. (Publishers) Ltd.,
41 Great Russell Street, London, WC1B 3PL
This paperback edition first published in 2024 by
C. Hurst & Co. (Publishers) Ltd.,
New Wing, Somerset House, Strand, London, WC2R 1LA
© Robert Ivermee, 2024
All rights reserved.
Printed in the United Kingdom

The right of Robert Ivermee to be identified as the author of
this publication is asserted by him in accordance with the
Copyright, Designs and Patents Act, 1988.

A Cataloguing-in-Publication data record for this book
is available from the British Library.

ISBN: 9781911723349

This book is printed using paper from registered sustainable
and managed sources.

www.hurstpublishers.com

CONTENTS

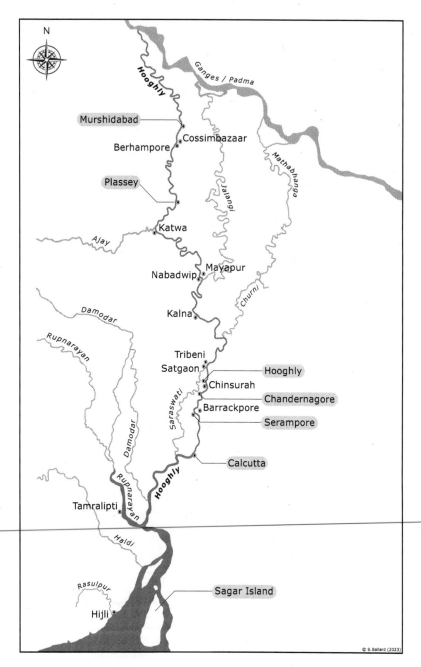

Map 1: The Hooghly and its key sites

Map 2: Bengal and neighbouring regions

ACKNOWLEDGEMENTS

The writing of this book, like most, has relied on the support and input of others. I would like to thank Michael Dwyer and his colleagues at Hurst for backing the project, the anonymous reviewers of the original manuscript for their efforts, and Rukun Advani at Permanent Black for his editing of the final draft. I am grateful to colleagues at SOAS University of London and the Institut Catholique de Paris for their interest and ideas, along with staff in the SOAS Library and the British Library for their help and guidance. Friends and family following the progress of the book have helped greatly. Above all, I would like to thank Jeanne, whose support is immeasurable and whose feedback on each chapter—not least in urging me to write more clearly and engagingly ('it's a bit dry, tell a story!')—has made this a better, more readable book.

INTRODUCTION

THE HOOGHLY IN GLOBAL HISTORY

The Hooghly River, a distributary of the Ganges, winds its way into the Bay of Bengal through the western deltaic flats of its parent stream. Today, it is unlikely to be considered one of the great rivers of the world: at about 500 kilometres, its length is modest; lacking natural depth, it has relied since the 1970s on waters dammed and distributed from the Ganges, like a middle-aged child dependent on the resources of an ageing mother.[1] There was a time, however, when the Hooghly was a waterway of truly global significance, attracting merchants, missionaries, statesmen, soldiers, labourers, and others from Asia, Europe, and elsewhere. As the principal artery between lower and upper Bengal, it facilitated travel and communication between the coast and locations inland. Its tributaries and distributaries afforded access to deltaic Bengal, the Gangetic plain, and the Mughal heartland of Hindustan, linking northern and eastern India with territories across the Indian Ocean and beyond.

This book shines a light on the remarkable period when the Hooghly was at the centre of global history. From the sixteenth century, successive external parties—among them Portuguese, Mughal, Dutch, British, French, and Danish—were drawn to the river. The Hooghly came to be integrated into networks of encounter and exchange spanning different cultures and regions and, at least until the turn of the twentieth century, was renowned not only in Bengal and India but across the world.

* * *

1

The Bengal delta, covering much of present-day Bangladesh and the Indian state of West Bengal, is the largest river delta in the world. Bordered by the Bay of Bengal to the south, and to the north by a series of hill ranges that separate it from the Himalayas, Assam, Burma, and the plains of upper India, the delta was formed over centuries by silt deposited in the sea by the Ganges, the Brahmaputra, and the Meghna—the rivers which determined its ancient sites of settlement and defined its cultural sub-regions.[2] Foremost among these was the basin shaped by the Hooghly on its descent through Bengal to the sea. For centuries, this was the main branch of the Ganges through which the larger stream entered the Bay of Bengal. From its source in the high Himalayas, the Ganges flowed in a broadly south-easterly direction across the Indian plains. After negotiating the hard rock of the Chota Nagpur Plateau, it descended onto the loose alluvial soil of Bengal and made a decisive turn southward towards the coast.

The Hooghly marks the start of deltaic Bengal. To the west, the lands immediately bordering the river in its lower reaches are low-lying and alluvial. Further west and north, the land rises and becomes hilly, with rocky hard clay ground, a milder climate, and fast-flowing rivers and streams creating conditions conducive to winter rice, sugarcane, tobacco, and potatoes. To the east is the delta, flat, swampy, and humid, its often-submerged soil used to produce spring rice and jute in the midst of jungle and mangrove swamps. On its descent, the Hooghly is reunited with the waters of the Jalangi and the Mathabhanga—lesser branches of the Ganges—and joined by the Damodar, the Rupnarayan, the Haldi, and the Rasulpur, all tributaries emerging from the Chota Nagpur Plateau to enter the river on its right. These contributions compensate for the Hooghly's loss of fresh water to the innumerable creeks and channels which branch off it into the Sunderbans, as well as its discharge of fresh water into the sea.

As the most fertile area of the ancient delta, the Hooghly basin was inhabited the earliest and became the most densely populated.[3] Archaeological evidence confirms that rice-cultivating communities were present more than 3000 years ago; by the eleventh century B.C. they were living in carefully ordered settlements and producing pottery. The earliest migrants into Bengal were probably Mongolian peoples from Burma and the Himalayas. In the fifth century B.C. they were joined by Indo-Aryans from the north and west, who brought with them their sacred Sanskrit texts and hierarchical Brahmanical society. The first large-scale government in north-east India, with its capital at Magadha in present-day Bihar, was established by the Mauryans in *c*. 320 B.C. The Hooghly basin was incorporated into the Mauryan Empire which, under its third ruler, Ashoka, embraced the doctrines of the Buddha.[4] While Buddhism claimed official patronage, however, it was Brahmanism that carried popular appeal in the territories adjacent to the Hooghly; Brahmans arriving from the Indian plains introduced new and successful methods of farming, encouraging the development of a productive but socially stratified agrarian order. After the collapse of Mauryan rule, a growing number of local rulers adopted and promoted Brahmanism, which, by the time of the Sena dynasty (*c*. A.D. 1097–1223), was entrenched as state culture and faith. Brahmans were responsible for cultivating lands granted by rulers, and for governing peasant society.[5]

Alongside agriculture, commerce thrived. Near the meeting point of the Rupnarayan and Hooghly, Tamralipti (on the site of present-day Tamluk) was a busy trading port dating at least to the Mauryan period: merchants from China, South East Asia, Ceylon, western India, and the Near East, including Alexandria, were attracted by its wares. Environmental historians suggest that trade across the eastern Indian Ocean—in rice, spices, salt, cloth, slaves, and other commodities—increased in volume from the ninth to the twelfth centuries before changes in average temperatures and monsoon winds forced it into decline.[6] The Hooghly basin was an integral part of this trade. Satgaon on the Saraswati—a distributary of the Hooghly which broke off from it at Tribeni—succeeded Tamralipti as the basin's main port.

The lives of the Hooghly basin's population were lived along a river of great sacred and temporal significance. In South Asia, the veneration of rivers as manifestations of the divine dates at least to the Indus valley civilisation (*c*. 3300–1300 B.C.). In the Rigveda, the belief was put down in word: the rivers of north-west India were denoted 'mother rivers' and stories of their descent from heaven to earth were recounted.[7] This Vedic myth of descent was repeated in various forms in subsequent Hindu epics, the most well known of which is the descent of the Ganges to earth narrated in the Ramayana and Mahabharata.

King Sagara of the Sun Dynasty, the story goes, released his horse into the wild in the expectation that wherever it wandered, his sovereignty would be recognised. When the horse disappeared, Sagara ordered his 60,000 sons to look for it. However, when the sons made the mistake of accusing a venerable sage, Kapila, of stealing the horse, he turned all 60,000 of them to ashes with a curse. On finding this out, Sagara was overcome with grief and remorse and sent his grandson Anshuman to make amends. After Anshuman had demonstrated his piety, Kapila consented to the sons being brought back to life, but with one condition: that the waters of the Ganges, which streamed through the heavens, be brought down to nourish the earth. This feat was finally accomplished by Anshuman's grandson, Bhagiratha, who became an ascetic in the Himalayas and pleaded with Lord Brahma to release the waters from heaven. To catch them as they fell, Bhagiratha enlisted the help of Lord Shiva, who cushioned the descending river in his hair before unleashing it onto earth.[8]

In Bengal, worship of the Hooghly and other rivers pre-dated the arrival of Indo-Aryans with their Sanskrit texts—perhaps not surprising when we consider that survival depended on the waters. Older folk beliefs and stories were then incorporated into the Brahmanical tradition as it spread.[9] Bengal occupied a position of great importance in the story of the descent of the Ganges. After it had been released from heaven, Bhagiratha led the Ganges out of the mountains and across the Indian plains to the Bengal delta, where it flowed into the sea next to the site of the sage Kapila's ashram on what is now Sagar Island. On viewing the great river on earth, Kapila kept his promise and brought Sagara's sons back to life. As the original course of the Ganges, the Hooghly is to this day known by many as the Bhagirathi, after Bhagiratha, or simply Ma Ganga (Mother Ganges).

In the mid-sixteenth century, the main flow of the Ganges moved away from the Hooghly basin towards what is now the Padma River and estuary in Bangladesh; below modern-day Kolkata, the Hooghly changed course.[10] Some accounts hold that when leading the Ganges across Bengal, Bhagiratha was misled by the sound of a conch shell down the route of the Padma, before realising his error and retracing his steps to lead the river through the Hooghly basin to the sea. Other versions of the story suggest that he deliberately led the Ganges down more than one route, realising that its force would otherwise be too great for the delta.[11] Whichever is believed, Hindus attach no sanctity to the Padma, whereas the Hooghly is the object of great veneration until its ancient course dries up just south of Kolkata.

From its source—Gangotri, high up in the Himalayas—until it enters the sea, the Ganges is worshipped. Pilgrims come from far and wide to bathe in its waters or achieve *moksha* (spiritual liberation) by dying on its banks. The story of the Ganges' descent is ritually re-enacted with the pouring of water on Shiva *lingams* (objects representing a deity); the descent has come to represent the opposite journey, from earth to heaven, when recounted in funerary rites.[12] The Hooghly is the Ganges at its most sacred. Every morning and evening, it is the site of worship, with passages of the Bhagavad Gita—a part of the Mahabharata—read by devotees on its banks and a glass of river water offered to the gods. Important occasions are marked with bathing festivals (*melas*) and the immersion of statues of gods in the water. Water is collected from the river and distributed to homes, where it is sprinkled in rooms at sunset to ensure a safe passage through the night, and used to celebrate auspicious occasions like births. Whereas along most of its course the Ganges is considered a gift from the gods, in Bengal it is usually worshipped as a god itself. *Puja* (ritual prayer) is performed to the river, whose names 'Mother Ganges' and 'Goddess Ganges' suggest love and nourishment. Across the Gangetic plain, it is common to see the Ganges depicted on temple doors, guarding sacred sites. On the Hooghly, however, whole temples are devoted to the goddess Ganga. During bathing festivals like the Berhampur-Murshidabad *mela*, clay models of Ganga being led by Bhagiratha are immersed in the sacred water.[13]

The holiest sites on the Hooghly are at its confluence and divergence with other waters. At Katwa, the river Ajay enters the Hooghly; further south, the now dried up Saraswati and Jamuna once separated from it at Tribeni. Both Katwa and Tribeni are revered pilgrimage sites. Between the two is the town of Nabadwip, where the Jalangi re-enters the Hooghly; the ancient capital of the Sena dynasty, it remains a centre of Sanskrit learning. Sagar Island, where both the revered and modern routes of the Hooghly reach the sea, is the final point on the river's sacred map, and the site of an annual *mela* attracting in excess of a million devotees.[14]

Over time, the development of new religious movements within the Hindu fold has led to the foundation of other spiritual centres along the river. Inspired by guru Chaitanya Mahaprabhu, Vaishnavism centres on the cult of Krishna as an incarnation of the Supreme Lord Vishnu and departs from Brahmanism by emphasising inclusiveness over caste, devotion over ritual, and the Bengali over the Sanskrit language. In the territories surrounding the upper Hooghly it produced a population of Krishna-following peasant cultivators distinct from the Brahmin owners of the land and turned Chaitanya's birthplace of Mayapur, facing Nabadwip across the river, into a major pilgrimage centre.[15] Kali, the four-armed black-skinned Goddess of Time, Creation, Destruction, and Power, was later singled out by other Bengali Hindus as the ultimate reality or Brahman. The centre of Kali worship became a temple constructed on the sacred original channel of the Hooghly in what is now the Kolkata suburb of Kalighat. The story of the descent of the Ganges was integrated into Kali worship.

These developments unfolded at a time when control of the Hooghly basin had been taken out of the hands of Hindu dynasties by the advent of Muslim rule. The earliest Muslims to reside in Bengal were long-distance traders from Arabia and Persia, their arrival precipitated by the incorporation of Bengal into the Indian Ocean economy in the tenth century A.D. Muslim rule was then established through the conquests of Muhammad Bakhtiyar, a Turkish cavalryman who arrived from northern India with 10,000 fellow horsemen in 1204. Bakhtiyar was in the service of Muhammad Ghori, a conquering Afghan who had captured Lahore and Delhi at the end of the twelfth century, expelling the original carriers of Persian-Islamic civilisation to the subcontinent, the Ghaznavids, and establishing the Delhi Sultanate.[16] Bengal was ruled as a province of the Sultanate until 1342, when the nobleman Shams al-Din Ilyas Shah engineered a separation of authority from the Tughluq dynasty at the imperial centre and established the city of Pandua, on the north bank of the Ganges as it enters Bengal, as his autonomous capital. The Bengal Sultanate, as the state established by Ilyas Shah became known, lasted under successive dynasties for more than two hundred years, reaching its peak under Husain Shah between 1494 and 1519. The capital, Gaur, just south of Pandua, is described in contemporary reports as an imposing and prosperous citadel controlling access between the Bengal delta and Hindustan.[17]

With Muslim rule came Sufi orders from upper India, such as the Chishti and Firdausi—spiritual leaders and their followers who promoted varieties of Islam more concerned with acts of devotion and the cult of saints than literalist adherence to Sunni doctrine. Encouraged by successive dynasts to settle in the province, many integrated local esoteric practices and cosmologies into their religious worldviews and were influential in the gradual embrace of Islamic monotheism by peasant communities east of the Hooghly.[18] During the sixteenth and seventeenth centuries, Bengal was then incorporated into the Mughal Empire. Conquered by Babur, it was lost by his son Humayun before being re-taken by Akbar and finally consolidated into the imperial system under Jahangir, a struggle that formed the backdrop to the arrival of Europeans on the Hooghly's stage.

* * *

In about 150 A.D., Ptolemy, the renowned Greek scholar resident in Alexandria in the Roman province of Egypt, produced his *Geographia*, an atlas and treatise on cartography featuring maps of different parts of the world. One depicted India and showed the Ganges crossing the subcontinent to enter the Bay of Bengal through a series of distributaries. An isle roughly corresponding with Sagar Island was sketched in the Bay where the most westerly of these distributaries reached the sea, confirming that Ptolemy and his contemporaries had a fairly good understanding of the Hooghly's course.[19] Almost fifteen hundred years would pass, however, before sustained European contact with Bengal began. In 1488—just four years before Columbus' discovery of America—Portuguese sailors rounded the Cape of Good Hope to enter the Indian Ocean, and European sea trade with Asia got underway. Vasco da Gama reached Calicut, on the western Indian coast, in 1498, laying the foundations for the Portuguese maritime empire—the Estado da India—operating out of Goa. The first Portuguese merchant to arrive in Bengal landed in 1517 and the following year an official expedition was sent to investigate the possibilities of trade with the delta.[20]

The Bengal that they encountered was a diverse mixture of ethnicities, languages, and faiths. Beneath the sovereignty of the Muslim rulers there existed powerful local courts and multiple alternative sources of political and spiritual authority. The Hooghly basin was the most densely populated region of the delta, with the highest levels of agricultural and commercial activity; its population had traded with other parts of the Indian subcontinent and across the Indian Ocean for centuries. The question arises: why, if the Hooghly was the site of such activity prior to 1517, should a global history of the river begin with the arrival of Europeans? To pre-empt the charge of Eurocentrism, we must take a step back and consider what it means to write the global history of a river.

As the title of this book suggests, its intention is not to study events worldwide, in the manner of some global histories, but rather to consider a particular geographical formation—the Hooghly—in relation to the global. Its focus is not on a single topic or theme of supposed universal importance but on a set of interrelated subjects central to understanding an age when events on the Hooghly were of global significance. As with many global histories, encounters and exchanges between peoples from diverse backgrounds are at the heart of the study. It takes as one of its main subjects the individuals and populations from distant locations who, at least for a period, made the Hooghly their home, and considers the commodities, ideas, and institutions that travelled with them across borders and boundaries. While parties from far and wide arrived around the Hooghly before 1517, the volume and frequency of foreign encounters with the river increased dramatically thereafter as Portuguese, Mughal, Dutch, British, French, and other peoples were attracted to its banks. Individuals who had spent time on the Hooghly, including those indigenous to Bengal, increasingly travelled to locations far removed from the river, carrying with them ideas and influences of their own— another way in which accelerating mobility closed the gap between local and global contexts.

Taking after Sebastian Conrad's excellent work on the subject, this book adopts as its starting point the insight that global history is not just about encounters and exchanges across cultures, territories, or regions but about processes of integration on a global scale—the increasing interconnectedness of diverse parts of the world.[21] As most historians recognise, Western expansion across the globe from the sixteenth to the twentieth century determined many of the systematic global networks and connections that we know today. European and

American imperialism shaped patterns of trade, migration flows, the spread of institutions, and the circulation of knowledge and ideas around the early modern and modern world. The causes of Western supremacy are debated but usually considered to include improvements in science and technology, which led to military and commercial dominance; the development of modern capitalist economies; war and conquest; and the institution of new techniques and practices of government. Recent scholars have stressed the importance of culture and ideas—democracy and the rule of law, for example—to the West's ascent, while others focus on biological and ecological explanations, like the influence of disease epidemics or climate change on patterns of migration and trade.[22]

An overarching concern of this book is the incorporation of the Hooghly into global networks for the regular and systematic transfer of people, commodities, institutions, ideas, and aspects of culture. No specific cause of that integration is privileged to the exclusion of others. Rather, diverse factors receive attention, from improvements in navigation that facilitated travel between Europe and India, to the practices of European trading companies through which Bengal was integrated into the global economy; from the military revolution that underpinned European expansion, to the intellectual currents that sustained colonial rule. A recurring interest is the contribution of cross-cultural exchange to growing interconnectedness between different peoples on the river, in ways that challenged existing identities and created new ones, even as yet other identities were emboldened. The 'English' army that established control over Bengal after 1757 was largely composed of Indian-born mixed race descendants of the Portuguese.

The integration of the Hooghly into global networks was not simply about the relationship between Bengal and Europe. As such, not all of the connections studied in this book involve European actors. One chapter is concerned with the encounter between Indo-Persian and Bengali cultural and religious forms and the syntheses that followed. Another considers the development of Calcutta into one of the world's largest cities, attracting migrants from across the globe. For better or worse, however, the integration of the Hooghly into global networks took place through diverse encounters during a time when Europeans were economically and geopolitically ascendant and, by the nineteenth century, dominant. It follows that encounters involving Europeans are the main focus here. Those encounters were shaped by specific global conditions and structures of power; the opening up of Bengali markets to European capital, for example, was decisively influenced by the exercise of colonial military power. While prevailing structures of power were often weighted in favour of Europeans, however, other parties were not entirely without agency and often played vital roles. The influence of Bengali businessmen like Dwarkanath Tagore on the integration of the Hooghly into the world economy, considered in chapter 6, provides an illustration.

A global history of the Hooghly must naturally prioritise some events, processes, people, and contexts over others, deliberately seeking out global dimensions of the river's past and elevating them over subjects without a definite global dimension. In focusing on the increasing interconnectedness of the Hooghly with the rest of the world, however, no teleology is implied—whether the European inculcation of progress and export of modernity across the globe, or the inevitability of globalisation. Integration is not assumed to be an inherently good or bad thing, and its consequences—ranging from the productive to the catastrophic—are enquired into. To guard against teleological thinking, it should be recalled that the integration of the Hooghly into global networks was not unidirectional. Just as global events and forces impacted on the river, developments on the river had global repercussions. As we will see, metropolitan political thought shaped the exercise of colonial power by the English and French trading companies on the Hooghly. Equally, that exercise of power had implications for economy, society, and politics in Europe; in France, as chapter 4 explores, it profoundly impacted the development of Enlightenment thought that would lead to the French Revolution.

The book devotes attention to a number of topics of global—and enduring—significance, among them modern economics and the power of large corporations; the relationship between trade and conquest; and processes of formal and informal imperialism. Others include slavery and migration; religious exclusivism and pluralism; the role of new technologies in revolutionising social relations; and the impact of humans on the natural environment around them. Some parallels with the world we inhabit today are made explicit while others are left for the reader to discern. While dealing with large subjects, however, the book is also a human history, focusing on some of the remarkable and more ordinary people who inhabited the Hooghly basin. During its time in the global spotlight, the Hooghly was witness to the best and worst of human nature. It saw curiosity, generosity, and friendship, along with beauty and creativity in the production of art and literature or scientific and technological innovation. Simultaneously, it witnessed violence, cruelty, greed, and exploitation, often accompanied by pretensions of cultural, religious, or racial superiority.

As Conrad reminds us, the discipline of history has traditionally been bounded by the category of the nation-state. To write history has meant writing the history of a nation—or, in some instances, of a civilisation like the West. In rejecting this compartmentalisation of how we know and understand the world in favour of a broader vision of connections or entanglements across national and civilisational boundaries—what Sanjay Subrahmanyam termed our 'connected histories'—global history has naturally redirected attention towards the 'alternative spatialities' where those connections have been made and forms of integration have taken place.[23] Some scholars have focused on borderlands or peripheries where different peoples meet, while others have studied regions or networks larger than individual states. Seas and oceans have been written about extensively, as spaces linking diverse territories and peoples, facilitating migration and other forms of exchange. Sunil Amrith's study of the Bay of Bengal as a region 'at the heart of global history' is one example particularly relevant to this work.[24]

Among the objects of this book is to make a claim for the importance of rivers as spaces for encounter and exchange—and, consequently, to argue the need for the further study of rivers by global historians. The fluidity of rivers draws our attention to connections between different locations.[25] On account of their natural wealth, rivers attract people from far and wide; as arteries for travel, communication, and exchange, they link separate territories and facilitate movement between coastal and inland sites. By crossing interiors, rivers provide access to local contexts, while their length and connection to seas allow them to be integrated into global networks. The Hooghly is an excellent example. As the most significant waterway linking lower and upper Bengal, it provided access to sites across the western delta, upriver via the Ganges to North India, and downriver to the coast, connecting the Bay of Bengal and more distant locations with eastern and northern India. Over the period of this study, the Hooghly was integrated into global networks. As the site of encounters and connections between heterogeneous peoples and cultures, it was at once a local and global space.

In what follows, the Hooghly is not only a stage but a participant, beyond the complete control of human parties. Essential for the transport of people and goods, the river was also vital for agriculture, its nutrient-rich silt fertilising the land, but its actions could never be fully predicted or regulated. Strong currents meant that it frequently spilled over its banks, particularly when water levels were high after the monsoon; if too much silt was deposited on surrounding fields, crops were ruined. From the mid-sixteenth century, the Hooghly's median water levels were in decline—a consequence of the eastward shift of the Ganges' main course. Without sufficient freshwater flows, the river was unable to flush out silt deposits to the sea; the build-up of silt along the river's course further reduced its irrigative capacity and navigability, making it more and more dependent on tidal inflows that over time pushed further and further upriver. Periodically, the Hooghly and other rivers of the delta changed course, depriving some areas of water and inundating others. The abandoned cities of Gaur and Rajmahal, once flourishing on the Ganges near its junction with the Hooghly but later several miles removed from the river, served as a melancholy reminder to subsequent generations of the fate of settlements without water. In this book, we will witness repeated human attempts to tame the Hooghly and turn it to productive use. Many would come to recognise, however, that complete human mastery of the river could never be achieved, an impression reinforced with each unexpected episode. In 1814 the Hooghly at Cossimbazaar suddenly shifted three miles to the west, away from the town. The swamps and stagnant water that it left behind led to an outbreak of fever from which three quarters of the local population perished.[26]

For people on the Hooghly, the climate of Bengal was also challenging. From March to October, temperatures and humidity were high; the build up of hot wind currents in the Bay of Bengal culminated in the heavy rainfall of the monsoon. Once the monsoon was over, dry land winds from the north provoked storms before the respite of lower temperatures and humidity through the winter months. Broad patterns of climate change were conducive to the growing European influence on the Hooghly. Shifts in the inter-tropical convergence zone accompanying the transition to what environmental historians have labelled the Little Ice Age (c. 1350–1850) caused the weakening and periodic failure of the Asian monsoon. The repeated droughts and famines that followed led to agricultural decline, negative population growth, and falling levels of trade in the Bay of Bengal, creating favourable conditions for the European trading companies to step in.[27] Once on the Hooghly, however, European parties were forced to contend like all others with its climatic extremes. Heat and humidity led to disease and low life expectancy, while earthquakes, cyclones, and tidal waves were commonplace. Just as the Hooghly was unmanageable, wider natural forces defied control.

* * *

The book focuses on seven locations along the course of the Hooghly. The intention is not to provide a comprehensive history of these various sites; rather, each provides the context for the exploration of themes related to the global history of the river. As the book progresses, first up and then down the river, it moves forward in time from the sixteenth century to the present.

Chapter 1 considers the flourishing and destruction of the earliest European settlement on the river, the Portuguese city of Hooghly. Drawing on surviving contemporary accounts, it considers the nature of life in the Portuguese settlement and seeks to understand why the Mughal emperor Shah Jahan considered it necessary to attack and destroy Hooghly in 1632—a decision that, it becomes clear, was closely related to the Portuguese traffic of slaves in the Bay of Bengal. Reflections are offered on the enduring legacies of the Portuguese at Hooghly for the global history of the river.

The second chapter focuses on the city of Murshidabad, christened the capital of Bengal by Murshid Quli Khan, an imperial officer who engineered the separation of Bengal from the Mughal Empire to establish an independent state under his personal rule. Charting the dynastic struggles and warfare that engulfed his successors, it offers a corrective to the commonplace politicised reading of Indian history as Hindu versus Muslim. The picture emerges of a kingdom characterised by its pluralism, in which encounters between heterogeneous peoples fostered the emergence of new and syncretic cultural and religious forms combining Islamic and other elements.

In chapter 3, the ascendancy of the English East India Company on the Hooghly is brought under scrutiny. The chapter examines how the Company took after its Portuguese and Dutch counterparts to press its trading claims and obtain commercial monopolies using force and coercion when required. It analyses the transformation of the Company from a commercial entity into a militarised territorial power and considers the great human costs of the warfare and famine that followed. Plassey—the site of the showdown between English forces and those of the Bengal ruler through which the Company assumed power—serves as a metaphor for this tragedy and offers a series of lessons for today about the extension and abuse of corporate power with the tacit permission and encouragement of nation-states.

The fourth chapter, on Chandernagore, turns attention to the state-sponsored French trading companies on the Hooghly. It aims to globalise the history of the French Revolution by showing how events on the Hooghly helped to bring about the revolution, and how, in turn, the revolution impacted Bengal. The actions of the French and English companies on the Hooghly, it is revealed, occupied an important position in metropolitan French anti-colonial thought and wider criticisms of the ancien régime. However, revolutionary ideas like freedom, democracy, and the rule of law would sustain as much as challenge European colonial practices on the river.

A small group of English Baptist missionaries who settled in the Danish town of Serampore are the perhaps surprising subject of chapter 5. What made the Serampore mission party so significant is that it operated one of the earliest and most influential printing presses in Bengal. The chapter considers the legacy of the mission and its press in areas including education, literature, journalism, political activism, and social and religious reform. It documents the missionaries' impact on the English government of Bengal and considers its influence on those who would contest and defy colonial rule.

INTRODUCTION

Chapter 6 focuses on Calcutta, which, it is suggested, deserves to be recognised as one of the world's first megacities. The chapter considers the manifold ways in which the development of Calcutta during the nineteenth century was dependent on human control of the Hooghly— for the transport of people and goods, food and water supply, hygiene and sanitation. This was an age of great innovations in science and technology, among them steamships and railways, pumping plants and new drainage systems, all of which appeared on the Hooghly. Despite these advances, however, the natural environment of Bengal, including the Hooghly itself, remained unruly and, as such, colonial confidence in the triumph of civilisation over nature was punctuated by self-doubt. The Hooghly would come to occupy an important position in Bengali nationalist responses to colonial rule.

By the turn of the twentieth century, Calcutta's status as the economic and political capital of India was under threat and the global importance of the Hooghly was in decline. The final chapter, Sagar Island, reflects on the Hooghly's global history and considers the potential significance of the river to the emergence of India as a global superpower today. It suggests that actors shaping the Hooghly's future must learn from the mistakes of the past if the great challenges of the twentieth-first century—among them the climate emergency and rising levels of inequality—are to be met.

1

HOOGHLY

THE RISE AND FALL OF THE PORTUGUESE

When Pedro Tavares stepped onto the bank of the Hooghly in the autumn of 1578, he had no idea what would happen next. Tavares was a merchant, the latest in a succession of Portuguese to visit the Bay of Bengal in search of quick profit. His aim was to unload a vessel's worth of produce on the markets of the Bengal delta, wait four months for the monsoon winds to change, and return to the Portuguese settlements on the western coast of India on a ship laden with merchandise from further east. However, events conspired against Tavares' plan, which had to be radically revised. In the imperial capital of Fatephur Sikri, a thousand miles to the north-west, a report of the activities of the Portuguese had reached Jalal-ud-din Muhammad Akbar, Emperor of Hindustan. Naturally inquisitive, Akbar had resolved to meet one of these strange foreign guests. Earlier that year, the emissary dispatched to Bengal with instructions to detain a Portuguese had arrived too late; with the trading season over, the European ships had departed for Cochin and Goa before the emperor's wishes could be conveyed. Akbar could not be disappointed again. No sooner had Tavares, the first Portuguese of the new season, reached dry land than a high-ranking local official appeared, carrying the imperial edict. With great ceremony, following the symbolic discharge of muskets, it was read out: his majesty desired the immediate presence of a Portuguese at his court. Tavares agreed voluntarily, though in reality he had little choice. Selecting three of the more respectable of his shipmates, and a large retinue of servants, he embarked on an escorted journey into the unknown.[1]

Tavares was an educated merchant, versed in politics and the affairs of state in the Portuguese East. Travelling upriver in a stately flotilla of boats, his party followed the turns of the Hooghly until it met the Ganges next to the ruins of the city of Gaur, once the capital of Muslim rule in Bengal. In contrast to the shallow and irregular Hooghly, the Ganges was immense. As Tavares and his companions were led further they passed through a flat, cultivated landscape of riverside villages to the busy port of Rajmahal, and on to the enormous and wealthy trading city of Patna. Here the river journey came to an end and the flotilla was exchanged for a caravan of pack animals and carts. After four days' travelling by land the party reached the holy city of Benares, packed with pilgrims, before continuing to Allahabad, where the Ganges and Yamuna converge. The route was well travelled, with small villages interspersing larger settlements and no shortage of amenities. Yet in spite of an overriding impression of prosperity, Agra must have come as a surprise. Its bazaars surpassed those of Patna, with goods and merchandise brought for sale from all over the subcontinent and Central Asia. On the back of thriving trade, merchants had built a city of mansions and gardens; the most prosperous transported their wares in two-wheeled carts studded with gold. The final day's journey from Agra to Fatephur Sikri proceeded along a route marked by a constant line of shops and market stalls selling silk, cloth, and precious stones.

Fatephur Sikri, the 'City of Victory', had been constructed in 1569 to celebrate the triumph of the imperial army over a string of independent rulers in Rajasthan. It occupied a site on the edge of a small chain of mountains stretching westwards to Ajmer. The walled citadel was two miles in circumference, with four entrance gates and a main bazaar more than half a mile in length. Visitors could not fail to be impressed by its 'great size and magnificent appearance'; its population exceeded that of London and was estimated to include 30,000 horses and 1000 elephants.[2]

In an elevated position in the middle of the city was the royal court, an elaborate assembly of palaces, courtyards, fountains, audience rooms, and mosques. Water was supplied from a great tank created by the damming of a low-lying piece of land that annually filled with water during the rains, an engineering marvel providing the additional benefit of a refreshing breeze when the northern Indian summer was at its worst. From the windows of his personal audience chamber, Akbar looked out on the city below. Beyond the northern or 'circus' gate, guarded by two life-size stone elephants with raised trunks, lay an arena for elephant fighting, gladiatorial contests, and polo.[3]

Tavares was to reside at Fatephur Sikri for a year. How often he and Akbar met during this period is unclear; the chronicles of Akbar's rule give little away. Akbar was perhaps disappointed that the Portuguese was unqualified to explain and debate with him the finer points of Christian theology, a task for which a succession of European priests was later summoned. There may be little doubt, however, that Tavares charmed the emperor. At their final audience Akbar bestowed on him lavish gifts and, more importantly, permission to found a Portuguese settlement in Bengal. The city of Hooghly was born.

* * *

Bengal in the late sixteenth century had only recently been brought under Mughal control. Since 1204 it had been ruled by a series of Muslim dynasties derived from Persia and Central Asia, the most successful of which, the Husain Shahi dynasty, stretched at its peak from Orissa in the west to Chittagong and modern-day Myanmar in the east. By the time Babur marched into northern India to establish Mughal rule, Husain Shah's kingdom was in decline. The Buddhist rulers of Arakan had seized control of substantial eastern territories. Gaur, the capital, fell to Sher Shah Suri, a renegade Afghan commander who, with his successors, ensured that the Mughal ruler Humayun was exiled from India for fifteen years. After the re-establishment of Mughal power in the north and Akbar's ascension to the throne, a decisive move into Bengal was made. In 1576, the imperial army crushed the forces of Daud Khan Kurrani, whose family had seized control after Sher Shah's demise, and the government of Bengal by autonomous Muslim rulers was brought to an end.[4]

Among European traders, Bengal's fertility and wealth were legendary. 'I find no country in all the East Indies,' wrote one, 'more abundantly supplied with all things needful for food, and with the riches of nature and art; and were not the navigation so dangerous, it would be the fairest, most pleasant, fertile, and profitable land in the world.'[5] The province's sought-after natural commodities included rice—the staple of the Bengali diet—sugar, and fruits which grew so profusely as to leave no doubt that Bengal was 'a very nursing mother'.[6] Fresh and salt-water fish, goats, sheep, pigs, and vegetables could be bought for next to nothing in riverside markets, where butter, oils, salt, pepper, and sweetmeats were also sold alongside the finest silk and cloth. On occasion, European travellers' descriptions of Bengal stretched credulity—one Frenchman in the first decade of the seventeenth century reported sightings of unicorns—but they are largely verified by other contemporary accounts.[7] A general in the Mughal army recorded that 'one can hunt as many game as his arm has strength to shoot', whether deer, buffalos, elephants, tigers, or rhinoceros.[8] A popular proverb asserted that on account of its abundance 'the Kingdom of Bengal has a hundred gates open for entrance, but not one for departure.'[9]

In the years immediately following the rounding of the Cape of Good Hope in 1488, Portuguese trading activities had been focused on the western Indian Ocean. A centralised trading empire operating out of Calicut and then Goa was consolidated under the governorship of Afonso de Albuquerque.[10] After the capture of Malacca in 1511, however, the Estado da India—the Portuguese government in Asia—turned its attention to the Bay of Bengal. In 1517 a trader by the name of João Coelho reached Chittagong on the ship of a Muslim merchant, and the following year three Portuguese vessels arrived in the port on an official expedition (or *carreira*) from Goa, which would be repeated annually thereafter.[11] The principal motivation of the *carreira* was trade, but establishing commercial privileges was inevitably a political business: from 1521 diplomats of the Estado visited the court of the Bengal sultanate in Gaur.[12] While the early *carreira* focused exclusively on Chittagong, labelled 'Porto Grande' in Portuguese sources, it wasn't long before a decision of lasting consequence was made: to explore the commercial possibilities of western Bengal. In the early 1530s an official Portuguese expedition first ventured up the Hooghly to the point where it met two smaller rivers, the Saraswati and the Jamuna. Here they began to trade in the port of Satgaon, an economic and spiritual centre dating to the first centuries A.D.

Alongside the annual official expeditions, a growing number of independent Portuguese merchants ventured to Bengal, some with a licence from the authorities in Goa and others unrecognised by the Estado. By the early 1540s private trading initiatives were more voluminous and profitable than official ones; the crown monopoly of trade of specific products, such as pepper, was lifted and the *carreira* ceased altogether. Increasingly, the eastern areas of Bengal attracted those who had struggled to find a place in formal Portuguese settlements in Asia.[13] Deserters from Malacca and Goa were employed by the king of Arakan, who appreciated their European firearms, navigation skills, and ships. Portuguese freebooters and pirates disrupted trade with Chittagong, forcing respectable traders to head instead for Satgaon, a city 'abounding in all thinges' that by the mid-1560s was attracting up to thirty-five European ships each year.[14]

Reaching Satgaon was itself no easy task. A Portuguese vessel setting sail from Goa would follow the Indian coastline to its southern tip, calling at the ports of Calicut, Colombo, and San Thomé, and then move northwards to the Bay of Bengal, possibly halting at Pipli before negotiating unpredictable tides and shifting sandbanks to enter the Hooghly estuary near Sagar Island. Seafaring boats advanced no further than Buttor, now a suburb in south Calcutta, where smaller crews boarded light vessels known as 'barks', waited for a favourable tide, and rowed upstream for a minimum of eighteen hours to their destination.[15] At the beginning of each trading season, the Portuguese arriving at Buttor constructed a village of straw houses which, in the absence of permission to build a permanent settlement, was burnt down when it was time to leave, an impractical arrangement as trading activity expanded. Akbar's curiosity and subsequent generosity on meeting Pedro Tavares had come at just the right time.

* * *

On his return to Bengal in late 1579, one of Tavares' first acts was to dispatch letters to the viceroy of Goa and bishop of Cochin reporting the new settlement's foundation. Hooghly had been selected by Tavares because of its strategic location at the point furthest north on the Hooghly before it became too shallow for larger ships to access. Rapidly it was populated by Portuguese traders from western India and

Chittagong, who brought with them wives and children or intermarried with the local population.[16] Under Tavares' governorship the town flourished. Houses and warehouses were erected on both sides of the river to cater for the increasing flow of people and goods. Hooghly's earliest traders focused on Portuguese sites on the Indian subcontinent and Ceylon. Textiles and rice were exported, while Malabari pepper, Ceylonese cinnamon, and cowrie shells—indigenous to the Maldives but popular in Bengal as a form of currency—were brought in. As trade at Hooghly grew, a link was quickly established with the ports of Gujarat, the Red Sea, and the Persian Gulf: cotton, silk, and sugar appeared in these areas; dried fruit, rosewater, and carpets arrived in Bengal. The greatest expansion of trade took place with Malacca and, through it, with locations further east. Cloves, nutmeg, and mace arrived from the Spice Islands; porcelain, pearls, jewels, and furniture from China; sandalwood from Timor; camphor and pepper from Borneo; and velvets, satins, and muslins from Sumatra.[17] The thriving trade of Hooghly attracted seafaring Persians, Turks, Arabs, and Malays, as well as Bengalis and other Indians. Though the Portuguese dominated each sea route, carrying produce as far as Europe and the Middle East, the exclusion of Asian traders was an aspiration rather than something achieved.[18]

In addition to long-distance voyages, inland trade with India attracted Portuguese interest. The foundation of Hooghly facilitated travel to Patna, where spices and porcelain were sold and cloth and carpets bought. The kingdom of Hijli, a semi-independent principality on the right bank of the Hooghly where it entered the sea, produced great quantities of salt for Portuguese ships to carry upriver and overseas. The annual duties paid by Portuguese merchants to the Mughal government, at the rate of 2.5 per cent, confirm that trade was phenomenally profitable: in one year, imports and exports amounted to more than 100,000 rupees.[19] Within two decades of its foundation, Hooghly was the commercial heart of western Bengal, annually attracting up to a hundred ships.[20]

A layered social hierarchy governed Portuguese cities in the east. At the top were officials of the crown, usually native to Portugal. Civilian traders who were long-term residents of the Estado, recognised by the authorities, were known as *casados*; lesser traders and mercenaries were referred to as *chatins*. Those who had had their passage from Portugal paid by the crown, in return for a commitment to fight for the Estado when wars broke out, were known as *soldados*; in times of peace they married with the local population and went into trade. Outlaws and pirates who failed to recognise crown authority were condemned as *arrenegados*. Mirroring this social hierarchy was a rigid racial one. Those born in Portugal to white parents were termed *homo blanco* or *firangis* (foreigners); pure Portuguese born in the East as *casticos*; and those of mixed Portuguese-Asian parentage as *mestizos*. At the bottom of both hierarchies were Asian and African slaves, on whose labours the functioning of economy and society depended.[21]

As the governor of Hooghly, Tavares was ultimately answerable to the crown; more directly, he and his successors reported to the captain-major resident at Syriam on the Burmese coast. By and large, however, the residents of Hooghly managed their affairs independently of the Estado. The position of *casado*, occupied by Hooghly's wealthier residents, was not always clear-cut. Official recognition of their status as traders carried the advantage of protection in law; it also meant the burden of a duty to assist the authorities in times of crisis. However, the distance of Hooghly from Goa meant that obligations to the Estado could easily be ignored. Unlike on the western coast of India, no large body of *soldados* existed to enforce the crown's will.[22] At Hooghly, influence was wielded by a gentry composed of the most successful traders, under whose authority lesser merchants and other civilians lived. The Dutch traveller Jan Huyghen van Linschoten observed in the 1580s that the Portuguese at Hooghly 'have no Fortes, nor any government, nor police, as in India [on the western coast] they have.'[23] This was a more informal, less militarised settlement than on the western coast, though distinctions of class and race remained.

* * *

Alongside the lay population, another significant constituency at Hooghly was the ecclesiastics. When Akbar granted Tavares permission to found the city he also permitted the construction of churches and monasteries and guaranteed the right to practice and propagate Christianity. While the settlement on the left bank of the river—with its bazaars and storehouses, residences and gambling dens—was dedicated to commerce and society, the right bank, known as Bandel, became a centre of faith.[24] As in many parts of India, the first Portuguese missionaries to arrive in Bengal were Jesuits. Their religious order present on the subcontinent—most notably on the Coromandel coast and Madurai—from 1542, a pair of Jesuit fathers, Antonio Vaz and Pedro Dias, first made the journey to Bengal in 1576, to reside at Satgaon. After the foundation of Hooghly they were joined by Francisco Fernandes and Domingo de Souza, under whose supervision a church and college were established.[25] The first Jesuit mission to Akbar took place in 1580.

At Hooghly, however, the main religious order was not the Society of Jesus but the Augustinians. On hearing of the founding of Hooghly, the viceroy of Goa had determined that Bengal would be a focus of Augustinian missionary endeavours; a first batch of priests was dispatched almost immediately, and others followed in 1599, when a church and convent were built. With the blessing of Akbar and his successor, his son Jahangir, who even offered financial support to the Christian orders, Hooghly developed into a mission centre from which priests set out to other parts of Bengal. Of the first five Augustinian brothers to arrive at Hooghly, two remained in the town to cater for the spiritual needs of its people, while the other three ventured out into the surrounding territories to propagate the faith.[26] Churches were erected in the kingdom of Hijli in Orissa, and later in Dacca, in spite of the opposition of Muslim clerics in the city.

Among the Augustinians sent to Hooghly was Frey Sebastian Manrique, a native of Porto who took orders in Goa in 1604 before being assigned to the mission in Bengal. His extensive narrative of his travels provides an invaluable first-hand account of early-seventeenth-century life on the Hooghly. After receiving his assignment, Manrique and a confrere, Frey Gregorio de los Angelies, were put on a merchant vessel, the *St Augustin*, carrying a cargo of cowrie shells and some two hundred Portuguese and Indian sailors and their families from Cochin to Hooghly. The voyage got off to an inauspicious start when the overloaded ship became stuck on a sandbank while on its way out of Cochin harbour. Only after a great deal of prayer, and the unloading of some of the cargo, did it make it to open sea. After thirteen days' sailing with a favourable wind, the coast of Bengal and Orissa came into view.

Approaching the Hooghly estuary, however, another sandbank was struck, this time with disastrous results: the hull of the ship was torn open and the storage decks began to fill with water. To the experienced sailors on board it quickly became apparent that the ship was going to sink, at which point Manrique sprang into action: after hearing the confessions of all Christians on board he ventured down to the lower deck, where the wives of the predominantly Muslim Indian sailors were housed, in an attempt to save their souls. Citing the Prophet Muhammad, one of the senior women told him firmly to go away.

As it turned out, Manrique needn't have worried. Caught by a strong wind, the sinking *St Augustin* drifted to the shore of the Hooghly estuary without loss of life. The crew had barely had time to prepare arms when a fleet of boats came into view. Raising a white flag to declare its peaceful intentions, one of the boats advanced towards the washed up *St Augustin*. The latter's captain came ashore and announced that the Portuguese had strayed into the kingdom of Hijli. Under the terms of a treaty between authorities at Hooghly and the prince of Hijli, the right of trading ships to travel unmolested up the Hooghly estuary was guaranteed; however, if a ship landed on the coast of Hijli, its cargo automatically became the property of the prince. To ensure that this term was enforced, the royal fleet was joined on the scene by one of the prince's cavalry regiments. After the captain of the *St Augustin* refused to hand over keys to all of the ship's chests and stores, he and Manrique, who happened to be standing closest, were stripped to their underwear and their hands tied behind their backs. In chains they and the rest of the ship's crew were escorted to the city of Hijli, a day's march away, and brought before the prince. Things took a turn for the worse when an officer of the nawab of Dacca, the Mughal-appointed governor of Bengal, arrived in the city to exercise his authority over the prince and claim the ship's possessions. Fearing that they would be sent as prisoners to Dacca, Manrique and Angelies, along with four Portuguese merchants and two slaves, stole away in the night, rowing in a small barge from Hijli back to the sea, before making upriver for the safety of Hooghly. On arrival, Manrique retired to the monastery of St Nicholas of Tolentino, his rather more adventurous than planned journey from Cochin at an end.

Manrique found Hooghly a city at its peak. By the time of his arrival, the mansions of the most successful Portuguese merchants spilled out for several miles down the banks of the river. Prosperous but less rich traders lived in stone houses in the city, while poorer residents lived in huts of straw reminiscent of the residences of the earliest Portuguese. Food, Manrique recorded, was plentiful and cheap: the rice was 'far superior to that of Europe', the sweetmeats delicious and the fruit, particularly mangoes, unsurpassed.[27] The climate was fair and the water of the Hooghly clean and healthy. Manrique cast a sharp eye on the social practices of the city's residents. In dress and manners, he noted, the Portuguese had in large part become Indianised: the men wore silk or cotton robes with jewellery and slippers; rice, meat, fish, vegetables, and pickles formed the basis of their diet. Sundays and festivals were celebrated extravagantly, with merry-makers taking to boats on the river or passing time in the orchards and gardens on its banks. Attendance at church was accompanied by great ceremony: the wealthy were carried in palanquins with their slaves and servants in tow. Music marked all important occasions: for their tradition of music-making, the Augustinian friars were renowned.[28]

The institution that perhaps offers the best insight into Hooghly society is the gambling house, where cards, dice, and other games of chance were played. Here, in different rooms reflecting social gradations, men competed with each other in the pursuit of wealth. Women were present only as entertainment for men, to sing and play instruments. Competition was fierce, but a strict code of honour prevented quarrels descending into violence. In gambling houses men would eat, sleep, and above all drink. The wealthiest indulged in wine imported from Portugal. Most settled for locally fermented rice liquor—'very potent ... the same effect on the senses as our wine when drunk to excess'—or a thicker arrack made with brown sugar.[29] Opium was taken as an aphrodisiac. Bhang, prepared from the leaves and flowers of the cannabis plant, was smoked, chewed, or drunk in water mixed with nutmeg, mace, cloves, and other spices. Manrique reports that it was also used to aid 'the attainment of that particular end to which all barbarous and bestial luxury is addressed'—sex—or, failing that, to induce 'a deep sleep, laughter and cheerfulness, driving away all thoughts of a depressing nature.'[30]

That men at Hooghly lived sometimes loose lives is perhaps not surprising when one considers the ever-present possibility of illness and death. Life in seventeenth-century Bengal was often short. Those arriving by sea suffered from dysentery and scurvy, as well as shortages of food and drinking water. On dry land, fever, malaria, cholera, and venereal disease took their toll. A journey up the Hooghly, and through the channels branching off from it, could involve encounters with crocodiles—reportedly immune to gunshot—sharks, tigers, mosquitoes, and leeches, not to mention greedy customs officials, angry villagers, and hostile piratical crews.[31] So unpredictable was the river that some preferred the arduous journey across land from the Bay of Bengal instead. Humour was one way of dealing with the danger: a joke recounted by the French physician François Bernier was that tigers always pounced first on the fattest person in a boat. If mortal danger was overcome, more trivial concerns, like sodden baggage, could become upsetting: on reaching Hooghly, Bernier reported that 'my wearing-apparel were wet, the poultry dead, the fish spoilt, and the whole of my biscuits soaked with rain.'[32]

* * *

Missionaries occupied an ambiguous social position in Hooghly. On the whole it would appear that they were accommodated by the city's merchants, who provided transport and supplies when needed. Patronised by the crown, their role as spiritual leaders and agents of evangelisation was officially endorsed. Each religious order claimed that its aims were spiritual rather than political—an important distinction when difficulties were encountered with foreign rulers. There can be no doubt, however, that missionaries did sometimes play political roles. In the 1620s one Augustinian friar was involved in an attempt to depose the king of Arakan.[33] Towards the end of his time in Bengal, Manrique acted on behalf of the viceroy of Goa in negotiations with the prince of Hijli over the production of salt at a cheaper rate than was supplied to western India by the Portuguese at Hooghly.[34] Manrique's position as a priest meant that occasionally he was called upon to act as negotiator in disputes between merchants, and once brokered peace during a hostile exchange between Portuguese and Mughal ships.

When they left Hooghly to propagate the faith in other locations, missionaries were closer to and more observant of Indian society than most Portuguese. Manrique's *Itinerario* contains a host of observations on the character, dress, living and eating habits, and religion of the people of Bengal. His reflections were not always very positive. The Bengalis, he recorded, are 'a languid race and pusillanimous ... mean-spirited and cowardly, more apt to serve than to command, and hence they easily accustom themselves to captivity and slavery.'[35] The women are 'naturally impetuous' and 'much addicted to sexual intercourse'.[36] The population was riddled with superstition, not least people listening for 'the songs and cries of birds and the actions of wild animals, and carrying out or abandoning their intentions in accordance with the good or evil they deduce from such foolish proceedings.'[37] Manrique's greatest condemnations were reserved for Bengali religion. The Hindu myths, he pronounced, are 'so stupid that I shall not record them ... vile beliefs, so full of abomination and cruelty, that a little rational consideration would show them to be repugnant to all reason.'[38] The sum of Hindu belief is 'attributing to cows that which they should attribute to their divine Creator.'[39] Worse still, Bengal was home to many Muslims, followers of that 'false' and 'wicked' prophet, the 'undoubted precursor of Antichrist'.[40]

Before Manrique is dismissed as a bigot, however, the context of his writing must be taken into account. The *Itinerario* was written and published in Rome after Manrique's return to Europe in the 1640s, at a time when the Roman Inquisition held sway. In this environment, to condemn non-Christian religions and peoples was necessary for approval by the Vatican's censors. Beneath the surface-level denunciations, Manrique's curiosity and fascination with Bengali social and religious practices spill out from the pages of his text. Repeatedly he describes the rituals and ceremonies of the Hooghly basin's Brahmanised population. He devotes page after page to explaining the doctrine of reincarnation—'the transmigration of souls'—and recounts his many visits to Hindu temples: 'fine, majestic structures ... richly decorated and filled with treasures ... in which sweet-smelling essences were burnt.'[41]

A particular fascination for Manrique—and indeed for many of his European contemporaries—was Bengali people's relationship with the Hooghly. He recorded in detail, albeit with errors, the rituals performed on the river's banks and in the water: bathing and ablutions, cremations and the practice of sati (widow immolation). The Ganges was at its most sacred in Bengal: people travelled from far and wide to bathe in the Hooghly's waters and die at its edge. The sight of partially cremated and half-burnt bodies floating downstream in the otherwise pristine river was commonplace. So sacred was the water of the Hooghly that it was bottled and sold in other parts of the subcontinent by Indian sailors working on Portuguese ships, until the authorities in Goa outlawed the trade as un-Christian in 1585.[42] In the course of observing these practices, Manrique interacted at close quarters with Brahman elites, and on occasion dined with the heads of villages. He befriended Mughal officials, travelled in small parties with Muslim traders, and admired the beauty of local mosques and shrines. The later condemnation of Hindus and Muslims in the *Itinerario* was more performance than conviction.

In the territories east and west of the Hooghly, what did propagating Christianity and making conversions mean? It could certainly be a dangerous enterprise. At one point, Manrique was shot at and his confrere, Frey Manuel de la Concepcion, poisoned after the pair had instructed recent converts to Christianity not to take part in a Hindu procession.[43] On some occasions, conversions to Christianity were preceded by meaningful theological conversation and debate. Members of the royal family of Arakan, for example, were persuaded through Manrique's efforts to quit the kingdom and relocate to Hooghly to raise their children as Christians. When one Muslim journeyman wished to become a Christian after Manrique had saved him from having a hand amputated—the punishment prescribed by a Mughal official after he had killed and eaten a peacock in a Hindu village—Manrique insisted that he first learn the rudiments of the faith.[44] However, incidences of this kind were a tiny minority within the official conversion figures sent back to Goa. Manrique periodically reported the conversion of Bengali heathens in tens of thousands. In this sense, conversion meant a number of things: a native woman married to a Portuguese was a convert, as were their offspring; slaves owned by a Portuguese were converts too. Whole settlements were converted by the building of a church or visit of a priest, without the merest hint of theological engagement.

In September 1628 Manrique was ordered to leave Hooghly to spread the word of God in the kingdom of Arakan. En route he stayed at the port of Dianga, near Chittagong, where he relieved a fellow Augustinian friar, Domingos de la Purificacion, who had been carrying out mission work there alone, amid a reportedly hostile Hindu population, for seven years. It was perhaps with regret that Manrique left the relative comfort and security of the monastery of St Nicholas of Tolentino for a journey across the wild deltaic regions of eastern Bengal and the Chittagong hills, yet in all probability the assignment to Arakan saved his life. Soon after his departure, Hooghly was besieged by the forces of the Mughal Empire and destroyed.

* * *

By 1632, half a century after its foundation, Hooghly lay at the centre of a network of Portuguese settlements in Bengal populated by traders and missionaries. Via the Hooghly, the Padma, and a labyrinth of smaller waterways it was connected with the cities of Dacca and Chittagong to the east, and Hijli and Tamluk to the south. Regular exchanges also took place with the Orissan ports of Pipli and Balasore to the south in the Bay of Bengal.[45] Hooghly was almost completely independent of Mughal control. The nawab of Dacca could enter the city only with Portuguese consent; on the Hooghly, even Mughal ships were subject to Portuguese regulations. The Mughal governor and his overlord in Agra satisfied themselves with the lucrative collection of custom duties from Portuguese trade.

Near-contemporary European explanations of the fall of Hooghly focus on the immorality of the Portuguese in Bengal. Writing a few decades later, François Bernier considered the destruction of the settlement an act of divine retribution provoked by the depravity of its inhabitants—their addiction to vice and sinful habits.[46] In the nineteenth century, British writers expounded a secularised version of this account—that the residents of Hooghly had become decadent, their moral decay precipitating economic and political decline.[47] Such a narrative reveals more about later British colonial anxieties concerning the effects of colonialism on the morality of the coloniser than it does about Hooghly's fall. If the Mughal conquest of the city is to be understood, the background to the events of 1632 must be looked at anew.

Shah Jahan, the grandson of Akbar, ascended to the Mughal throne in 1628. Less open-minded than his predecessors, he reversed the official policy of patronising Hindu and Christian institutions and oversaw the destruction of Jesuit churches in Agra.[48] Persian records of his rule, in particular the *Padshahnama*, describe the siege of Hooghly as a battle between infidels and warriors of Islam.[49] In truth, however, the decision to attack Hooghly was more about personal antipathy and realpolitik than religion. Shah Jahan's dislike of the Portuguese dated to his first attempt to seize the Mughal throne. In 1619 the prince had instigated a rebellion against his father, Jahangir, engaging the imperial army in battle first in the Deccan and later in Bengal. After the capture in 1622 of Burdwan, eighty kilometres north-west of Hooghly, Shah Jahan sought the support of the Portuguese for his coup and secured a promise of loyalty from Michael Rodrigues, Tavares' successor as governor. When it became clear, however, that the imperial army was going to defeat the rebellious prince, Rodrigues and his compatriots switched sides; Shah Jahan was thrown out of Bengal, his insurrection at an end. The prince's antipathy towards the Portuguese was accentuated when, six years on, no emissary was dispatched from Hooghly to congratulate him upon his finally securing the throne.[50]

As emperor, Shah Jahan attempted to tighten Mughal control over Bengal, appointing a trusted lieutenant, Qasim Khan, as governor. On the western coast of India, trade from the port of Surat had been brought more closely under imperial supervision; Shah Jahan considered wresting control of the overseas Bengal trade from Portuguese hands.[51] Particularly troubling to the emperor as he contemplated the Bengal scene was the evidence of growing links between the residents of Hooghly and officially unrecognised but increasingly powerful Portuguese further east. A strategic reason why successive Mughal governors had encouraged Portuguese settlement at Hooghly was the conviction that respectable duty-paying traders would keep the Bay of Bengal free of lawless pirates. However, the presence of *arrenegados* in the eastern parts of the bay had continued to grow. On the island of Sandwip, near Chittagong, an outlaw called Sebastian Gonzales had installed himself as the ruler of a heavily militarised independent Portuguese colony that engaged in piracy and repeatedly defeated Mughal naval forces stationed at Dacca. Before his demise, Gonzales had made overtures to Goa and Hooghly about the incorporation of Sandwip and coastal eastern Bengal into the Estado da India.[52]

The clearest and most vexing indication of co-operation between Portuguese pirates and the residents of Hooghly lay in the capture and trade of slaves. Of course, slavery was not an institution brought new to Bengal by the Portuguese; the possession of slaves was a feature of Bengali society preceding even the advent of Muslim rule in the thirteenth century. As Portuguese pirates had gained in number and influence, however, the aquatic slave trade had grown. Bernier writes of whole settlements captured and enslaved by piratical crews:

> As they were unawed and unrestrained by the government, it was not surprising that these renegades pursued no other trade than that of rapine and piracy. They scoured the neighbouring seas in light galleys, called galleasses, entered the numerous arms and branches of the Ganges, ravaged the islands of Lower Bengal, and, often penetrating forty or fifty leagues up the country, surprised and carried away the entire population of villages on market days, and at times when the inhabitants were assembled for the celebration of a marriage, or some other festival. The marauders made slaves of their unhappy captives, and burnt whatever could not be removed. It is owing to these repeated depredations that we see so many fine islands at the mouth of the Ganges, formerly thickly peopled, now entirely deserted by human beings, and become the desolate lairs of tigers and other wild beasts. [53]

A Bengali poet of the time, Kavikankan Mukundaram Chakravarti, recorded that a journey around the coast was filled with dread on account of slave-capturing pirates. [54] Slaves were sold to the Portuguese at San Thomé, Ceylon, Goa, and Hooghly, 'who bought whole cargoes at a cheap rate'. [55] Hooghly's slave market was in the centre of the town: men, women, and children were displayed for inspection before sale, with the younger, healthier, domestically skilled, and virgins commanding a higher price. The number of slaves possessed by a trader was an indication and advertisement of his wealth. The sale and purchase of slaves blurred the boundaries between Hooghly's traders and illegal profiteers further east. To police the capture of slaves in the eastern delta was beyond the scope of Mughal power, but preventing their sale and possession at Hooghly was possible. The *Padshahnama* confirms that this was the main incentive for the attack on the city. [56]

On the orders of Shah Jahan to Qasim Khan, Mughal forces assembled at Dacca: a fleet of 600 ships, and an army of 90 elephants, 14,000 horses, and a large body of infantry attracted by the promise of plunder.[57] The hardened Afghan general Bahadur Khan was put in command. As the build-up of men and equipment escalated at Dacca, the Portuguese in the city sent a warning to their compatriots at Hooghly. A further warning was sent by the Jesuit fathers in Agra, where word of the impending attack had spread. Both were dismissed, perhaps because the Mughal disinformation that the kingdom of Hijli was to be attacked was believed.[58] In mid-June 1632 the naval force set sail from Dacca, entering the Hooghly estuary and advancing upstream to assemble again at Cancarole, just south of modern-day Calcutta, where it was met by the army a few days later.

The best eyewitness account of what followed is that of Father John Cabral.[59] Born in Colorico, Portugal, in 1599, Cabral had entered the Society of Jesus in 1615 before arriving at Hooghly in 1624. In 1627 he was sent with a fellow Jesuit, Father Stephen Cacella, to Tibet. From Bengal, the pair travelled through Cooch Bihar to the foothills of the Himalayas and on to Ü-Tsang in the eastern Himalayan range, only to return to Hooghly when they ran out of wine for Mass. Cabral tells us that the Portuguese defending Hooghly totalled 300, plus an unknown number of servants and slaves. The city possessed no fortified walls, just a small ditch filled with water from the river. When the approaching Mughal forces were first sighted on 26 June 1632, makeshift barricades were erected from house to house, and muskets and cannons shared out among the Portuguese residents. Many of the free Indian inhabitants took the opportunity to flee.

Hopelessly outnumbered, Hooghly's remaining residents resolved to negotiate. After the Mughal forces set up camp just a few kilometres from the city, Cabral was sent with two Bengali gentlemen to speak with Bahadur Khan. From the conversations that ensued it became clear to the Portuguese that the main source of Mughal antagonism was their possession of slaves: if all slaves were given up, Bahadur Khan intimated, conflict might be averted. When Cabral relayed this message to his compatriots a division emerged among the Portuguese. To the majority, including the vast number of merchants, handing over the slaves was prudent: as long as Bahadur Khan could be trusted, paying off the Mughals with a part of one's assets was a sensible business move to ensure the security of the rest. For most of the missionaries and a small number of others, however, giving up the slaves was unthinkable.

By entering into the Portuguese community, albeit as unpaid labour, they argued, the slaves had become Christians; abandoning them to the Mughals would mean their forced conversion to Islam. With the imperial army at the gates, Hooghly's Portuguese descended into a quarrel between factions favouring pragmatism and principle, self-preservation and faith.

With the question undecided, the siege of Hooghly began. At sunrise on 2 July, Mughal land and river forces were unleashed. The Church of Our Lady of Mercies, located on the right bank of the Hooghly, quickly fell, a symbolic victory for the Mughal soldiers, who triumphantly carried away the statues of saints and threw them in the river. Armed with their superior weaponry, however, the Portuguese in the other buildings on the right bank, and in the main part of the city on the left, held out. At the end of the first day of fighting, twenty-five Portuguese and Indian defenders had been killed, compared to approximately 600 Mughal troops. A second round of negotiations followed. Antonio de Christo, the Augustinian prior of Hooghly, visited Bahadur Khan's camp, accompanied by a female interpreter, a Muslim lady of high rank. Despite the protestations of Cabral and others, ninety slaves were handed over, along with four merchant ships. When Bahadur Khan responded to this offering by demanding the astronomical sum of 700,000 *patacas* (the main currency of Portuguese trade in Asia) and all Portuguese goods, it became clear that continued conflict would not be avoided. The settlement on the right bank of the river—which included the residences of the Society of Jesus and the Augustinians— was abandoned to concentrate on the defence of the city. Bahadur Khan and his officers made the Jesuit college their home.

The siege of Hooghly lasted two and a half months. Conscious of the power of Portuguese muskets, Bahadur Khan opted for attrition, starving as much as fighting the city into submission.[60] Cabral's account is full of heroic episodes—the defence of a row of houses by sixty Portuguese commanded by Father Manuel Rodrigues against 1500 Mughal troops, for example. Eventually, however, it became clear to the Portuguese that they could not hold out much longer, as casualties mounted and the city's usually abundant stores of food ran low. They would have to either surrender or break through the siege. With its strong current, and the possibility of a favourable wind, the Hooghly was the obvious escape route. Just outside of Hooghly, however, a large pontoon of boats had been erected to blockade the river; a flotilla of fire ships lay in wait; and further south, near Buttor, a huge iron chain had been secured from one side of the river to the other, at one of its narrowest points. On top of this, the riverbanks were lined for more than twenty kilometres downstream with trenches filled with troops ready to fire on those making an escape.

Before sunrise on 24 September the remaining inhabitants of Hooghly made their way down to the river and boarded those small merchant boats and barges that had survived the siege unscathed. By the time that they were full, each carrying approximately thirty people, Mughal troops had realised what was happening. Under heavy bombardment, twelve vessels made it out into the middle of river, where they returned fire with light cannons. At this point, the Mughal commanders made a huge mistake, interpreted by Cabral as an act of God. A fire raft composed of sixteen burning ships was directed at the Portuguese fleet but veered off course into the pontoon of Mughal ships, setting it alight. A gap opened up in the blockade big enough for the Portuguese vessels to pass. For a day and a half the Portuguese fleet drifted downriver, the boats returning the fire they received from the trenches on the river banks and the ships giving chase. Several boats ran aground, including that of Gomez Barreiros, one of Hooghly's wealthiest traders, which carried two Jesuit priests. A chest full of gold and silver was lost to the riverbed. Among those killed was Frey Gregorio de los Angelies, who had arrived at Hooghly with Manrique, when his ship got stuck on a sandbank and was destroyed by fire. Only six Portuguese vessels made it as far as the iron chain cast into the river near Buttor. One succeeded in breaking through, and a further three followed; after a day of fighting, the other two were sunk. In total, some 100 Portuguese died in the siege and flight, alongside many more servants and slaves. Mughal casualties were conservatively estimated at 4000 on land and on the river, with the loss of 100 ships.[61]

Those residents of Hooghly who did not die or escape—among them Father Antonio de Christo and three other priests—were taken prisoner and escorted to Agra. On account of the large numbers of sick, injured, and elderly the journey took eleven months; 400 made it to the imperial capital, where they were presented to Shah Jahan. The female prisoners were distributed as slaves around the Mughal court and the men interned in jail. Special treatment was reserved for the priests who, after being given the chance to convert to Islam, were tortured, paraded in the street, and condemned to death. Legend has it that the priests were spared execution when the elephant that was to trample them to death in Shah Jahan's presence instead knelt reverentially before them.[62] Some of the surviving prisoners were permitted to return to Bengal. Antonio de Christo spent a further nine years in captivity, until Sebastian Manrique visited Agra disguised as a Muslim merchant and secured his release.

* * *

The fall of Hooghly was not the end of its history as a commercial port. One year on from the siege, Shah Jahan, missing the income reaped from Portuguese trade, permitted the return of Portuguese merchants and missionaries; their commercial and religious privileges were confirmed in an imperial decree.[63] Jesuit and Augustinian churches were rebuilt, the latter on a northerly site on the right bank of the river, where its more recent incarnation stands today. The Society of Jesus retained a seminary at Hooghly, famous for the beauty of its gardens, until the middle of the eighteenth century; the last Augustinian prior died in 1869.[64]

After the fall, however, Hooghly no longer belonged to the Portuguese. Instead, it became an imperial port, governed by a Mughal official appointed directly by the emperor. The history of the city thereafter signposted the fate of Bengal. In 1635 a fleet of Dutch ships first sailed up the Hooghly, securing licence from the nawab of Dacca to establish a trading post at the port. Hooghly developed into a major station for Dutch maritime trade, in particular the purchase of silk and cotton for shipping to Japan. Representatives of the English East India Company had first visited Bengal in 1620, travelling across India from Surat. Five years after the Dutch, the Company established itself at Hooghly—the centre of its Bengal trade until the foundation of Calcutta fifty years on.[65] When the merchant Thomas Bowrey arrived in the 1660s he found a flourishing settlement of fine stone buildings and a large bazaar.[66] Portuguese trade had not entirely been wiped out; records testify to the fortunes made by a small number of Portuguese,

Arab, and Indian traders until the end of the century. However, the Dutch and English companies devoured a growing proportion of Hooghly's trade.

The arrival of the Portuguese on the Indian subcontinent signalled the first sustained contact between Europe and India in the early modern age. Whereas in Goa monumental cathedrals, churches, forts, palaces, and mansions testify to the Portuguese presence, in Bengal little visible evidence remains. The Augustinian church at Hooghly was destroyed by an earthquake in 1897 before being rebuilt for a second time. Many descendants of the Portuguese later exchanged Catholicism for Protestantism and anglicised their names, becoming indistinguishable from mixed race Anglo-Indian communities. On close inspection, however, lasting impacts of Portuguese imperialism on the Hooghly can be identified. For at least a century after Hooghly's fall, Portuguese remained one of the major spoken languages of Bengal. Everyday words such as *chai* (tea) and *biskut* (biscuit) entered Bengali and other Indian vocabularies, in addition to religious terms. The first Bengali work of prose, a Christian tract, was written by a Portuguese missionary, Father Sousa, in 1599; the first Bengali-language printed books were later produced (in the Roman script) in Lisbon. The most likely derivation of the name 'Hooghly' is from the Portuguese word *gola*— the term for a storehouse found on the river's banks.[67]

One ubiquitous way in which the Portuguese presence at Hooghly continues its impact on Bengal is in relation to diet. Portuguese traders introduced plants from Asia, Africa, and the Americas that became essential parts of Bengali cuisine: potatoes, tomatoes, chillies, maize, and papaya, to mention just a few. However, the most significant consequence of the rise and fall of Portuguese Hooghly was to set a precedent for other European powers seeking to profit from Bengal. Dutch and English parties had viewed with envy the produce and earnings derived by the Portuguese from trade at Hooghly. After Shah Jahan's destruction of the city, they spotted an opportunity and set sail for the river.

2

MURSHIDABAD

THE KINGDOM OF THE NAWABS OF BENGAL

In the early 1670s, Haji Shafi Ispahani, a Mughal officer, was travelling through the Deccan in central southern India, when he purchased a young boy sold into slavery by his impoverished Brahmin parents. Quitting Mughal service, he returned to his native Persia with the boy, who was given the name Muhammad Hadi and raised a Muslim. When Haji Shafi died, Muhammad Hadi was forced to seek a living elsewhere. Now in his twenties, he returned to India and entered the service of the *diwan* (chief revenue officer) of the Mughal province of Berar. As an assistant in the revenue office, Muhammad Hadi acquired a reputation as an efficient and hard-working administrator, attracting the admiration of Emperor Aurangzeb himself. Aurangzeb, son of Shah Jahan, had spent the best part of a decade attempting to bring the Deccan plateau under Mughal control. After the fall of the Golconda Sultanate in 1687, competent and trustworthy officials were required; Aurangzeb installed Muhammad Hadi as *diwan* of the newly conquered territory. For a child born to destitute Brahmin parents it was a meteoric rise, but Muhammad Hadi's acquisition of reputation and power did not end there. After fifteen years of service in the Deccan, he was transferred by Aurangzeb to the *diwani* of Bengal and Orissa and awarded the prestigious title Murshid Quli Khan. The elderly Aurangzeb had just three more years to live. After his death, Quli Khan would be responsible for the breaking away of Bengal from the Mughal Empire and the establishment of an independent dynasty under his personal command, governed from a city of his making: Murshidabad.[1]

The separation of Bengal from the Mughal Empire—on first view a process of disintegration rather than integration—may appear contrary to the idea of growing interconnectedness between the Hooghly and other locations with which this book is concerned. As we shall see, however, the establishment of an independent Muslim kingdom governed from Murshidabad facilitated the embedding of Indo-Persian culture into Bengal and the development of new religious and cultural forms. Despite recent attempts to re-read Indian history as Hindu versus Muslim, the rule of the nawabs was not the Muslim oppression of Bengal's predominantly Hindu population, nor was it the spread of Islam at the point of a sword. In spite of the external threats faced, the kingdom of the nawabs of Bengal was consistently cosmopolitan and pluralist, witnessing encounters between heterogeneous peoples and cultures through which striking new syntheses emerged.

* * *

From the moment of its incorporation into the Mughal Empire under Akbar, Bengal had been viewed by Mughal officers as a territory like no other. While its trade offered possibilities for enrichment and nature in it was abundant, most imperial administrators dreaded being sent to the province, which, with its terrain of rivers and swamps, appeared so foreign to those accustomed to the northern and central Indian plains. The people of Bengal differed in language, dress, and diet from those of Hindustan and were consequently dismissed as uncivilised. The wet climate was feared for the grave threats to health that it appeared to present. Aurangzeb, who never visited Bengal, insisted that it was a 'paradise'.[2] A common saying among his officers, capturing their mixture of apprehension and expectation, had it that the province was 'a hell filled with good things'.[3]

Aurangzeb's decision to send Murshid Quli Khan to Bengal has its origins in the summer of 1696 when Subha Singh, a landowner in the Midnapore area of western Bengal, joined forces with Rahim Khan, an Afghan commander in Orissa, to instigate a rebellion against the

Mughal governor, Ibrahim Khan. Aurangzeb's response to the rebellion was to send his grandson, Muhammad Azim al-Din, to restore imperial authority, which he duly did. Once victory had been secured, however, Azim al-Din proved an unsatisfactory ruler, monopolising inland trade from the province's ports and failing to send remittances to Delhi. Aurangzeb issued repeated warnings to his grandson and downgraded his rank in an attempt to enforce submission, before resolving to assign his trusted Murshid Quli Khan to the government of Bengal and Orissa.

By the latter stages of Aurangzeb's rule, a clear distinction had been confirmed between two key administrative positions in each Mughal province: the *subahdar* (governor) and the *diwan* (chief revenue officer). While the *subahdar* held general responsibility for a province's management, maintaining order and quashing rebellion, the *diwan* was authorised to handle all fiscal matters, including the collection, remittance, and spending of revenue; the keeping of accounts and records; oversight of the treasury; and the administration of land grants, endowments, and salaries.[4] As *diwan* of Bengal and Orissa, Quli Khan's first task was to curb the corruption of Azim al-Din's government. To do so, he brought the province's revenue officials under his direct control and deputed them to make a new assessment of the revenues to be collected from each segment of land. By reclaiming some of the more prosperous lands for the crown, he created a revenue surplus for remittance to Delhi.[5]

While Aurangzeb was delighted by Quli Khan's reforms, Azim al-Din was—unsurprisingly—provoked, his authority and licence for the acquisition of wealth having been reined in. One morning, when he was riding alone in Dacca, Quli Khan was surrounded by a body of troops ostensibly demanding arrears of pay. Refusing to rise to their provocation, he promised that the matter would be investigated and quickly exited the scene. On enquiry it became clear that the troops' demonstration had been organised by Azim al-Din, who had planned for one of the soldiers to incite Quli Khan's anger and then kill him during the ensuing melee. When Quli Khan reported the episode to Aurangzeb, the emperor's response left no doubt as to whether it was the *subahdar* or the *diwan* that he favoured. '[Murshid Quli Khan] is an officer of the Emperor,' he wrote to his grandson, and 'in case a hairbreadth injury, in person or property, happens to him, I will avenge myself on you.'[6] Soon after, Azim al-Din was sent away to act as *subahdar* in Bihar.

A measure of the extent of Quli Khan's authority, just a year after his arrival in Bengal, is his decision to relocate the capital of revenue collection in the province from Dacca in the east to the banks of the Hooghly. His chosen site was the town of Maksudabad, sixty kilometres downstream from the Hooghly's separation off the main branch of the Ganges. Maksudabad had been founded during the reign of Akbar, when Makhsus Khan, the brother of one of Akbar's governors, built a *serai* (guesthouse) on the route from Hooghly to northern Bengal. It developed into a local seat of Mughal administration, with a modest walled city bounded by land on three sides and the river on the west. From the early seventeenth century Maksudabad gained a reputation as a centre for the manufacture of silk, before being plundered in 1697 by the rebellious army of Subha Singh.[7]

Murshid Quli Khan settled on Maksudabad as his capital because of its strategic importance. To the north-west, the passes of Sakrigali and Tiliagadhi controlled access to and from Bihar. By travelling up the Hooghly and crossing to the northern side of the Ganges, Rangpur and Cooch Bihar were accessed. To the south-west lay the forests and hilly passes of Jharkhand, forming a natural barrier with Central India. Southwards by river and road were Hijli, Orissa, and, within easy reach of the city the European trading stations at Cossimbazaar and Hooghly. From Maksudabad, Quli Khan could exercise authority over both western and eastern Bengal, Orissa, and Bihar. Renaming the town Murshidabad, he made a statement of his dynastic intentions.

* * *

Among Quli Khan's first actions on arrival at Murshidabad was to order the rebuilding of the city's walls, which had fallen into disrepair since Akbar's time. The office of the *diwani*, known as the *kachari*, was constructed, along with a treasury, a mint, and a customs house overlooking the river. As the centre of administration, Murshidabad was swiftly populated by government servants, landowners, and others arriving to support the new official population. Meanwhile, Quli Khan moved swiftly to consolidate his position, appointing new deputy revenue officers in Bengal and Orissa and finding official positions for fourteen relatives from Persia.[8] Before long, a relative by blood or marriage occupied almost every post of importance; the Delhi court's appointment to Bengal of civil and military officers had been brought to a halt. When Aurangzeb died in 1707, Quli Khan's occupation of the *diwani* was put in doubt; the new emperor, Bahadur Shah, instructed him to return to the Deccan. The following year, however, he was back at Murshidabad, and the work of consolidating his independence from the imperial court recommenced.

As that court splintered after Aurangzeb's death into a host of competing factions, Quli Khan's strategy was wise. Each time a war of succession flared up, he waited patiently for the outcome before declaring loyalty to the new emperor and submitting gifts of elephants, horses, ivory, musical instruments, silk, cloth, and curiosities from Europe in a show of deference. A portion of the province's revenues was sent annually to Delhi; coins were minted in each emperor's name, and ships of the Mughal navy were saluted with great ceremony on their visits to Murshidabad from Dacca.[9] Alongside this outward recognition of Mughal sovereignty, however, Quli Khan took further steps to concentrate power in his hands. The fortifications of Murshidabad were extended and the Bengal army increased to such a size that in 1712, when one of the pretenders to the Mughal throne—the Aurangabadi Farrukhsiyar—marched his army into Bengal uninvited, Quli Khan could dispatch a force to defeat him on the Karimabad plain near Murshidabad.

According to one Persian chronicler, Quli Khan displayed no anxiety on hearing that Farrukhsiyar's troops were approaching the city. Instead, he passed a few hours engaged in his favourite morning activity of copying out verses of the Qur'an in his own hand, leaving a Hindu commander, Mir Bangala, to engage the enemy. Quli Khan's appearance on the battlefield in the afternoon then inspired his troops to victory: on sight of the *diwan*, 'the courage and boldness of Mir Bangala and his army increased ten-fold and hundred-fold.'[10] Mir Bangala rushed towards the enemy, killing the opposing commander, Rashid Khan, with an arrow, and a 'glorious victory' was won.[11] A minaret containing the skulls of Farrukhsiyar's slain soldiers was erected on the Bengal side of the Sakrigali pass to serve as a warning to other possible invaders from Hindustan. When, in spite of this set-back, Farrukhsiyar succeeded to the throne in Delhi, Quli Khan was in a position strong enough to pay him off. The emperor declared him not just *diwan* but nawab (ruler) of Bengal, still theoretically subordinate to the Mughal throne but effectively independent so long as the annual tribute was paid.

With independence from Delhi assured, Quli Khan turned his attention to the administration of his territories. In the Mughal agrarian system, introduced to Bengal by Akbar, three main types of land existed: *khalisas*, administered directly by the government through its revenue officers; *jagirs*, assigned to officers for the maintenance of soldiers or some other specific purpose; and *zamindaris*, on which the owner, or zamindar, paid a certain proportion of revenues to the crown.[12] Quli Khan organised a new survey of the lands in his territories, calculating precisely, plot by plot and estate by estate, what each zamindar and the peasant farmers (*raiyats*) on his estate should pay. Responsibility for the collection of annual dues was placed on zamindars, supervised by revenue officials.[13] The result of the new land assessment was a dramatic increase in the revenue return, which, coupled with customs revenues and tolls on rivers and roads, greatly increased the resources at the disposal of the Bengal state. If reports are to be believed, this achievement was accomplished without an increase in the tax burden on individual *raiyats*.[14] The two decades of Quli Khan's rule included no serious instances of famine, suggesting rising prosperity. Zamindars who had previously remained autonomous from the Mughal system, such as the rajas of Assam and Cooch Bihar, were forced to recognise the Murshidabad government's authority and submit revenues. Those who defaulted were imprisoned in the fort at Murshidabad or stripped of their land, with compliance enforced by a standing army of 2000 cavalry and 4000 infantry.[15] In this way, Quli Khan's rule over Bengal, Bihar, and Orissa was secured.

Alongside the collection of revenues, it was the administration of justice for which Quli Khan became renowned. Civil disputes were resolved according to Muslim law by a group of jurists (*qazis*) headed by Muhammad Sharif, a favourite scholar of Aurangzeb's respected for his piety and learning. Quli Khan placed himself in personal command of criminal justice. Twice each week he held sessions at court where complaints and grievances could be raised, thereby gaining a reputation for the application of justice, irrespective of wealth and power, to zamindar and peasant alike. To prevent murder and robbery in the countryside, police posts were established on important routes and one of Quli Khan's trusted enforcers, Muhammad Jan, was deputed to hunt down criminals and bring them to justice. Zamindars were charged with maintaining law and order on their estates.[16]

In his fort at Murshidabad, the Qila Nizamat, Quli Khan ordered the construction of a palace known as the Chehil Satoon, modelled on the grand audience halls found in palaces in Persia and named for its forty intricate pillars. This was deliberately conceived as a royal palace. Within it was installed a throne carved from a single slab of black marble. Ceremony and etiquette were vital to the functioning of Quli Khan's growing court. When important guests arrived, their entrance into the palace was marked by the playing of drums, trumpets, and cymbals in a specially constructed drum house (naubat khana), imitative of the one at the Red Fort in Delhi. Lesser zamindars were denied access to court audiences, while all those admitted were required to remain standing. A multitude of court servants ensured that the correct ceremonies and rituals were carried out.[17]

Quli Khan was not merely a talented administrator. From the accounts of contemporaries and the course of his actions a picture emerges of a shrewd and intelligent individual who was well educated, eloquent, physically imposing, and pious. Every morning he rose early and, after prayer and breakfast, passed the morning copying out verses of the Qur'an, which would be sent with other offerings to Mecca or an alternative holy site. In the afternoon he held audiences at court, consulted advisers, and engaged in conversations with Qur'anic scholars and learned men. According to one estimate, 2500 scholars and chanters of the Qur'an were hosted in the fort, including Shia and Sunni clerics.[18] In his lifestyle and personal spending, Quli Khan was austere. He employed no singers or dancers and showed no interest in women except his wife. For three months each year, including Ramadan, and on the twelfth and thirteenth days of each lunar month, he fasted. Beyond that, he ate simply and avoided wine. He did, however, have one major weakness: 'sweet and delicious' mangoes.[19] Revenue officers surveying lands were instructed to keep a close eye on the quality and quantity of mangoes on zamindars' estates. The best were to be sent immediately to Murshidabad at the zamindars' expense. The zamindars of those estates whose mangoes tasted the best—at Malda, Katwa, and Akbarnagar—would cut down a tree at their peril.

Important as expressions both of piety and political authority were celebrations of religious festivals and the building of mosques. As Shias, Quli Khan and his Persian relations celebrated Muhurram, while Eid and Shab-e-Barat (the night of forgiveness) were also observed. The largest festivities, however, were reserved for the birthday of the Prophet, stretching over twelve days during the third month in the Islamic calendar. Each night a feast would be organised in the Chehil Satoon and food distributed to the residents of the city. On the main route through Murshidabad, along the left bank of the Hooghly, huge lamps displaying verses of the Qur'an and pictures of important religious figures were erected. After sunset, the lamps were lit simultaneously on the firing of a gun, 'producing an illusion as if a sheet of light had been unrolled, or as if the earth had become a sky studded with stars.'[20] The lamps were so impressive that the Qur'anic verses could be read by observers watching from the opposite bank of the Hooghly.

The mosques built at Murshidabad during Quli Khan's reign combined a traditional Perso-Islamic style with elements specific to Bengal—in particular the use of brick rather than stone and the erection of covered rather than open courtyards.[21] The most striking example was the Katra Masjid, east of the Qila Nizamat, completed in 1723 on the site of a residence for travelling merchants. The mosque sits on a raised courtyard with a turret in each corner; Quli Khan was later buried under the steps leading up to the courtyard. Similar in style were the tomb of his daughter, Azimunissa, to the north of the fort, and the Begam Masjid, shared between Shias and Sunnis. Attached to the Katra Masjid was a madrasa for Islamic education focused on the Qur'an, hadith, jurisprudence, astrology, and Muslim law. The expansion of Persian learning during Quli Khan's reign is evidenced by the increasing number of Persian-language books published at Murshidabad, Patna, and Dacca.[22]

* * *

How did the predominantly non-Muslim population of Bengal respond to the transformation of the Mughal province into an independent territory under Quli Khan's command? From the beginning, Muslim rule in Bengal was dependent on the support of others. Hindu landowners participated in the administration of the Bengal Sultanate; when their support was withdrawn, the sultanate was thrown into upheaval.[23] Mughal policy was to continue the employment of Hindus in civil and military positions; indeed, among the governors of Bengal appointed by Akbar was the Raja of Amber, Man Singh I. That Aurangzeb reversed some of the policies of religious tolerance introduced to the Mughal Empire by Akbar is well known. Most infamously, he reintroduced *jizya*, a tax levied on all non-Muslims in his territories, which was collected from Hindu and European traders on the Hooghly in the early 1680s. Under Quli Khan, *jizya* was lifted, and, after control of the customs of Hooghly had been wrestled from Diya al-Din Khan—an officer directly appointed from Delhi—discrepancies in the customs levied on non-Muslim traders were removed. The records of the European trading companies show that Hindu merchants were among the richest operating on the river.[24]

In India today, a particularly toxic form of nationalist historiography depicts Muslim rulers of the subcontinent as religious zealots fired by their bigotry to repress their Hindu subjects. In this vein, several episodes have been highlighted by those seeking to demonstrate Quli Khan's animosity towards Hindus and Hindu culture. In 1713, for example, the nawab ruthlessly supressed the zamindar of Bhushna, Sitaram, whose court has subsequently been valorised as a great centre of Bengali literature and the arts.[25] He also stripped of his zamindari Udai Narayan of Rajshahi, who was defeated in battle by Muhammad Jan.[26] However, the circumstances of these depositions differ little from those of other defaulting or rebellious zamindars, whether Hindu or Muslim. Both Sitaram and Udai Narayan defied Quli Khan's authority, refusing to submit revenues, resorting to armed opposition, and making incursions into other zamindars' estates. Their suppression followed a very similar course to that of the insurgent Afghan zamindars Shujat and Najat Khan. Though Quli Khan's revenue settlement in Bengal may have displaced members of a pre-Mughal Hindu landowning elite whose position had been confirmed under Akbar, the zamindars who stepped

into their shoes were more often Hindu than Muslim. The successors to
Sitaram, Udai Narayan, Shujat Khan, and Najat Khan were all Hindu.[27]

A further case is that of Darpa Narayan, a prominent Hindu official
in the Murshidabad court responsible for scrutinising revenue collection. Towards the end of Quli Khan's reign, Darpa Narayan was
arrested and killed—proof, some might suggest, of Quli Khan's consistent antipathy towards Hindus. During an earlier part of his rule,
however, Darpa Narayan had flourished not just as a government official but also as the holder of a zamindari in Malda. His execution followed an attempt by him to extort 300,000 rupees from Quli Khan,
demanded as payment before he would sign off the revenues to be
remitted to Delhi.[28] Of course, the reign of Quli Khan was arbitrary
and often bloody, involving the violent suppression of criminals and
political opponents. This, however, was directed as much against
Muslims as Hindus. On one occasion, Quli Khan intervened personally
to try to prevent the execution of a Hindu villager accused of mistreating a Muslim fakir.[29]

Any number of examples might be produced to demonstrate the
employment of Hindu elites in the revenue and executive branches of
Quli Khan's administration. Below the most senior positions, Hindus
were the majority. They included Lahori Mull, a high-ranking revenue
official; and Raghunandan, for some time head of the Murshidabad
mint. Several of Quli Khan's close advisers were Hindu, including
Kishen Ray, one of his private secretaries. By far the most remarkable
incidence of the flourishing of non-Muslims under Quli Khan, however, is the story of the Jagat Seths, a family of Jain Rajput merchants
belonging to a caste of jewellers.[30] The Jagat Seth family had become
wealthy when one of their number, Hiranand Galera, flourished as a
banker and saltpetre merchant at Patna. His son, Manikchand, was sent
to oversee the family business at Dacca, where he became acquainted
with Quli Khan when the latter was first sent to Bengal. According to
the family history, Manikchand was influential in convincing Quli Khan
to move the *diwani* from Dacca to Murshidabad in 1703, rationalised as
a measure to increase revenue collection and consolidate his rule. At
Murshidabad, Manikchand was appointed deputy *diwan*, with authority
over the state treasury and mint. He oversaw the annual transfer of
revenue to Delhi and acted as Quli Khan's personal banker.

When Manikchand died he was succeeded by his nephew Fatechand, under whom the power of the Jagat Seths reached its peak. The Jagat Seth bank financed not only the Mughal aristocracy but the imperial court at Delhi as well. When drought struck northern India in 1715, causing widespread crop failure, fiscal disaster was averted through the bank's distribution of loans to farmers, secured against their land. Fatechand's monopoly on the minting of coins at Murshidabad allowed him to manipulate the price of bullion and trade old currency for new, reaping huge profits for loan to Quli Khan and nobles at his court. Little wonder that he became the richest merchant in Bengal, protected by a personal guard of 2000. Fatechand was awarded the title Jagat Seth—'banker to the world'—in 1723.[31] In addition to an imposing mansion, constructed in the north Murshidabad suburb of Nashipur, he left his mark on the city by patronising a set of Jain temples that remain pilgrimage centres today.[32]

Notwithstanding his personal devoutness, enthusiastic endowment of mosques, and support of Islamic learning, Quli Khan also articulated his political authority in ways reflecting the heterogeneity of the population under his rule and the strong Hindu representation in his government. The completion of the collection of revenue was marked each year by an elaborate ceremony known as *punya*, inherited from the earliest Hindu kings of Bengal. The highest award of recognition granted to state officers bore the distinctly Bengali emblem of a fish.[33] A particularly revealing insight into the extent to which Hindu authorities accepted Quli Khan as head of state, and even as a spiritual leader, is found in the appeal of a group of Vaishnava pandits from Nabadwip for his judgment in a dispute with their counterparts in Rajasthan over the doctrine of *parakiya*. According to this doctrine, divine love can only be understood through analogy with a particular form of human love—that which precedes marriage and therefore defies social convention.[34] Quli Khan resolved in support of the Nabadwip scholars, who favoured *parakiya*, disappointing those pandits who had travelled all the way from Jaipur and Benares to hear his answer.

* * *

Murshid Quli Khan died in 1727, well into his sixties. He had achieved a remarkable amount, rising from slave to government officer and ending as the undisputed autonomous ruler of Bengal. After him, the position of nawab was hereditary. Only after succession had been secured on the ground was the symbolic confirmation of the Mughal emperor sought. Quli Khan had no male heirs. However, his only daughter Azimunissa, who had married a native of the Deccan, Shuja-ud-din Muhammad Khan, had a male child named Mirza Asad Allah. This child, Quli Khan's grandson, had been raised at the Qila Nizamat in Murshidabad as his heir. In the years before his death, Quli Khan attempted to strengthen the position of Mirza Asad Allah at court, granting him a zamindari, awarding him the title Sarfaraz Khan, and appointing him *diwan* of Bengal.[35] When Quli Khan lay dying, however, the heir apparent's father Shuja-ud-din acted quickly to seize the throne from his son. Informed that Quli Khan had just five or six days to live, he marched to Murshidabad from Cuttack, where he was serving as deputy governor of Orissa, and arrived at just the right moment to announce his succession. Sarfaraz meanwhile decided to heed the advice of his grandmother, Quli Khan's widow, who suggested he wait until his own ageing father had died before ascending the throne: 'Your father is old; after him, the Subahdari as well as the country with its treasures will devolve on you. To fight against one's own father, is cause of loss both in this world and the next, as well as of ignominy.'[36]

The reign of Shuja-ud-din—which in fact lasted twelve years—was one of growing wealth at Murshidabad and the development of the capital into a city fit for a king. The business of government was entrusted to a small council headed by the Jain banker Fatechand, allowing the nawab to indulge in more pleasurable pastimes. Religious scholars and readers of the Qur'an who had been patronised in the court of Quli Khan were retained, but joined by singers and musicians. The buildings of the Qila Nizamat were dismantled and newer, grander ones built in their place: a palace in which the nawab could live in 'magnificent splendour'; a public audience hall; a revenue house and court; and a gateway through which he could 'ride out in right regal state'.[37] Every guest to Murshidabad with 'the air and language of a gentleman' was hosted generously at court; Shuja-ud-din kept a list of all his acquaintances in an ivory-leaf notebook and bestowed gifts on a selected few each evening before bed.[38] 'The kingdom of Bengal, which in books is called the terrestrial paradise,' wrote one Indo-Persian historian later in the century, 'came to enjoy so much prosperity, as to exhibit everywhere an air of plenty and happiness quite analogous to the title it bore.'[39] The crowning glory of Shuja-ud-din's beautification of Murshidabad was the construction on the right bank of the Hooghly, facing the royal fort, of a new palace and mosque called Dahapara, set in a garden of reservoirs, canals, and fountains compared flatteringly with the famous Mughal gardens of Kashmir. Here the nawab regularly entertained guests and held state banquets, until the report reached him that 'owing to the superb charmfulness of that garden, Fairies used to come down there for picnics and walks, and to bathe in its tanks.'[40] On hearing this news, Shuja-ud-din ordered that the tanks be filled with earth and the parties stopped. Fairies, even picnicking ones, could not be countenanced.

When Shuja-ud-din died in March 1739 his son finally succeeded to the throne. Sarfaraz's reign, however, lasted just one year, for he was deposed by a usurper known as Alivardi Khan. A native of the Deccan, Alivardi and his elder brother Mirza Ahmad had acquired reputations as talented soldiers and administrators while serving under Shuja-ud-din in Orissa. On Shuja-ud-din's ascension to the Murshidabad throne, Alivardi had been appointed judge of Rajmahal and, shortly after, deputy governor of Bihar. At Patna, he added to his natural intelligence and charms a talent for efficient and occasionally ruthless government, becoming notorious for his uncompromising repression of unruly zamindars and military officials.[41] The deputy governorship of Bihar was perfect preparation for a bid on the throne of Bengal, Bihar, and Orissa.

The plot to depose Sarfaraz and install Alivardi in his place was led by Mirza Ahmad, Fatechand, and Rayrayan Alamchand—the last being the *diwan* of Bengal under Shuja-ud-din. With the imperial court at Delhi in turmoil following the invasion by the Persian Nadir Shah, the trio persuaded Sarfaraz to mint coins in Nadir Shah's name and have him declared emperor during the Friday sermon in Bengal's mosques. Concurrently, they arranged for Alivardi to send gifts and money to the ailing emperor, Muhammad Shah, who announced in return that Alivardi was the rightful nawab of Bengal.[42] Why exactly Fatechand and Alamchand withdrew their support from Sarfaraz and schemed for his replacement is a matter of conjecture. Some have painted a picture of an incompetent ruler more interested in devotional religious practices than the affairs of state. Another story has it that Sarfaraz lost the indispensable backing of Fatechand when he insisted on seeing the wife of the banker's second son without a veil, a grave breach of decorum at court.[43]

Initially reluctant, Alivardi was persuaded to seize the throne when the backing of Muhammad Shah was received. In April 1740, on a day determined auspicious by his astrologers, he assembled his troops on the outskirts of Patna and convened a meeting of the generals. Each of them was made to swear an oath of loyalty to Alivardi—the Muslims while holding the Qur'an and the Hindus while drinking from a jug of Ganges water—and the plan to depose Sarfaraz was revealed.[44] By the time Sarfaraz became aware of Alivardi's intentions, the latter's army had marched from Patna along the Ganges and through the Rajmahal hills into Bengal. Mirza Ahmad had escaped from Murshidabad to join his brother, while Fatechand and Alamchand waited in the city, feigning ignorance of events to come. On 6 April, Sarfaraz set out from the capital at the head of an army of 4000 cavalry and a large infantry body. At Geria, a village on the Hooghly twenty-two miles north of Murshidabad, the two forces camped facing each other on opposite banks of the river. At dawn the following day, the battle commenced. Alivardi divided his forces into three. By crossing the river on a bridge of boats, one third of his army was able to surprise Sarfaraz from the rear while the rest approached the nawab front-on. Aware that he was surrounded, Sarfaraz mounted an elephant and, with the Qur'an in one hand, rode in the direction of Alivardi. He was killed by a musket shot, possibly fired by a traitor in his own camp, 'and the bird of his soul flew to heaven'.[45]

After the battle, Mirza Ahmad returned to Murshidabad to announce the death of Sarfaraz and the ascension of Alivardi. The city was thrown into a 'general and deep convulsion'.[46] To curb disorder, Mirza Ahmad installed troops in the palace and other important buildings and promised a pardon to all those soldiers and officers who had served under the deceased nawab. Three days later, Alivardi entered the city in a triumphant procession. On arrival at the Qila Nizamat, his first act was to visit Sarfaraz's mother, Nafisa Begam, to request forgiveness for what he had done. He then proceeded to the Chehil Satoon and formally ascended the throne to the sound of ceremonial drums. The dynasty of Murshid Quli Khan was at an end and a new one—the Afshars—had begun.

* * *

In the early months of his rule, Alivardi followed the time-honoured strategy of appointing relatives to key positions in state: his son-in-law, Nevazish Muhammad Khan, was made *diwan* of Bengal; his nephews, Salat Jang and Zainuddin, deputy governors of Orissa and Bihar, respectively.[47] This, however, was only the beginning of his struggles to have his authority recognised throughout Bengal, Bihar, and Orissa. In 1741 he was forced into a major military campaign to defeat the forces of Rustam Jang, deputy governor of Orissa under Sarfaraz. The following year, just as peace beckoned, the Marathas invaded Bengal.

A Hindu warrior group from the western Deccan, the Marathas had risen to prominence in the mid-seventeenth century under the leadership of Shivaji Bhonsle, who led his people in prolonged guerrilla wars against the Mughal Empire and other dynasties.[48] In the 1670s Shivaji established a Maratha territory near the Western Ghats, in present-day Maharashtra, which expanded strikingly as the Mughal Empire shrank. During the reign of Shivaji's grandson Shahuji, an army of Marathas marched as far as Delhi, securing a treaty in 1714 recognising their state and guaranteeing it a portion of the revenues collected from Mughal territories in Gujarat, Malwa, and the Deccan. In the 1720s and 1730s, under a succession of hereditary ministers known as *peshwas*, the Marathas expanded their control over large portions of Central India and plundered Delhi again in 1737, as Muhammad Shah watched helplessly from the Red Fort. In conquered territories, the rulers installed were obliged to pay *chauth*, a tax of 25 per cent on produce and revenue, to the Maratha capital at Pune.

Raghuji Bhonsle, chief of the Maratha province of Nagpur, was the most powerful of these rulers. In 1742 he resolved to invade Orissa and Bengal with the object of incorporating them into the Maratha dominions.[49] His prime minster, Bhaskar Ram, was deputed to the task and set out for Orissa with an army of twenty-three commanders and 20,000 cavalry. Easily overrunning the Orissan court at Cuttack, he continued to Burdwan, on the Damodar river, less than a hundred miles from Murshidabad. Here the first engagement between the Marathas and Alivardi's troops took place. As Alivardi camped on an embankment on the outskirts of the city, with an army of just 3000 cavalry and 5000 infantry, he was surrounded at night. Skirmishes followed in which the horses and elephants of the nawab's army were captured and its food supplies cut off. The situation was desperate: with his soldiery dwindling and hungry, Alivardi had no choice but to retreat from Burdwan to Katwa, where the Ajay and Hooghly rivers meet, with the Marathas in pursuit.[50]

At this juncture it dawned on the pursuing Maratha commanders that Murshidabad was undefended. If a force were sent at high speed it could arrive at the city before the nawab's troops and sack it. On the morning of 6 May 1742, 700 Maratha horsemen arrived in the suburbs of Murshidabad on the Hooghly's right bank. The bazaar of Dahapara was burnt to the ground, the river crossed, the city entered. Its wealthiest quarters were pillaged, the inhabitants fleeing as the Marathas 'swept clean the houses of numerous residents with the broom of plunder.'[51] Fatechand's mansion was robbed of 300,000 rupees in gold and silver. Carrying their booty, the Marathas quit Murshidabad and retreated towards Katwa, avoiding Alivardi and his army, which arrived back at the capital the following day.

In the summer of 1742, Maratha authority was established over large parts of western Bengal. Around Katwa, taxes were collected from the local zamindars; incursions were made into Midnapore, Burdwan, Birbhum, and Rajmahal, and, particularly troublesome for Alivardi, Hooghly was occupied with a Maratha governor installed to collect the port's customs duties. The Hooghly River served as a natural boundary beyond which Maratha forces strayed only once, before an English East India Company warship scared them off. Alivardi's territory was reduced to the eastern side of the river and a small pocket on the west, opposite Murshidabad. The rainy season provided a break in hostilities during which the nawab's army was able to rest and regroup. Money was found to pay troops, the artillery was expanded, boats purchased from Dacca, and soldiers transferred to Murshidabad from Patna.

With the arrival of these reinforcements, Alivardi resolved to launch a surprise attack on the Marathas before the rains came to an end,

From Murshidabad, his army marched southward to a spot on the left bank of the Hooghly, opposite the Maratha force, which was found camped near Katwa on a piece of land formed by a loop of the Ajay River just before it entered the Hooghly.

For eight days the opposing armies cannonaded each other across the water. Before dawn on day nine, a bridge of boats was assembled on the Hooghly and the nawab's army crossed. The bridge was then dismantled and the boats floated downstream into the Ajay, where the bridge was reassembled. Alivardi's plan appeared in jeopardy when this second bridge of boats capsized as his army was crossing it, casting 1500 troops into the river. However, the remaining 3000 made it safely across, and now stood just a mile from the Maratha camp, on the same patch of land. The Marathas were encircled by the Hooghly to the east, the Ajay to the north and west, and the nawab's forces to the south. A rout ensued, in which the fleeing Maratha soldiers were hunted down and killed.[52] A turning point in the first Maratha invasion of Bengal, the massacre was not, however, the end of the Maratha threat to Alivardi and his subjects. The following spring, Bhaskar Ram, the Maratha prime minister and commander, was back with his army, this time accompanied by Raghuji Bhonsle, the chief of Nagpur. For the next eight years, Maratha forces raided Bengal, extorting zamindars and pilfering pockets of land, repeatedly defying Alivardi's efforts to vanquish them.

Like the rule of the nawabs of Bengal, the rise of the Marathas has been reinterpreted in recent years through a communalist lens, another episode in the supposed interminable conflict between Muslims and Hindus. Right-wing Hindu nationalists depict the Maratha ascendancy as a religious response to Muslim domination of the subcontinent, elevating Shivaji, the first Maratha ruler, to the status of a crusader fighting to establish Hindu self-rule.[53] Shivaji's eldest son, Sambhaji, who was captured and killed by Aurangzeb, is widely celebrated as a Hindu martyr. Such narratives can only be sustained if historical fact is forgotten or wilfully ignored. Despite modern reinterpretations, Shivaji and his successors did not view their military campaigns as religious wars. In Bengal, the conflict between the Marathas and Alivardi Khan was anything but Hindu versus Muslim.

For one, the civil and military branches of the nawab's government contained, as already noted, a large number of Hindus; Hindu commanders such as Raja Jankiram, a chief minister in Alivardi's court, fought against the Maratha invader.[54] The Maratha force, moreover, contained a number of Muslim generals; some felt no difficulty switching from one side to the other, as the case of Mir Habib confirms. During the retreat from Katwa in 1742, Mir Habib, a resident of Murshidabad hailing from Shiraz and a commander in Alivardi's army, was captured by Bhaskar Ram's troops. Instead of suffering at the hands of his captors, he immediately switched sides and headed the unit of Maratha cavalrymen that sacked Murshidabad in April that year. Some contemporaries were convinced that the first Maratha invasion of Bengal had been encouraged by relatives of Sarfaraz Khan, the deposed nawab, who had taken refuge in the Deccan after Alivardi's seizure of power. Though this claim cannot be proven, it is clear that for the protagonists the Maratha–nawab wars were principally about power, wealth, and dynastic struggle rather than religion, as subsequent events confirm.

The second Maratha invasion of Bengal began in early 1743. Instead of sending his army to fight Raghuji Bhonsle's forces, Alivardi enlisted the support of Balaji Bajirao, a *peshwa* in the Maratha Empire. For the past three years, Raghuji and Balaji had been bitter rivals for supremacy among the Marathas. By promising Balaji a portion of the revenues of Bihar, Alivardi was able to set the two Maratha leaders against each other. This strategy was not without its drawbacks; instead of one Maratha army ravaging the land there were now two. By joining forces with Balaji near Birbhum, however, Alivardi was able by the close of the year to defeat Raghuji and force his army out of Bengal for a second time.[55]

The Afghan general Mustafa Khan had served Alivardi faithfully during the first two Maratha wars, commanding a body of Afghan troops that had been influential in Alivardi's victory at Katwa in 1742. During the third Maratha invasion, in 1744, Mustafa devised and carried out a plan to lure Bhaskar Ram into Alivardi's camp on the pretence of negotiating peace, before hacking the Maratha general and his commanders to death. However, a split then opened up between Mustafa and Alivardi, reportedly because the nawab reneged on his promise to grant the Afghan the deputy governorship of Bihar in reward for the assassination.[56] Mustafa launched a rebellion. Gathering 8000 Afghan troops, he considered seizing Murshidabad before quitting the city and marching to Patna. Warned of Mustafa's approach, the deputy governor of Bihar, Alivardi's nephew Zainuddin, assembled an army of 15,000 and defeated Mustafa's force near the town of Arrah, south of Patna, in June 1745. Mustafa's body was carried back to Patna, cut in half and suspended from two of the city's gates.

While the nawab's troops were engaged in defeating Mustafa, Raghuji Bhonsle's Maratha army invaded Bengal for a fourth time. From Orissa, they reached the outskirts of Murshidabad, destroying the settlements on the left bank of the Hooghly once again. For Alivardi the situation was grave. After the death of Mustafa, there existed in Bengal and Bihar a huge number of armed Afghan soldiers who owed no loyalty to Alivardi and had no qualms about siding with the Marathas to defeat him: 3000 of them took control of Patna, murdering Zainuddin and torturing Mirza Ahmad to death.[57] The loss of Patna, the return of the Marathas, and the deaths of his nephew and brother amounted to a personal and political crisis for Alivardi. This should not, however, be considered a Hindu retaliation against Muslim rule. In April 1748 Afghan and Maratha troops, the former predominantly Muslim and the latter predominantly Hindu, fought alongside each other at Ranisarai on the Ganges, east of Patna, in a showdown against the forces of the nawab involving as many as 80,000 men. Alivardi's key commander was a Hindu, Raja Jankiram, and the leader of half of the Maratha forces was a Muslim, Mir Habib.

The suffering caused by nine years of warfare between the Marathas and Alivardi's government affected Hindu and Muslim indiscriminately. In one of his best-known poems, the Bengali writer Gangarama describes the population of a small town responding to news that the Maratha army is approaching: pandits flee in terror with their books under their arms; Rajputs are so frightened that they forget to pick up their swords before they bolt; Hindu shopkeepers abandon their stores; and higher-caste women who have never set foot in public desert their homes with bags on their heads.[58] Residents of Murshidabad also fled for cities further east. The human cost of the conflict is evocatively summarised by one Persian historian: 'When the stores and granaries were exhausted, and the supply of imported grains was also completely cut off, to avert death by starvation, human beings ate plantain-roots, whilst animals were fed on the leaves of trees. Even these gradually ceased to be available. For breakfasts and suppers, nothing except the discs of the sun and the moon feasted their eyes.'[59]

* * *

By 1751, Alivardi's army and the Marathas were exhausted by almost a decade of military campaigns. Large parts of western and southern Bengal had been devastated. The nawab's lieutenant, Mir Jafar, travelled to the Maratha court at Nagpur to sign a treaty surrendering Orissa to Mir Habib but securing peace at last. Alivardi could finally retire to the comforts and pleasures of his capital. In the Qila Nizamat he passed his time listening to the conversations of religious scholars, to storytellers, and to recitations of poetry—or in the company of his wife Sarfunnissa Begam, who had been influential at court while he was away. Alivardi loved food and took great interest in the recipes prepared by the chefs he imported especially from Persia; he was also fascinated by animals and collected a menagerie of horses, dogs, and cats in the fort. In his final years, the nawab left Murshidabad only for an annual hunting expedition in the Rajmahal hills.[60]

The nawab's court developed into a renowned centre of learning in the Muslim world. Venerated scholars attracted by Alivardi's patronage included the Persian philosopher Muhammad Ali Tajrid, the physician Hakim Taj al-Din, and the revered scholar Muzaffar Ali Khan who turned down the post of *wazir* at the imperial court in Delhi to travel to Bengal.[61] In Murshidabad, writers of Persian poetry and historical works flourished and some of the first Urdu literature on the subcontinent was produced. Alivardi's friend Mir Bakhar composed an affectionate set of Urdu verses (ghazals).

Court painting flourished too. The earliest portrait of one of the nawabs dates to 1720 and depicts Quli Khan holding court on a terrace with his grandson Sarfaraz at his side. In the background is the Hooghly at night, with barges floating past and fireworks illuminating the sky. In its formality and understated colours, the painting is very similar to the court style at Delhi during the latter part of Aurangzeb's reign. By the time of Alivardi's rule, however, a distinctive Murshidabad style had emerged, more opulent and colourful and increasingly influenced by European painting techniques.[62] One striking painting from the early

1750s depicts Alivardi hunting on horseback, a spear in his right hand, pursuing a roebuck fleeing into the water. Its eye-level perspective marks a departure from the Indian miniature tradition in the direction of European landscape painting. While almost all Murshidabad painting during the first half of the eighteenth century depicted aspects of the life of the nawabs, the final years of Alivardi's reign saw a diversification of subject matter to include festivals at Murshidabad and scenes from the Hindu epics.[63] The most prominent painters at Alivardi's court, such as Dip Chand, were Hindu.

The countryside of Bengal recovered from the ravages of war. On zamindars' estates, agriculture and manufacturing revived: silk, cotton, jute, sugar, and opium were produced alongside less valuable food-stuffs. Wealthier zamindars, including Raja Ramakanta of Rajshahi and Maharaja Krishnachandra of Nadia, established courts that rivalled Murshidabad for splendour. They constructed temples, built schools, and patronised Bengali and Sanskrit authors. Maharaja Krishnachandra hosted the writer Bharatchandra, whose *Annada Mangal*, a eulogy to the Hindu goddess Annapurna, is the most famous Bengali narrative poem of the period. According to Bharatchandra, the maharaja was so rich that he spent 100,000 rupees on the marriage of a monkey.[64]

Examples of what today is considered Hindu–Muslim syncretism were so widespread as to be unremarkable. At an elite level, Hindus learnt Persian and Muslims Bengali; many words passed from Persian into the Bengali vocabulary, and works of literature and history were translated from one language to the other. In dress and manners Hindu and Muslim elites in government service were almost indistinguish-able. It is known that some Brahmins wishing for divine protection consulted the Qur'an before setting out on journeys, while Vaishnava and orthodox Hindu notions entered Muslim thought.[65] At Murshidabad, the Persian poetry of Sayyid Murtaza was heavily influ-enced by Hindu mystical and yogic ideas. The greatest sharing of Hindu and Muslim beliefs and practices at a popular level took place through the influence of Muslim mystics who had first settled in Bengal in the thirteenth century. Members of Sufi orders such as the Chishtis, Madaris, Qalandars, and Naqshbandis made the Murshidabad area their home, propagating ideas of world-rejection and the cult of saints, often with the encouragement of the ruling power.[66] Some Sufi leaders emphasised the distinctiveness of Islam compared to Brahman and Vaishnava religions, but others integrated elements of Bengali esoteric practices and cosmologies into their religious worldviews.[67] As a result, Hindus revered Muslim saints and offered *puja* at their shrines. Muslims in turn prayed at Hindu temples and celebrated Hindu festivals. In Bengali folk literature and tradition, the cult of the *satya-pir* developed—a spiritual leader endowed with supernatural powers, deified by both Muslims and Hindus. Adherents of both religions considered the water of the Hooghly sacred.[68]

The question of why an overwhelmingly Muslim population developed in the rural areas east of the Hooghly during the course of the eighteenth century is contentious. While Bengal under the nawabs attracted Muslim migrants to its towns and cities from northern India and further afield, migration cannot account for the emergence of a Muslim peasantry in the east. A popular cliché has it that Islam was spread by the sword, with Muslim rulers forcing conversion on their helpless Hindu subjects. However, the nawabs of Bengal showed very little interest in the spread of Islam in their territories. An agrarian Muslim population developed in remote rural areas far removed from Murshidabad and other centres of power.[69]

A counter-narrative attractive to Muslims today is that Islam, with its egalitarian theology, was a source of social liberation for lower-caste Hindus, who converted voluntarily to escape the rigid hierarchies of the Hindu social order. Putting to one side the fact that in the eighteenth century Indian Islam was hardly ever articulated in egalitarian terms, geography runs counter to this explanation too. A Muslim peasantry developed east of the Hooghly in deltaic areas where Brahmanist religion had made very few inroads and no caste system existed. West of the Hooghly, where Brahmanism had flourished from the third century B.C., very few Hindu peasants became Muslim.[70]

As Richard Eaton has shown, the emergence of a Muslim peasantry east of the Hooghly can only be explained if the concept of 'conversion'—implying as it does an abrupt and absolute change in religious affiliation—is abandoned.[71] The peasantry of deltaic Bengal became Muslim through a gradual process of the admittance of Allah, Muhammad, and other venerated Islamic characters into local Bengali cosmologies alongside other superhuman agencies. Over time,

Muslim figures became identified with local divinities and slowly eclipsed them to create worldviews more recognisably Islamic.[72] This process is captured in Bengali literature invoking folk and Muslim deities and identifying them as one and the same before later elevating the latter. The support offered by the nawabs of Bengal to Sufi religious orders indirectly facilitated this change; Sufi holy men (*pirs*) moving through the Bengal delta introduced the Islamic characters and ideas that would gradually incorporate and supplant local deities.[73] Islamisation, however, was a long-term process without conscious state design. Well into the nineteenth century, when the arrival of print technology spurred the rationalisation of religion and fixing of religious identities as definite, immutable categories, local cosmologies existed alongside Islamic precepts.[74]

Murshidabad in 1755 was a city at its peak. At its heart, the Qila Nizamat stood as an imposing edifice dominated by the Chehil Satoon. South-east of the fort, the Motijhil palace stood on the edge of a pearl-shaped lake, its grandeur amazing visitors. Nearby was the palace of Sarfaraz Khan, where his body had been returned and buried after the battle of Geria, and a grand but unfinished mosque, the construction interrupted by his death. North of the fort were the neighbourhoods of Mahimpur and Nashipur, the latter containing the house of the Jagat Seths. To the east was the Katra Masjid of Quli Khan, and west, on the opposite bank of the river, the palace, mosque, and enchanted gardens of Shuja-ud-din. Further afield, seven kilometres downstream on the Hooghly, were the European trading posts at Cossimbazaar. The villages of Jiaganj and Azimganj, centres for the production of cotton and silk, lay a similar distance upstream.[75]

The city's population was an impressive 700,000.[76] At the top of the social tree were the zamindars and high government officials, wealthy bankers, and merchants. They included Persians, Afghans, Arabs, Turks, Hindustanis, Bengalis and Deccanis, Hindu and Muslim, Sunni and Shia. Below them were lower-ranking government officials, soldiers, and religious clerics, plus a multitude of occupational groups, some predominantly Muslim or Hindu, their names revealing the diversity of the city's manufacturing and trade. Distinctly Muslim occupations included weaving, fishmongering, livestock herding, and tailoring. Hindu caste groups worked as craftsmen, potters, jewellers, woodcutters, and boatmen. All would come together for festivals such as Holi, Diwali, and Muharram.

The annual event that perhaps best captured the spirit of Murshidabad at the end of Alivardi's reign was the festival of Khwaja Khizr, an Islamic mystical figure who in Bengal was revered both by Muslims and Hindus as a saint of the waters. Often depicted in green, riding on a fish, Khizr was believed to preside over the well of immortality and for some Hindus represented an incarnation of Vishnu. The Khwaja Khizr festival was celebrated spectacularly at Murshidabad. Thousands of tiny ships made of plantain or bamboo were floated on the Hooghly after dark, carrying sweetmeats and a lamp. Illuminating the river, they floated downstream towards the nawab's palace. Fireworks were discharged from a raft in the middle of the Hooghly, their reflection in the water dazzling onlookers, while boats took part in a musical procession towards the fort.[77] A veneration of Khizr, the festival was also an exuberant celebration of the river.

When an English officer, Robert Clive, visited Murshidabad shortly after Alivardi's death in April 1756, he found a city 'as extensive, populous, and rich as the city of London, with this difference, that there are individuals in the first possessing infinitely greater property than in the last.'[78] This recognition of the wealth of Murshidabad was the beginning of the city's end. Within fifteen years its political authority would be stripped, its economy undermined, its population decimated, and its cultural heart ripped out.

3

PLASSEY

THE ENGLISH EAST INDIA COMPANY'S ASCENT

Thirty miles south of Murshidabad, as you travel downriver, the Hooghly sweeps around to the right and then immediately to the left, forming a 'S' in the landscape. Today, the fields are green but austere. On the river's left bank, nothing remains of the mango grove—the Laksha Bagh (or Garden of a Hundred Thousand Trees)—mentioned in English imperial histories. There is no longer any trace of the trees with bright orange flowers, the palash, that gave the nearby village, Palashi, or Plassey, its name. In the history books, Plassey is remembered chiefly as a battle rather than a place. Here, in the summer of 1757, Siraj-ud-Daula, nawab of Bengal, was defeated by the English East India Company in an encounter marking the end of the independent authority of the nawabs and the rise of the English in their place. In truth, however, Plassey was not much of a battle at all. Less than a quarter of the troops that Siraj-ud-Daula had stationed at Plassey fought on his behalf. The English 'victory' was attained not primarily through military engagement but by the efforts of William Watts, representative of the Company at Siraj's court, who had convinced the nawab's commander, Mir Jafar, and other leading generals to switch sides.

In the nineteenth century, as Victorian imperialists reflected on the origins of British rule in India, the history of events at Plassey was rewritten. Plassey was removed from the realm of fact into fiction and celebrated as the moment when the moral, intellectual, and technological superiority of England over India was confirmed and the imperial task of raising the subcontinent from degradation to civilisation began.[1] From our contemporary vantage point, a different understanding of the meaning of Plassey stands out. Rather than a battle, Plassey should above all be considered a metaphor for the transplanting of competition between European powers onto the extra-European stage; for the ruthless pursuit of profit and enforcement of monopoly by European trading companies; and for the accrual of European wealth at the expense of the non-European world. Plassey represents empire at its ugliest: the over-extension and abuse of corporate power in the pursuit of wealth; the cynical politics, deception, and naked aggression involved in the transformation of a trading company into a territorial state—and the devastating consequences that followed.

* * *

The English East India Company was founded in 1600 in response to the petitioning of Queen Elizabeth I by a body of London merchants. Its royal charter granted a monopoly on trade to the East Indies, roughly defined as everything east of the Cape of Good Hope. A first voyage to the Indian Ocean set out in February 1601, calling at Madagascar, the Nicobar Islands, Aceh, and Bantam before returning to England two and a half years later without the loss of a single ship. Over the next two decades, trading links were established with Java, the Spice Islands, Siam, Cambodia, and Japan, and the import of pepper and other spices to English markets began. The earliest Company merchants showed little interest in the trading possibilities of India. Their attempts to exchange English woollen cloth for spices in South East Asia met with little success, however; the only textiles accepted by spice traders were Indian. To sustain the import of spices to Europe it was essential that a market for selling English cloth and buying Indian silk and cotton be found.[2]

With this object in mind, the fleet of the third Company voyage to the East Indies was instructed to investigate the trading possibilities of the Arabian Sea en route to islands further east. Under the command of William Hawkins, one ship separated from the fleet and headed for the port of Surat on the north-west coast of India. The largest port of the Mughal Empire, Surat was found to be rich in cottons and calicoes. Spotting an opportunity, Hawkins left his vessel behind and travelled overland to Jahangir's court at Agra to secure permission for trade. The establishment of a Company trading post, or 'factory', at Surat was followed by a second at Masulipatam, halfway up the east coast of India, four years on. A third came soon after at Pulicat, not far from the Portuguese fort of San Thomé, adjacent to which, on the site of a small fishing village, the Company would construct Fort St George and found the city of Madras. At each of these trading stations, the best cottons and silks were discovered to originate in Bengal. The idea of trading directly with the province was first mooted in 1616, with the enthusiastic backing of Thomas Roe, English diplomat and scholar, who had been sent as the ambassador of James I to Emperor Jahangir.[3]

The first visit of an Englishman to Bengal actually preceded the foundation of the East India Company by fifteen years. In 1585 gentle-man-merchant Ralph Fitch journeyed through Aleppo, Baghdad, and Ormuz—where he was detained by the Portuguese as a spy—to India, stopping at Fatehpur Sikri before joining a convoy down the Yamuna and the Ganges to Hooghly. In 1618, two representatives of the Company were then sent to investigate the possibilities of the Bengal trade. Robert Hughes and John Parker stayed at Patna for three years, sending samples of Bengali silk to the English deputations at Agra and Surat and arguing the viability of trade with Bengal, until the Company's directors vetoed the plan.[4] Their interest was revived in the early 1630s when widespread famine in north-west and central India forced a redirection of attention to trade on the eastern coast. Scarcities of food made dealing in Bengali sugar, rice, and butter poten-tially lucrative. Moreover, the supply of silk and cotton from Bengal to Surat and Masulipatam had all but dried up.

Fearful of the great Mughal, who had just recently expelled the Portuguese from Hooghly, a party of eight Englishmen sailed from Masulipatam to the upper reaches of the Bay of Bengal in March 1633. On reaching the mouth of the river Patali, they exchanged their seafar-ing vessel for a smaller one and ventured upstream to the court of the Mughal governor, Aga Muhammad Zaman, at Cuttack; the governor granted the party permission to establish a factory on the Orissan coast at Haripur, from where access to Bengali markets would be attained.[5] The Haripur factory was in large part a disaster. Within a year, five of the six English factors stationed in this malarial spot were dead; Arakanese pirates captured a boat carrying replacements, killing some and taking the rest prisoner. However, the efforts of the Company at Haripur were not entirely in vain: the profitability of trade with Bengal was confirmed and the consent of Emperor Shah Jahan for English mercantile activity secured.

Under the terms of Shah Jahan's imperial decree (*firman*), large English ships were prohibited from sailing upriver from the coast of Bengal or Orissa. The Company satisfied itself by relocating from Haripur to Balasore, next to the mouth of the Hooghly—a more convenient base for accessing Bengali markets. From the Balasore factory, light English vessels set off on expeditions up the Hooghly estuary. In 1651 they made it to Hooghly, where an English post was established. Others followed at Cossimbazaar, Malda, Patna, and Dacca with the encouragement of the Company's authorities in London: 'Whereas it is the designe of our Masters of the honourable Company to advance and increase the trade in these parts of Orexea [Orissa] and Bengal, you are by all possible means to endeavour more and more to informe yourselves how best and most profitably to carry out the trade thereof.'[6]

During the course of the 1650s, regular trading patterns were established. At Hooghly the English procured saltpetre—shipped downriver from Patna by Indian merchants and agents of the Company—along with sugar and other foodstuffs. At Cossimbazaar they invested in silk and cloth. Loaded onto light single-mast sloops, these goods were carried to Balasore, transferred to bigger vessels, and exported further afield. Saltpetre was taken back to England for use in the manufacture of gunpowder; sugar was also sent home to meet the demand of changing domestic tastes, or sold in the Persian Gulf. In England, Bengali silk was considered inferior to French and Italian. However, it was also much cheaper and became popular among a wider section of the English populace. When the import of French products to England was banned in 1678, the demand for Bengali silk received a boost. To pay for its Bengal purchases, the Company imported woollen cloth and broadcloth, lead, copper, iron, firearms, and other goods, but these never equalled the amount it spent. The balance, which could amount to more than three-quarters of annual totals, was paid in bullion.[7]

In 1669 Shah Jahan conceded the right of the English to bring larger seafaring vessels up the Hooghly. The necessity of loading and unloading ships at Balasore, a time-consuming and costly process (on account of the commission taken by Mughal officials), was removed. However, a major obstacle to efficient trade remained: navigation of the river. In the absence of accurate charts, the Hooghly was considered too dangerous and capricious to be negotiated by large boats. In spite of a financial incentive—the Company's directors promised an additional ten shillings per tonne for goods conveyed 'within the bar of the Ganges'—English captains refused to take the risk.[8] The Company therefore commissioned the building of a ship, the *Diligence*, specifically to survey the river; six men trained in the techniques of river charting—taking soundings, recording shoals and channels, measuring distances and depths—were sent out to Bengal especially for the task. They produced the first known navigational and topographical charts of the river, along with detailed instructions on how to pilot a ship as far as Cossimbazaar, avoiding perilous spots such as the sandbanks at the mouth of the river where Sebastian Manrique had earlier been shipwrecked. In 1672 an English vessel of 200 tonnes, the *Rebecca*, made it safely to Hooghly, guided by the *Diligence*. A 600-tonne ocean ship then completed the voyage for the first time in 1679. After navigation of the river had been mastered, Hooghly became the main port of English commerce and the profitability of trade soared: Company investment in Bengal increased almost tenfold between 1670 and 1690.[9] 'Our operations are growing so extensive', wrote one English merchant, 'that we shall be obliged to build new and large warehouses.'[10]

* * *

It is widely held, perhaps it is even a truism, that the histories of imperialism and capitalism are intertwined—that the origins of European empire in the early modern world lay in the development of capital. Capitalism, it is assumed, provided the impetus for the expansion of European trade and power to the non-European world, sustained by the search for new products to import and for new export markets overseas.[11] In a crucial yet overlooked sense, however, this contention is wrong. The abstract logic of capital is of course the free circulation of money, commodities, and people—the freedom of markets from political intervention. In the Indian Ocean, however, the trading companies of Europe were anything but free-market merchants and entrepreneurs. Unlike the Arab, Persian, and Indian traders who preceded them, they did not seek the unfettered movement of goods and capital from one port and market to the next. Instead, their object was the creation and enforcement of trading monopolies, often violently. Rather than operating within a free-market economy, they usurped existing markets and imposed monopolistic conditions, enlisting the diplomatic and military power of European states towards that end. Close and mutually beneficial relationships existed between the trading companies and their respective national governments: monarchs supported the pursuit of the company's profits, which in turn financed the development of the state. As one scholar emphatically puts it, the development of European imperialism in the Indian Ocean was not the triumph of capitalism but its 'stillbirth'.[12]

The earliest example of a European trading organisation allied to its national government was the Portuguese Estado da India. Under the flag of the Estado, merchants employed directly by the state were joined by those operating under licences bought from it. The trade of both was backed by the fiscal and military power of the Portuguese (and during the period of the Iberian Union, between 1580 and 1640, the Spanish) crown. To capture and preserve its spice-trade monopolies, the Estado attempted to police the seas: major trading routes were controlled from fortified strongholds; any vessel not carrying a trading permit, known as a *cartaz*, issued by the authorities in Goa, was liable to be seized or destroyed. As early as the 1520s, Indian and Arab ships setting off from Bengal to trade in South East Asia were captured and their cargoes confiscated, though, despite Portuguese efforts, a complete monopoly of Indian Ocean trade was at no point achieved.[13]

Like the Estado da India, the Dutch East India Company (VOC) involved crown and private entrepreneurs working in alliance. Dutch merchants had sailed into the Indian Ocean for the first time in 1595, establishing a trading post at Bantam in western Java. Other expeditions followed, with the establishment of control over Banda Neira, the main nutmeg site in the Banda Islands, a major coup. In 1602 these private single-voyage initiatives were consolidated into the royal-chartered VOC, with the express intention of wrestling the spice trade from the Portuguese.[14] Domination of the straits of Sunda and Malacca and the seas between Borneo and Sumatra meant that by the middle of the seventeenth century this aspiration had largely been achieved. However, Dutch attempts to monopolise trade were accompanied by the violent acquisition of islands from their indigenous inhabitants and the brutal enforcing of treaties exacted under duress. Dutch ships resorted to arms to exclude other Asian and European traders, and in the pursuit of maximum returns determined the precise amount of different spices to be produced, destroying surpluses. Competition between the Dutch and English companies led to outright conflict, most infamously on Ambon Island, when twenty men accused of spying against the VOC—ten of whom were servants of the English Company—were tortured and executed in 1623.[15]

The alliance of the English East India Company with its monarch began with the royal charter of 1600 but did not end there. In its early years the Company was reliant on subscriptions to fund each new voyage east; early subscribers included officials at the court of King James I, alongside City of London merchants. The relationship between Company and state was strong. In good years, Company trade provided substantial customs revenue to the crown; the Company, in turn, was dependent on the monarchy for diplomatic and political support, as Thomas Roe's royal embassy to Jahangir shows. Notwithstanding occasional disruptions, not least during the English Civil War, it remained in the interests of both Company and state that the English share of global trade expand. The preservation of a Company monopoly on English trade with the East appeared the most effective means of securing that expansion. In contrast to its Portuguese and Dutch counterparts, the Company was not initially heavily armed. Over time, however, this changed dramatically.

As in many parts of the Indian Ocean, the Dutch established a presence in Bengal several years before the English. In 1615 they first entered Bengali waters, siding with the king of Arakan in a short war leading to the downfall of Portuguese pirate-ruler Sebastian Gonzales.[16] Within two years of the banishment of the Portuguese from Hooghly, a Dutch factory had been established among the town's ruins; when the English arrived in 1651, Dutch trade was booming. The main incentive for this trade was the purchase of Bengali textiles; silk was shipped by the VOC to Japan, as well as to Europe. Japanese gold and copper were imported into Bengal, in addition to pepper, nutmeg, and other spices from South East Asia and cinnamon from Ceylon. When their Hooghly factory was flooded in 1654, the Dutch moved their Bengal headquarters a few miles downriver to Chinsurah, where a major settlement developed.

By the final third of the seventeenth century, the Hooghly had become one of the principal theatres of commercial competition between European trading companies. Attracted by the profits to be made and the relative peace that prevailed under the sovereignty of the Mughals, the Dutch and English were joined by Armenians who settled near Cossimbazaar; by the French who built a factory just south of the Dutch at Chandernagore; and by the Danish who resolved on a site next to the French, which they named Dinemardanga (the land of the Danes).[17] When those Portuguese merchants who had returned to Hooghly after 1632 are added, along with traders from Arabia, Persia, Central Asia, and the Indian subcontinent, the picture emerges of a remarkably cosmopolitan collection of peoples concentrated on the river's banks. To procure goods from the cheapest markets in territories either side of the Hooghly, the European companies employed Indian brokers to act as intermediaries in return for a small commission; their factories employed hundreds of local workers in the storage and transport of goods. Until the 1680s, the VOC commanded the greatest volume of trade. Thereafter, however, the English Company was predominant. In Europe, the Nine Years' War (1688–97) and the War of Spanish Succession (1701–14) marked the emergence of England as the largest commercial economy. By 1710, the volume of English trade in Bengal exceeded that of all the other European companies put together.[18]

* * *

The reaction of the Mughal authorities to the arrival of other European companies in the decades after the expulsion of the Portuguese from Hooghly was largely positive. To the Mughal state, the companies were a source of revenue, extracted in the form of transport tolls and customs dues, and annual payments that permitted them to trade custom free. Europeans could be useful allies when conflicts arose with other Indian parties, providing troops, weapons, money, and diplomatic aid. Their exotic goods and knowledge, including the latest European medical practices, were welcomed by the more curious Mughal statesmen. To Mughal officials on the ground, European trade provided an unprecedented opportunity for enrichment; pockets were lined at the same time as state coffers were filled through bribery and extortion. Government officers had long reaped profits from the inland trade of goods between Bengal and upper India; the arrival of the European companies provided a stimulus to this trade.

The extent to which Mughal officials sought to profit from the activities of the European companies is evident from East India Company records, which catalogue the growing English frustration at the regular payments expected by Mughal officials, from the *subahdar* down to lowly customs officers on the river. Among the most demanding was one of Aurangzeb's governors, Shaista Khan, who instructed his officers to prevent all English boats travelling to and from Patna to trade in saltpetre until substantial bribes had been paid; when the English factors refused, he attempted to bring the saltpetre trade under his own exclusive control.[19] The agreement reached with Shah Jahan permitted the English to trade custom free in return for an annual sum of 3000 rupees. Under Aurangzeb, a new firman was secured, granting the East India Company trading rights on payment of customs dues of 3.5 per cent. In reality, however, the success of attempts to trade depended on the amenability of the Bengal governor and his officers: in the words of one English factor, trade would only be profitable if 'the oppression of the Nabob [nawab] could be prevented'.[20]

In 1661, the East India Company was awarded a new royal charter. In addition to granting the Company exclusive rights to English trade with the East Indies in perpetuity, the charter empowered it to seize unlicensed English merchants, erect fortifications, maintain troops, and make war with non-Christians.[21] As a text, it reflected growing domestic confidence about the role of Britain overseas, inspired by the growth of British trade and power in the New World as well as in the Indian Ocean. It sprung from the unarguable fact that the use of force had been a major contributor to Portuguese and Dutch trading success. For Company servants in Bengal, the charter was well timed. The growth of English trade meant that for the first time the Company had a substantial economic interest to protect. Frustrated by Mughal officials' repeated financial demands, the English in Bengal sketched a plan for a fortified Company settlement on Sagar Island, a strategically important site at the mouth of the Hooghly.[22] Company servants were directed to acquire knowledge of army discipline and new commissions were introduced for those with specialist military training.

In the latter part of Aurangzeb's reign, tensions between Mughal and Company officials erupted into a conflict that threatened the presence of the English in Bengal altogether. At Cossimbazaar, the Bengali silk weavers and merchants trading with the Company complained to Shaista Khan that the English levied a charge for the pricing of goods before purchase and regularly took samples without paying for them. The governor sided with the complainants and dictated that compensation be paid. For the Company's Court of Directors in London, this demand was one act of aggravation too many. With the blessing of King James II, they declared war on the Mughal Empire and dispatched a company of infantry to Bengal. Against the forces at Shaista Khan's disposal, the Company stood little chance: 400 English soldiers made it to Hooghly (three of the six ships carrying them from England were lost en route), where they were met by 3000 Mughal troops. An uneasy standoff followed, until three English soldiers were beaten and imprisoned while shopping for supplies in the bazaar. A day of inconclusive fighting followed, after which the English force took to the river and regrouped at Sutanuti, twenty-six miles downstream. Led by Job Charnock, who had been responsible for English operations at Cossimbazaar, the Company attempted to negotiate; Charnock requested Shaista Khan's consent for the resumption of custom-free trade and the construction of a fortified English base on the river. The *subahdar* returned the Company's articles unsigned and instructed his officers to drive the English out of Bengal.[23]

The Mughal–Company war of 1686 ought to have come to an end in May the following year. By this point, the English contingent in Bengal had fled further down the river to a small island next to the coast of Hijli, where the Hooghly enters the sea. With their numbers dwindling, they held out against the besieging Mughal force in the swamps of Hijli for five days before a fleet of reinforcements arrived from Madras. With each side now fearing the other, Charnock and the Mughal commander Abdul Samad negotiated peace. However, the Court of Directors, more than five thousand miles away, had other ideas. Determined to teach the Mughals a lesson, it dispatched a fleet of battleships to Bengal under the command of William Heath with instructions to procure a fortified settlement. The mission was a farce. Intending to sail up the Hooghly, Heath and his party lost their way in the Bay of Bengal and instead struck upon Chittagong, three hundred miles to the east. Finding the town heavily fortified, they attempted without success to form an alliance with the king of Arakan, returning dejected to Madras. A simultaneous attempt to fight the Mughals in western India met with similarly disastrous results—the loss of the Company's possessions in Surat and on the island of Bombay. With its tail between its legs, a Company delegation travelled to Delhi to plead for Aurangzeb's pardon. It was granted on condition that the Company pay the significant sum of 150,000 rupees in damages and promise to be better behaved.

On the west coast of India, the most significant long-term conse-quence of the war was the Company's decision not to return to Surat and concentrate its trade on Bombay instead. In Bengal, a new firman was granted permitting the English to resume custom-free trade in return for 3000 rupees per year. Three subsequent events in short succession then transformed the Company's position. The first was the decision of Job Charnock not to reopen an English factory at Hooghly but to found a new settlement next to Sutanuti, where his party had taken refuge during the war. Sutanuti was unremarkable: a collection of small villages next to the Hooghly, just above the Mughal fort of Thana and by a stream known as Adi Ganga, revered by local Hindus as the original route of the Ganges. However, it possessed major strategic advantages: here the waters of the Hooghly were deeper and easier to negotiate; and, located on the left bank of the river, Sutanuti was much harder to attack by an opponent approaching it from the plains of India. Charnock's return to Sutanuti gave rise to the city of Calcutta.

The second major event transforming the Company's position was the outbreak of Subha Singh's rebellion in 1696, which, as we have seen, precipitated the arrival of Murshid Quli Khan in Bengal. An unintended consequence of the rebellion was that the East India Company, under the pretext of protecting itself from Subha Singh's rampaging forces, could at last fortify one of its bases without opposition from the governor of Bengal. During the rebellion, the Company leant its support to the Mughals by stationing a ship in the Hooghly next to Thana fort to deter Subha Singh's general, Rahim Khan, from crossing the river. Concurrently, the first bricks of Fort William at Calcutta were laid. Possession of the fort, which was gradually strengthened and enlarged, gave the Company's Bengal factors a new confidence on the eve of Murshid Quli Khan's arrival. When his predecessor, Azim al-Din, ordered Company goods to be seized in an attempt to extort bribes, the governor of Fort William, John Beard, responded by blockading the Hooghly for nine days, preventing Mughal ships from travelling seawards on to Surat and Persia.[24]

Azim al-Din's most significant act before Aurangzeb ordered his replacement by Quli Khan was to award the English Company zamindari rights over three territories surrounding Calcutta—Govindapur, Sutanuti, and Kalikata (which gave the English settlement its name). Through this monumental decision, motivated by the governor's short-term need for revenue, the Company became for the first time a territorial power in Bengal. In the Mughal system, zamindars collected revenues from their estates and submitted a portion of them, sometimes as much as 90 per cent, to the crown. The arrangement negotiated between Azim al-Din and the Company was a little different. The Company would pay a fixed sum of 1200 rupees per year; thereafter, it would be free to govern the territories as it wished and retain all profits. An English collector, Ralph Sheldon, was appointed with an Indian deputy and the Company began to extract revenue from the land: rent was collected from occupied plots; unoccupied plots were sold or leased; and inland customs duties were levied along with road and river tolls.[25]

In the first Company settlements on the Hooghly River, at Hooghly and Cossimbazaar, all English employees had lived within the walls of the factory, which in the regulation of the lives of its residents resembled a college or prison, with set hours of work, meals, and bed. At Hooghly, an English chaplain ensured that his compatriots didn't swear, drink, or quarrel too much, and that bedtimes were observed. (One eyewitness was convinced that the reason that mortality rates were so high was not because of the Bengal climate but because so much 'bowl-punch'—'the plague of body and health'—was drunk.[26]) With the growth of Calcutta, however, it was no longer tenable for all Company officials to live in the factory: the more senior were given permission to rent land and build residences in the town. Barracks were constructed for the growing number of soldiers employed by the Company, many of whom were mixed-race descendants of the Portuguese. A hospital was built next to the European burial ground and the Church of St Anne was consecrated in 1709. To maintain order, a small police force was assembled with jurisdiction over both European and Indian inhabitants. During times of peace, a standing army of 150 patrolled the river, protecting English trade. A court of justice was inaugurated to begin administering English civil and criminal law. By the end of the first decade of the eighteenth century, the metamorphosis of the Company in Bengal from a body of merchants into a colonial government was well under way.

* * *

Murshid Quli Khan's appointment to Bengal coincided with an order by Aurangzeb that English trade be embargoed. The emperor had been incensed by the violation of Muslim pilgrims en route to Mecca by English sailors in the Persian Gulf. After this sanction was lifted, English trade on the Hooghly resumed. An astute administrator, Quli Khan appreciated the revenue to be collected through the Company's annual payments in lieu of customs and the regular ad hoc 'gifts' made to his treasury. Nonetheless, impediments to trade remained: English saltpetre boats were periodically stopped on their descent from Patna by local officials eager to extract bribes; tensions escalated with the *faujdar* of Hooghly, whose demands for additional customs provoked the Company to prepare for war again in 1710.[27] From this point on, the English changed tactics. Instead of negotiating with the court of Quli Khan through Indian intermediaries they approached the *diwan* and de facto governor directly, establishing lines of communication that would prove vital as the century wore on. They also determined that the best way of ensuring trade unmolested by the Bengal administration would be the receipt of a new imperial firman from Delhi.

When Farrukhsiyar ascended the Peacock Throne in 1713, bringing to an end a year of turmoil at the Mughal court in Delhi, the Company's efforts to secure the firman began. Robert Hedges and Samuel Feak, representatives of the Company at Cossimbazaar, lobbied Quli Khan to submit a request for the firman to the emperor. Frustrated by the *diwan*'s recalcitrance, the Company's council at Calcutta then resolved to approach the emperor directly: an embassy under the leadership of John Surman, accompanied by three other Englishmen and an Armenian, Khwaja Sarhad, whose knowledge of Persian was vital, set off for the imperial court. The embassy's main demand was the right of the Company to trade custom free in return for an annual payment of 3000 rupees. Added to this was a request that the Company be permitted to purchase other villages around Calcutta, to complement the three over which it acted as zamindar, and that it might coin money in the mints of Murshidabad, Dacca, and Rajmahal without being charged. This final demand was particularly significant. Before the death of Aurangzeb, the Company had imported Madras rupees into Bengal, where they were accepted as currency. Under Quli Khan, however, recognition of the Madras rupee was withdrawn. If the English could not coin money in a Bengal mint, they would have no choice but to import silver bullion and exchange it for local currency at rates dictated by Indian bankers such as the Jagat Seths. Only the right to coin money freely would ensure the long-term profitability of the Company's Bengal trade.[28]

To the delight of the English party, most of its requests were granted. Farrukhsiyar issued a firman for each of the Company's three trading areas—Bengal, Madras, and Bombay. The Bengal firman reiterated that the English could trade custom free in return for an annual sum; it granted the Company the right to purchase thirty-eight villages around Calcutta and to use the mint of Murshidabad for three days each week. Subsidiary stipulations included the right to punish local officers seizing Company property and to pursue debtors beyond the Company's territorial jurisdiction. News of the firman reached Calcutta in March 1717 and was greeted jubilantly with a public dinner, a bonfire, and the ceremonial firing of a cannon. However, the celebrations were short-lived. When Samuel Feak presented a copy of the firman to Quli Khan he acknowledged the Company's right to trade custom free—already the accepted practice—but refused out-right the sale of the thirty-eight villages or use of the mint. Ever dis-cerning, the *diwan* knew that these concessions would undermine his authority and place the Company in a position of superiority. Moreover, his days of taking orders from Delhi were at an end. Not even the dangling of a 40,000 rupee bribe would change his mind.[29]

The terms of the 1717 firman remained only partially implemented when Quli Khan's dynasty ended and Alivardi Khan seized control. Like his predecessors, Alivardi appreciated the financial benefits of European trade on the Hooghly. The annual payment of 3000 rupees continued and, when funds for his campaigns against the Marathas ran dry, the European companies were turned to as a source of additional revenue. In 1744, Alivardi secured 350,000 rupees from the English Company to fund his war effort, without conceding the Company's right to purchase the thirty-eight villages or use his mint, but wariness about the presence of the European companies remained. The nawab's greatest concern was the possible outbreak of war between the com-panies in Bengal. He followed carefully the reports of events in south-ern India, where the French and English were fighting for political supremacy, and responded with an edict forbidding hostilities in his territories.[30] The neutrality of the Hooghly was briefly violated in January 1749 when French troops occupied the Dutch garden of Champonade, between Chandernagore and Chinsurah, but conflict was otherwise avoided during his reign. To ingratiate themselves with Alivardi, the French and English competed to offer him presents from overseas, including Arab horses and Persian cats. The nawab was not naïve enough, however, to think that these were disinterested gifts. According to one source, he compared the European settlements on the Hooghly to hives of bees: their honey could be reaped 'but if you disturbed them they would sting you to death'.[31] It would be for his grandson and successor, Siraj-ud-Daula, to discover just how apt the metaphor was.

* * *

In English accounts of the East India Company's takeover of power in Bengal, Siraj-ud-Daula has been portrayed as a drunken tyrant who terrorised his subjects—particularly the Hindus—and harboured an irrational hatred of the British. Writers have dwelt upon supposed instances of the young nawab's cruelty, reporting that he enjoyed torturing birds and animals and once tipped a boatload of people into the Hooghly to watch them drown.[32] An alternative English narrative suggests that Siraj was not mad but greedy and driven by this base instinct to seize the Company's trade.

The truth is that the nawab had a number of legitimate reasons to fear that the English presented a growing threat to his authority. From late 1755, the Company had begun to extend the fortifications of Fort William without seeking his consent. Krishna Das, a high-ranking revenue officer guilty of defrauding the nawab's treasury, had been granted asylum in Calcutta on payment of hefty bribes to the English council. Moreover, a growing number of Company servants were cheating the nawab by misusing the permits (*dastaks*) that he had granted to guarantee the Company's duty-free overseas trade. This latter problem most seriously undermined Siraj. For most English employees, the measly salaries offered by the Company hardly compensated for the risks and hardships involved in travelling to India: Company servants expected that while in Bengal they would have the opportunity to profit from private trade. Periodically the Company directors in London condemned the private trading of their employees, suspecting that it eroded their returns, but by and large the practice was condoned to attract recruits to India. Siraj was not the first nawab of Bengal to protest against the participation of Company officials in the province's inland trade; objections had been raised about English activity in domestic markets for salt and other foodstuffs as early as the 1680s. What particularly troubled him, however, was that permits meant to guarantee only the English Company duty-free import and export were also being used to bypass the payment of duties on commodities bought and sold in domestic markets for the private profit of Company officers. Indeed, some officers had even taken to selling or leasing their permits to other Indian and European merchants, and to charging for the carrying of private goods on Company ships, so that customs and river tolls could be avoided. English corruption was subverting one of the key revenue pillars of the Bengal administration.[33]

Siraj repeatedly requested the English council at Calcutta to clamp down on *dastak* abuse. In May 1756, he then demanded that the building of additional fortifications around the city be stopped. The council refused, stating without the decorum normally used in addressing the nawab that the fortifications were necessary to protect against the French, whom the English would declare war on in Europe that month. Siraj responded by seizing the English factory at Cossimbazaar and taking the chief factor, William Watts, prisoner. The nawab was at this juncture open to negotiation but the council, headed by the belligerent Roger Drake, rejected his advances, so Siraj resolved to take Calcutta as well. The city was defended by just 250 troops—English, Armenian, and Indo-Portuguese—mostly armed residents rather than professional soldiers. In spite of recent efforts, it remained poorly fortified, the most effective protection being a ditch dug in the previous decade to defend against a possible Maratha invasion. After holding out for four days, Calcutta fell. Its residents evacuated Fort William and fled to ships on the river—an undignified scramble during which several overloaded vessels ran aground. While Drake got safely away—an escape later condemned as 'absconsion'—those who remained were taken prisoner by Siraj's troops. An episode followed which would enter English lore as the 'Black Hole'. According to the most influential English account, 146 prisoners were detained in a small cell in Fort William overnight. By the morning, all but 23 had suffocated to death.[34]

The stage was now set for the military intervention of Robert Clive. Beginning Company service as a low-paid clerk in Madras, Clive had made a name for himself during the Anglo-French wars in the south as a skilful if sometimes reckless military officer: this in spite of his recurring nervous depression, opium habit, and suicide attempts. After a brief spell in England, he returned to India in 1756 as the head of an English force anticipating renewed hostilities with the French. Two days before his arrival at Madras, Calcutta had fallen to Siraj. With naval commander Charles Watson, Clive was selected to lead the expedition to retake the city. A fleet of five ships carrying 800 Europeans and 1000 Indians set off from Madras for the Hooghly. The voyage did not go to plan. Monsoon winds carried the fleet across the Bay of Bengal to the coast of modern-day Myanmar before they eventually arrived in December 1756 at Fulta, south of Calcutta, where the Rupnarayan joins the Hooghly. At Fulta, those who had fled Calcutta when it fell to

Siraj had regrouped and passed six months waiting, their supplies and number dwindling, for relief to arrive.

Clive's minimum aim as he set foot in Bengal for the first time was to recapture Calcutta and restore the privileges granted to the Company by the imperial firman of 1717, yet from the outset he believed that more might be achieved. A decisive military victory over Siraj and the French, he recorded, would leave the Company 'in a better and more lasting condition than ever.'[35] From Fulta he dispatched a letter to Siraj with an unmistakably threatening tone: he was, he claimed, at the head of 'such a force [as] was never seen before in your province … all things may be made up in a friendly manner by restoring to the Company and to the poor inhabitants what they have been plundered.'[36] Watson followed up Clive's dispatch with a bullying missive of his own: 'I will kindle such a flame in your country as all the water in the Ganges shall not be able to extinguish.'[37] Two weeks later the English offensive began. The forts of Budge-Budge and Thana were taken with ease and on 2 January 1757 Calcutta was once again in English hands. Demoralised and unpaid, Siraj's troops had failed to put up a fight. Some historians suggest that their commander, Manik Chand, was bribed by Clive.

Sensing an opportunity to ram home the English advantage, Clive and Watson pushed on. A force of 350 was dispatched from Calcutta to Hooghly, which was also found to be undefended. Its fortifications were blown up and the principal buildings razed to the ground. 'The capture and destruction of Hughly,' wrote one English participant, 'was essential to strike a terror in the Suba's [nawab's] troops … this we have reason to believe has had the desired effect and thrown the Country into a vast consternation.'[38] Siraj's response was to march again on Calcutta. On 5 February, the Company's troops met those of the nawab on the outskirts of the city. Clive's dawn attack took Siraj's forces by surprise: 1300 were killed and the fact of English military superiority was confirmed.[39] The nawab had little choice but to sue for peace, committing to a treaty confirming the Company's 1717 rights and paying compensation for all damages incurred during the previous nine months.

The treaty marked a break in hostilities on the Hooghly but not their end. What Clive and Watson most feared was an alliance between Siraj and the French against the now ascendant English. News of the outbreak of war between England and France in Europe had reached Bengal in December 1756 but on the Hooghly neutrality had been observed. French officers had even acted as negotiators between the English and Siraj to produce the February treaty. Clive, however, was convinced that this neutrality would not last: a pre-emptive strike against the French was required, one that would nullify their military threat without antagonising Siraj and encouraging the French–nawab co-operation that he most dreaded. At Murshidabad, William Watts lobbied Siraj for permission to attack the French and in early March 1757 obtained word from the nawab that 'the enemies of the English are my enemies, whether they be Indians or Europeans.'[40] This ambiguous pronouncement was taken as consent. On 14 March, Clive and Watson struck against the French settlement of Chandernagore. French arms were no match for the English heavy artillery on the river and following sustained bombardment the town fell. The Company was now the undisputed European power on the Hooghly.

The Bengal 'revolution', as it later became known, might have ended there but in the weeks following the capture of Chandernagore it became clear that Siraj had lost the support of influential figures in his court. His aunt, Ghasiti Begam, the eldest daughter of Alivardi Khan, had always opposed his rule, as had his cousin Shaukat Jung, the deputy governor of Purnea. Now it transpired that Amir Chand (the wealthiest Indian merchant in Calcutta), Rai Durlabh (Siraj's *diwan*), and Mahtab Rai (head of the Jagat Seth family of bankers) desired his removal. Together they negotiated with Watts to depose Siraj and install Mir Jafar, a senior court nobleman and respected military commander, in his place. For the English, the scheme was attractive. The council at Calcutta had little confidence that Siraj would stick to the terms of the February treaty. A new nawab whose authority depended on the Company would be more compliant and extra privileges could be extracted. Mir Jafar committed to a secret treaty with the council confirming the Company's trading and territorial rights, including the ceding of the thirty-eight villages. New promises were added: the nawab-in-waiting would reward the Company and its senior officers with cash gifts and support the Company's army from his own exchequer.[41]

With the treaty signed, the countdown to Plassey began.[42] On the pretext of going on a hunting trip near Cossimbazaar, Watts escaped from Murshidabad. Clive moved his army of 3000—a mixture of English, Indo-Portuguese, Armenian, and Indian—from Calcutta to Katwa, the Europeans travelling by boat and the rest marching along the bank of the river. The nawab's fort at Katwa was taken without resistance but doubts now began to set in. Twenty miles away, in the fields outside Plassey, Siraj's army was reported to have 50,000 troops, if those under the command of Mir Jafar were counted. If the general went back on his word and sided with the nawab, the Company force would be routed. On the afternoon of 22 June, however, Clive received a message from Mir Jafar that he would stick to the deal. The Company's troops were ordered to cross the river and march north.

Siraj's army was camped on a piece of land formed by a loop in the Hooghly, two miles north of Plassey, protected by the river on three sides. A mile south, a stone hunting lodge stood on the water's edge. Here Clive set up his headquarters and placed 500 troops. The rest were stationed in a grove of mango trees that provided camouflage and shade. At 8 a.m. on 23 June 1757 fighting began. Siraj's army—which actually numbered 35,000 infantry and 8000 cavalry, plus heavy artillery under the supervision of 50 Frenchmen—advanced from its camp and began to encircle Clive's force; cannon fire pushed the Company's troops further into the mango grove and by noon a real danger existed that the English would be encircled. They were saved by a monsoon storm which interrupted the artillery bombardment for an hour. When the rains stopped, the Frenchmen found their heavy weapons drenched and useless. Seizing the moment, one of Clive's officers, Major Kilpatrick, advanced without permission and seized the dug-in tank next to the French guns. Siraj's forces began to splinter; Mir Madan, the nawab's leading general, was killed. Against his instincts, Siraj took the advice of Mir Jafar and Rai Durlabh to retreat, and the Company's army moved forward. Fearing that the battle was lost, Siraj mounted a camel and returned to Murshidabad.

The day after the encounter, Mir Jafar met Clive at the hunting lodge. The general was instructed to proceed to Murshidabad to announce his succession and occupy the palace. On hearing of his approach, Siraj left the city like a fugitive, boarding a boat to take him upriver in disguise. At Rajmahal, he was betrayed by one of the boatmen and captured by Mir Jafar's brother-in-law, Mir Qasim. The nawab was returned to Murshidabad and paraded through the streets as a criminal before being hacked to pieces in an execution arranged by Mir Jafar's son, Miran. At his death, he was just twenty years old. Mir Jafar was ceremoniously installed on the throne on 26 June. Three days later, Clive entered Murshidabad, accompanied by 700 soldiers, as the city's residents lined the streets and watched on.

* * *

Accounts of the events of 1757 regularly condemn specific instances of duplicity on the part of English officers in Bengal—the composition of a second version of the treaty with Mir Jafar, which the Company had no intention of observing, promising Amir Chand £300,000 for his role in the deposition of Siraj, for example.[43] This rather misses the point: that greed and deception were not regrettable add-ons to the English takeover of power but its fundamental characteristics. After Plassey, 200 country boats were loaded with money from Siraj's treasury and floated down the Hooghly to Calcutta; Clive profited personally to the tune of £234,000 and other members of the Calcutta council received up to £80,000 each.[44]

The greatest deception following the installation of Mir Jafar was the pretence of the continued sovereignty of the nawab and, by extension, the Mughal emperor in Delhi. Admittedly, opinion differed on this question: one English official wrote earnestly about the need to respect Mir Jafar's authority while ensuring the profitability of Company trade.[45] Most, however, had no qualms over the idea that the sovereignty of the nawab was a mask for English power—a convenient way of deterring other European countries from committing aggressions in Bengal and sidestepping the tricky constitutional question of whether or not, in English law, a trading company could be a sovereign power. Clive described Mir Jafar as 'a mere pageant' and 'a name and a shadow' for English rule.[46] The financial and territorial commitments that Mir Jafar made to the Company before his installation would undermine any aspirations of independence that he held on assuming the throne. The Company's development as a revenue-collecting territorial power and its trespassing on the inland trade of Bengal were processes in motion before Siraj's removal. After Plassey, both were accelerated until trade was monopolised, the Company-state embedded, and the power of the nawabs reduced to the symbolic.

The states of eighteenth-century Europe are today recognised as fiscal-military entities.[47] Within the context of a revolution in military technology, producing devastating but expensive new weaponry, they required expansion across Europe and overseas in order to remain financially afloat but became locked into ever deepening spirals of conquest and debt. Avoiding bankruptcy was a major motivation for imperial expansion and explains, in large part, the close alliance between trading companies and their domestic governments. During and after the Seven Years' War (1756–63), the profits remitted by the East India Company had never been more important to the British crown: Bengal helped to service the English national debt.[48] Ironically, however, the Company itself increasingly resembled a fiscal-military state. The usurping of existing governmental structures in Bengal compelled the Company to maintain a dramatically enlarged standing army; military costs had grown significantly in the year before Plassey and thereafter continued to rise. To cover escalating costs and to profit from its presence on the Hooghly, the Company used its stranglehold over Mir Jafar to claim revenue-collecting rights over a growing portion of the nawab's territories. However, the costs of administering new lands consistently outweighed the revenue gained, leading the Company, like the states of Europe, into a worsening cycle of war, expansion, and debt.[49]

One of the first tasks of the Company's Bengal council after Plassey was to ensure a reliable return on the thirty-eight villages around Calcutta on which it finally had its hands. Instead of administering the territories directly in a similar fashion to Govindapur, Sutanuti, and Kalikata, its earliest territorial possessions, it determined to let out revenue collection to private profiteers. The villages were divided up into fifteen lots and auctioned at Calcutta town hall. Bidders paid the Company a fixed sum and bought the right to collect and retain land revenues for three years—a venture in speculative capitalism encouraging the extraction of as much revenue as possible from the ryots on the land. Of the fifteen lots auctioned in May 1759, eleven were purchased by Indians and four by English servants of the Company.[50] Simultaneously, the extraction of revenue directly from Mir Jafar got under way. In addition to 'gifts' to members of the council, the nawab had promised to pay the Company one million pounds sterling as compensation for the destruction of Calcutta and half a million for the military expenses incurred by the Company in fighting his predecessor. When Siraj's treasury was captured, however, it contained only a fraction of the forty million pounds that Mir Jafar and the English had reckoned on. If the new nawab's financial commitments to the Company were to be observed, the zamindars of Bengal and Bihar would need to recognise his rule. Mir Jafar and Clive set out together for Patna to enforce the submission of Ram Narayan, the deputy governor of Bihar, and of a succession of zamindari holders, but the financial position of the nawab went from bad to worse. He pledged his jewels to the Company as insurance against his debt and in September 1760 three more territories—Burdwan, Midnapore, and Chittagong—were handed over to the Company in place of cash.[51]

Financial demands followed by territorial encroachment had bankrupted the nawab; in October 1760, just after Clive's return to England, he was removed from the throne. The Company had tried to make Mir Jafar's government work only to extract profit from it. That pursuit had ruined his court and made him insolvent, and so he was deposed. Escorted by English soldiers, he was put on board a barge, carried downriver to the outskirts of Calcutta, and lodged in a house at Chitpur. His replacement was his son-in-law, Mir Qasim, a wealthy noble who had earlier coveted the deputy governorship of Bihar. In the first few months of his rule, Mir Qasim raised enough revenue to pay off a large portion of his administration's debt to the Company. But then, with his treasury running dry, he began to resist the harsh terms imposed by the English. Reversing the Company's rhetoric, he demanded compensation for the damages inflicted on his government by the financial straitjacket in which it had been placed. He withdrew his court from Murshidabad to distant Monghyr, on the banks of the Ganges in Bihar, and commenced preparations for war.

The deposition of Mir Jafar had proven a mistake. Though insolvent, he had shown no inclination to oppose the Company's demands. In July 1763, the Company declared war on Mir Qasim and returned Mir Jafar to the throne. An English force of 5000 besieged Monghyr and captured the makeshift capital. Mir Qasim was driven out of Bihar and took refuge in the kingdom of Awadh, where he formed an alliance with Shuja al-Daulah, the Lucknow nawab, and Shah Alam II, the titular head of the Mughal throne, who sought the recognition of his authority at Delhi. A combined force of the three fought the Company's army just outside Patna in May 1764 and then again four months on at Buxar, further west. The Battle of Buxar was decisive. Unlike Plassey, it was a large-scale military engagement in which unprecedented numbers on the English side—more than 800 of a force of 7000—were killed, but the Company prevailed again.[52] Shuja al-Daulah returned defeated to Awadh, while Shah Alam sought terms of accommodation with the English and the threat posed by Mir Qasim was extinguished. On hearing of this victory, Clive remarked: 'It is scarcely a hyperbole to say that the whole Mogul Empire is in our hands.'[53]

The final step in the transformation of the Company into a territorial revenue-collecting power in the decade after Plassey was then enacted. When Mir Jafar died naturally in February 1765, his son and successor Najmuddin Ali Khan signed a treaty guaranteeing the Company possession of the districts of Burdwan, Midnapore, and Chittagong. Six months later, in an agreement with Shah Alam known to posterity as the Treaty of Allahabad, the Company became the *diwan* of Bengal. Clive had arrived back in India just in time to negotiate this conclusion. In return for recognition of his claims to the imperial throne, Shah Alam awarded the Company revenue-collecting power over the entirety of Bengal, save for those districts that it already effectively owned.[54] The nawab was still legally sovereign and, in accordance with the Mughal system, responsible for the administration of justice and preservation of order. In reality, however, just as Quli Khan and Alivardi had assumed de facto power while symbolically honouring the sovereignty of the emperor in Delhi, the Company had emptied the position of nawab into a ceremonial shell. The English controlled all revenue and maintained an army for which the revenues of the province would pay. Clive was in no doubt about the significance of the *diwani*, writing to the Company's directors in London:

> By this acquisition, your possessions and influence are rendered paramount and secure, since no future Nabob will either have the power, or riches sufficient, to attempt your over-throw, by means either of force or corruption. All revolutions must henceforth be at an end ...

The power is now lodged where it can only be lodged with safety to us, so that we may pronounce with some degree of confidence that the worst which will happen in the future to the Company will proceed from temporary ravages only, which can never become so general as to prevent your revenues from yielding a sufficient fund to defray your civil and military charges, and furnish your investments.[55]

When news of the *diwani* reached England, shares in the Company went through the roof and the systematic drain of money from Bengal to London began in earnest.[56]

Mir Jafar's first administration (1757–60) was probably destined to result in bankruptcy from the moment that he conceded the right of Company officers to engage in private trade. After Plassey, abuse of the *dastak* system intensified and became more systematic. Company officers employed Indian agents, known as *banians*, to organise inland trading on their behalf and oversee the transportation of goods on the Hooghly. The boats of these agents, which carried the British flag, increasingly resorted to force not only to escape customs payments and tolls but also to monopolise the purchase and sale of particular commodities in Bengali markets—salt, betel nut, and tobacco in particular. Agents of the English seized villages and forced the production of certain goods, such as raw rather than manufactured silk.[57] One Company officer conceded in 1762 that oppressions were being carried out by boats on the Hooghly carrying the British flag—most by agents employed by the English and the rest by Indian interlopers who had simply adopted the Union Jack. 'The great power of the English,' he explained, 'intimidates the people from making any resistance.'[58] Pre-existent Bengali trade was ruined as English officers and their agents undersold Bengali merchants and undercut them when it came to purchasing goods for manufacture. Within a decade, English control over lucrative private trades in salt, opium, indigo, cotton, and tobacco was virtually unchallenged.

Recognising the crippling effect that unregulated private English trade was having on his court's revenues, Mir Qasim attempted to act where his predecessor had failed. In the closing months of 1762, he installed new customs posts on the Hooghly and began stopping and searching English boats. Henry Vansittart, the president of the Company's council, negotiated a compromise with the nawab by which

English merchants would pay a 9 per cent duty on all goods in transit (compared to the 30–40 per cent expected of Indian traders), but the terms of the agreement were rejected by the rest of the English council.[59] It was the issue of private trade that then provoked the descent into war that would lead to Mir Qasim's demise, with the English siege of Monghyr sparked by the seizure of a Company boat at Patna by the nawab's officials.

When Clive returned to Bengal in 1765, he arrived with a brief from the Court of Directors to rein in the private trade of Company officials. Instead of bringing that trade to an end, however, he simply organised it and redirected its profits to those at the top of the Company tree. A Society of Trade was founded, a body controlled by the Calcutta council in which all civil and military officers above a particular grade received a share of trading profits reflective of their station. The whole of the salt trade of the Hooghly was brought under the society's supervision.[60] When the society collapsed a couple of years later, inland trade simply reverted to private English hands. The directors in London lamented: 'An unbounded thirst after riches seems to have possessed the whole body of our servants to that degree, that they have lost all sight of justice to the Country Government, and of their duty to the Company ... The vast fortunes acquired in the inland trade have been obtained by a scene of the most tyrannic and oppressive conduct, that ever was known in any age or country.'[61]

* * *

In August 1768 it rained heavily across Bengal and Bihar but then suddenly, without warning, the rains stopped. Drought led to the failure of the autumn rice harvest, which usually provided 70 per cent of the annual yield.[62] The following summer it hardly rained at all and by September shortages and rising prices had turned to famine. From the countryside, which was most severely affected, reports were received of scarcity and widespread starvation. 'The fields of rice,' noted one English officer, 'are become like fields of dried straw.'[63] Peasants turned to selling off their goods, including their ploughs, eating grass and bark, and 'feeding on the dead'.[64] Thousands flocked to the cities, where supplies were rapidly dwindling. By March 1770, an estimated 150 were dying each day in Patna. Murshidabad was even more seriously affected: rice changed hands at incredibly high prices and 500 perished daily.[65] By summer, bodies were piled high in the streets of both Murshidabad and Calcutta: 'There was not a corner in the city, or any lurking place in the vicinity of Calcutta, where the living, the dying and the dead, were not mingled or heaped together in melancholy confusion.'[66] In an attempt to avoid disease, bodies were disposed of in the Hooghly rather than buried. 'At this time, we could not touch fish, the river was so full of carcasses; and of those who did eat it, many died suddenly.'[67]

The famine was a natural disaster but it was exacerbated by the Company's system of revenue collection and monopolising of trade. After assuming the *diwani* the Company had resolved to keep responsibility for the collection of revenue in the hands of Indian officers already experienced in it: Muhammad Reza Khan, the deputy governor of Bengal during Najmuddin Ali Khan's nawabship, was appointed chief revenue officer, tasked with organising Indian collectors in each *diwani* district. To place the districts under the supervision of English officials would have entailed a huge administrative task and a fresh assessment of the land revenue, for which the Company was not at this point prepared. Beneath the outward appearance of continuity, however, the traditional Mughal revenue system was changed. Previously, revenue collectors in a district enjoyed a close connection to the zamindar; returns were agreed between the two and deficits in a year of shortage could be compensated for in years of glut. Zamindars and ryots could borrow money from local lenders if necessary, as well. With the English assumption of the *diwani*, this flexible local system for ensuring revenue returns and the long-term prosperity of the land was broken up. When a zamindar was unable to remit the expected revenue in full, an officer external to the district, known as an *aumil*, was sent in. With no connection to the zamindar and no concern for the welfare of the estate, he prioritised the short-term extraction of revenue over the longer-term cultivation of land.[68]

In the years immediately before the famine, complaints reached the English that zamindars were no longer in a position to invest in their estates. Roads, bridges, and ghats—which zamindars had traditionally been responsible for maintaining—fell into disrepair. Complaints also began to emerge about the violent and intimidating tactics used by *aumils* to collect taxes directly from peasants, rather than zamindars—that torture, including genital mutilation, was not uncommon.[69] The records of the Company reveal a concern, rhetorical at least, to ensure that peasants were not excessively burdened by revenue demands. In response to the accusations of torture, it dictated that Indian officers must be of 'good character'.[70] However, the revenue collection procedures that the Company had introduced made the oppression of zamindars and ryots very likely. Almost no leeway was afforded to collectors in the returns that they were expected to produce. From the Court of Directors in London down to Indian agents in the field, the maximisation of revenue to pay off the Company's spiralling debts in Bengal was the order of the day. The total revenue collected by the Company as *diwan* increased steadily between 1765 and 1769.[71]

When the famine broke out, the Company failed to respond. Reports of scarcity were ignored by the Calcutta council, which believed that its Indian agents might be attempting to cheat them out of revenue. No temporary remissions were given to the land tax in 1769 and in the spring of 1770 the tax was increased by 10 per cent. Grain continued to be sent out of Bengal to the English settlement at Madras. Only in May 1770 did the council realise the scale of want, because by this point it had reached Calcutta, noting that 'the mortality and beggary exceed all description'.[72] The council had agreed in mid-1769 to appoint English supervisors to *diwani* districts to oversee the work of the Indian collectors. By the time they arrived at their stations the famine was well under way. Instead of ameliorating the situation, they made it worse. Some very small remissions of the land tax were granted in badly affected areas. The private hording of grain and its trading from one district to the next were banned. An attempt was made to requisition supplies from peasants and send them to the areas of most want, such as Murshidabad, where daily hand-outs began. However, these charitable efforts were pitifully inadequate: a total of just £9000 was set aside for the purpose.[73] By preventing the movement of grain between districts and compelling ryots to hand over supplies, the Company's servants prevented the transfer of grain from areas of surplus to want (as a minority on the council realised too late).[74] Charges surfaced that some Company employees had turned the famine into a source of profit, requisitioning grain only to sell it on, or in some instances back, at exorbitant prices later. Though accusations against particular Company agents, English and Indian, were never proven, the Court of Directors later concluded that profiteering had undoubtedly been carried out by those who 'could be no other than persons of some rank in our service'.[75] Grain was consistently requisitioned to feed English civilians and the Company army. Throughout the famine, meanwhile, the collection of revenue continued. In April 1769 the stock market bubble caused by the Company's assumption of the *diwani* had burst and shares in the Company had crashed. For investors, securing a steady return from Bengal was vital. In spite of the human tragedy unfolding, the total revenue collected in 1770 was more than ever before.[76]

At first, heavy rains in the Murshidabad area in the summer of 1770 added to the suffering rather than relieving it: large tracts of low-lying land around the Hooghly were flooded. Relief was only secured in the autumn when a good rice harvest was reaped. The Bengali peasantry had not accepted the famine without a fight: peasants travelled long distances in search of food, pleaded with English officials, and sold possessions to purchase rice. Zamindars attempted to organise relief— Shitab Ray of Patna, for example, sent boats to Benares to purchase 30,000 rupees worth of rice—and the nawab, Najabat Ali Khan, distributed grain to the poor.[77] In total, however, one-third of the population of Bengal and Bihar—approximately ten million people—were dead.[78] A smallpox epidemic accompanied the widespread starvation. The worst affected areas were those adjacent to the Hooghly— Birbhum, Burdwan, Hooghly, Nadia, Murshidabad, and Calcutta—plus several districts in Bihar. In many parts of the countryside there were no longer sufficient numbers of people to farm the land; formerly cultivated estates reverted to jungle. Of the towns on the Hooghly, Murshidabad was the most terribly hit. Its population after the famine was just a fraction of the 700,000 before and its silk industry was in ruins. Already threatened by the rise of English power, the agricultural and manufacturing economies of western Bengal fell into seemingly irreversible decline.

* * *

The transformation of the East India Company on the Hooghly from a trading corporation into a territorial state attracted much criticism in England in the decade after Plassey. How, metropolitan observers asked, could a body of merchants function as a government? Wasn't there a fundamental contradiction between the pursuit of profit and the duty of a government to the subjects under its rule?[79] The Bengal famine appeared to confirm critics' worst fears and expose the dangers of the monopolisation of trade. Condemnation of the Company did not, however, result in audible calls for the withdrawal of the English from the Hooghly: the phenomenon of empire was not itself called into question. Rather, each criticism of the Company provoked a rethinking and rearticulation of the way that empire would work. Scrutiny of the Company's abuses of power ushered in a new organisational structure with closer supervision of the Company by the British state. The critique of monopoly shifted attention towards the idea of an empire of free trade, outlined most influentially by Adam Smith in *The Wealth of Nations* (1776). In England, expressions of sympathy for the plight of the people of Bengal during the famine were in part a rhetorical device allowing Company misgovernment to be critiqued, but in a very real sense the famine also contributed to the development of a perception of Indians as physically, intellectually, and morally inferior to Europeans.[80] An understanding of empire as a benevolent force for the protection and improvement of non-European peoples—that the English had a moral responsibility to rule over India—began to emerge.

In the century after 1757, Plassey would serve as a template for the Company's treatment of other Indian rulers, as a succession of territories across the subcontinent was swallowed into the Company-state. Today, the events of Plassey offer a warning about the consequences of the unrestrained exercise of power by corporate bodies motivated solely by profit, with the complicity of national governments.

4

CHANDERNAGORE

THE FRENCH REVOLUTION IN BENGAL

In February 1790, a ship called the *Bienvenue* arrived at the French settlement of Pondicherry on the Coromandel coast, carrying news that in France a revolution had begun. In Paris, the Third Estate of the Estates General, representing the common people, had declared itself a National Assembly and passed an unprecedented Declaration of the Rights of Man and of the Citizen. The royal fortress and prison, the Bastille, had been stormed and angry protesters had besieged Louis XVI's palace at Versailles. Pondicherry's residents greeted the outbreak of the revolution with joy. For decades they had complained about the lack of attention bestowed by the French crown on its Indian territories and the inadequate military and financial support they received. A General Assembly modelled on France's new National Assembly was formed to share power with the settlement's royally appointed governor. A list of grievances was composed and a deputation of the General Assembly was sent to represent Pondicherry's interests in Paris.

The reception of the revolution at Chandernagore, France's settlement on the Hooghly, was more dramatic still. Like their Pondicherry compatriots, Chandernagore's citizens were disillusioned with the court of France because of its indifference to their plight. When accounts of the revolution reached their ears, they distributed cockades of liberty and established a General Assembly of their own. Unlike his Pondicherry counterpart, the governor of Chandernagore, François Emmanuel Dehaies de Montigny, refused to recognise the assembly's legitimacy and tensions that could have been defused escalated rapidly. Dehaies de Montigny and his supporters occupied the chateau of Goretty, the governor's country residence just south of Chandernagore. Through the summer of 1790 they claimed to represent the only legal government of the French in Bengal, a claim countered by the General Assembly in the town. The climax of this showdown arrived when the assembly armed Chandernagore's sympathetic citizens and laid siege to the chateau. Dehaies de Montigny surrendered and was imprisoned. A constitution was composed enshrining the principle of representative government.[1]

In France the revolution was a seismic overhaul, sweeping away the ancien régime and instituting ideas of freedom, democracy, and the rule of law. The revolution was not, however, only a European affair. Its repercussions would be felt across the world, including in Bengal, where revolutionary ideas encouraged social and religious reform while simultaneously sustaining and challenging European colonialism. Events on the Hooghly, meanwhile, contributed to the intellectual currents and concrete realities—political, social, and economic—that brought the revolution about.

* * *

France's trade in the Indian Ocean got off to a slow start compared to that of its major European rivals. After several failed ventures a Compagnie des Indes was formed with substantial state backing in 1664. Four years later an initial factory in India was established at Surat and in the following decade the foundations of Pondicherry were laid, 150 kilometres south of Madras. The lucrative prospects of trade with Bengal were first outlined to the Compagnie by the physician François Bernier, whom we encountered earlier at Hooghly: Bernier recommended the establishment of a French factory at Cossimbazaar to take advantage of the manufacture of silk.[2] In the end, it was Hooghly itself that the Compagnie selected for its inaugural Bengal base. A warehouse was opened in the town in the 1670s, before Aurangzeb granted permission for the establishment of a separate French *comptoir* (trading post) on the Hooghly in 1688. A site immediately to the south of the Dutch at Chinsurah was chosen. Chandernagore began as a single storeroom before a more extensive brick factory was constructed, with residential quarters and a chapel tended by two Jesuit priests. When Subha Singh instigated his rebellion in 1696, square fortified walls were built around the factory and Fort d'Orléans was born.[3]

Despite Dutch and English resistance, France had succeeded in gaining a foothold in Bengal. In comparison with the other two companies, however, French trade was very modest. Sales of imported cloth, firearms, and wine failed to meet the costs of the produce that the Compagnie sought to export, while money to fund purchases rarely arrived from Pondicherry when promised. Chandernagore stagnated; there were some years when no French ships arrived at all. The financial problems of the Compagnie were not confined to Bengal and in 1712 its directors decided that they could no longer afford to dispatch vessels to India. The Compagnie's monopoly of trade with the Indies was leased to a body of merchants in Saint-Malo, who sent ships to Pondicherry and Chandernagore for the next six years.[4] The main problem faced by the Compagnie had been a lack of consistent support from the French crown. When Louis XIV died, however, royal interest in the potential of Indian trade was revived. The Sun King was discovered to have left behind an astronomical public debt of more than two billion francs. To pay it off, his ministers resolved to launch a new Compagnie des Indes that might pay handsomely into the state coffers. For its early success, the French court had a Scotsman named John Law to thank. Appointed Controller General of the finances of the French state, Law, from a family of bankers in Fife, established France's first national bank and arranged for the sale of Compagnie shares, creating capital of some 100 million francs.[5] The first signs of prosperity at Chandernagore emerged soon after. French debts in Bengal were liquidated and a regular supply of bullion was used to purchase silk, saltpetre, and foodstuffs for shipping to Pondicherry and Europe. The Compagnie purchased additional villages around Chandernagore as the *comptoir* began to grow.

One of the new arrivals attracted to Chandernagore in this period was a Monsieur Albert, who sailed up the Hooghly in September 1725. Albert found the settlement a bustling and commodious town constructed of stone buildings more beautiful than those of Calcutta and Chinsurah. Along the bank of the river and inland, residents had constructed sturdy single-storey houses with gardens and courtyards. Fort d'Orléans had grown to include a barracks and magazine; a large tank collected water for the town next to the fort's western wall. The riverside marketplace served as a centre of commerce and gossip. Albert estimated that the population of the *comptoir* numbered 500 Europeans, served by approximately 1500 slaves, plus a large number of free Hindus and Muslims. There were two churches: one run by the Jesuits for European and Indian residents, the other by Capuchin friars admitting Europeans alone. A host of Hindu temples lay dotted around the town. During his three-and-a-half month stay, Albert complained about the rain, the heat, and the quality of air but he left convinced about the abundance of the Bengali countryside and the profits to be made, particularly from textiles. He was fascinated by the spectacle of Durga Puja, when, he tells us, the town's Hindus painted images of the goddess Durga on wooden boards, prayed to the images for eight days, and then immersed them in the Hooghly.[6]

It was during the governorship of Joseph François Dupleix that the growth of Chandernagore reached its peak. Born in Flanders in 1697, Dupleix had been sent to India as an official of the old Compagnie aged eighteen. With his father one of the Compagnie's directors, he was always likely to be favoured when it came to appointments: he served as second-in-command at Pondicherry before being appointed governor of Chandernagore in 1731.[7] Prior to Dupleix's arrival, the main source of income for Frenchmen at Chandernagore was the Compagnie's trade between India and Europe. Dupleix realised, however, that wealth could be created in the *comptoir*, as it had been at Pondicherry, via inland and overseas trade conducted by individuals on their private account. Dupleix utilised the fortunes he had made through private trade at Pondicherry to establish an extensive commercial network in which the residents of Chandernagore were encouraged to participate: boats were bought, cargoes freighted, and links established with merchants in Bengal and further afield. For each trading expedition, monies were advanced and a new company of Chandernagore residents was formed. Early ventures went to Dacca, Chittagong, and Patna, as well as Pondicherry and Mahé, the small

French *comptoir* on the Malabar coast. More ambitious voyages followed to Surat, the Persian Gulf, the Arabian Peninsula, China, and South East Asia, as Dupleix and his peers grew in confidence.[8] Among the subscribers to the voyages that Dupleix organised were a number of Englishmen and Dutchmen—indeed, English private capital was essential to get some of the expeditions off the ground. Relationships between merchants of different European nations were often strong. Not only did they undertake private trade together, they collaborated to return profits to Europe on each other's ships and protested jointly against obstacles to trade erected by the nawabs and their officials.

In December 1739, Dupleix quit Chandernagore to take up the governorship of Pondicherry. The timing of his appointment was propitious. That year, storms in the Bay of Bengal had disrupted trade and one of Dupleix's ships returning from Manila laden with cargo had been lost. Inland trade with Patna and northern India had been interrupted by Nadir Shah's conquest of Delhi. It is for his time as governor at Pondicherry that Dupleix is best remembered in history. Shortly after he took up his post, France and England found themselves on opposite sides in the War of Austrian Succession in Europe. The declaration of war between the two countries provided an opportunity for the rival companies in India to check the growing trade and wealth of the other. Dupleix the enterprising trader and efficient administrator was now replaced by Dupleix the ambitious and uncompromising war leader. With the aid of a fleet of warships dispatched from the Isle de France (Mauritius), he seized Madras before turning his attention to the subsidiary English station of Fort St David further down the Coromandel coast at Cuddalore. The Treaty of Aix-la-Chapelle brought hostilities in Europe to a close and secured the return of Madras to the English. In southern India, however, Anglo-French competition for supremacy was only just getting under way. The death of the Nizam of Hyderabad, Asaf Jah I, in 1748 provoked a scramble for control of the Deccan plateau. Dupleix's intervention to install a candidate on the throne sympathetic to French interests inaugurated the European practice of securing dependent Indian rulers in the subcontinent's regional seats of power. The extension of this policy to the Carnatic kingdom of Arcot provoked an English response. In a decisive battle at Arcot in 1751 an English army under the command of Robert Clive defeated the combined forces of the French and Chanda Sahib, Dupleix's nominated nawab. Muhammad Ali Khan, son of the late Nawab Anwaruddin Khan, became ruler with English backing.[9]

Clive's experiences fighting the French in the Carnatic fuelled his conviction that Chandernagore would have to be captured when, after his arrival in Bengal and retaking of Calcutta from Siraj-ud-Daula, war once again broke out between England and France in Europe in 1756. As the conflict between the English and Siraj unfolded, Pierre Renault de St Germain, successor to Dupleix as Chandernagore's governor, adopted a position of neutrality, refusing to side with either party. The governor had just a tiny military force at his disposal, some 140 Europeans and 300 Indians. An alliance with Siraj would have ensured the destruction of Chandernagore in the event of the English defeating the nawab, while supporting the English was out of the question with France and England at war domestically. Renault de St Germain acted quickly to prepare the defences of Chandernagore when he realised that the English were advancing up the Hooghly to attack. Ships were sunk in the river south of Fort d'Orléans to block the passage of the English men-of-war. Batteries were erected on the walls of the fort and the Church of St Louis was demolished because it interfered with the line of fire from the fort to the river. However, the English possessed overwhelming numerical superiority. The men-of-war negotiated their way through the river blockade using information passed on by a treacherous French artillery officer. After a three-hour bombardment and the loss of a hundred men, Renault de St Germain raised the white flag of surrender.[10]

In southern India, Anglo-French hostilities dragged on. In January 1760 English forces under the command of Eyre Coote recorded a major victory at Vandavasi, between Madras and Pondicherry, over the French army of Thomas Arthur, the Comte de Lally, and the following year Pondicherry and Mahé were in English hands. By the end of the Seven Years' War, all French possessions in India had been lost. For his capitulation to the English, Lally would be tried for treason and executed in Paris.

* * *

As the Seven Years' War took its toll, major intellectual and philosophical developments were unfolding in Louis XV's France. Individuals influenced by the rise of Enlightenment thought, with its emphasis on the use of reason, began to question established social, political, economic, and religious practices and ideas. The collective name given to these individuals was *'lumières'*. In the political sphere they questioned absolute monarchy and the doctrine of divine right, arguing for representative institutions, the rights of man regardless of social status, and the obligations of rulers to their subjects. In economics, they contested the prevailing emphasis on mercantilism and monopolistic trade, advocating a return to agricultural production and free unfettered trade. When it came to religion, they emphasised rationality over superstition, rebelling against the imposition of uniformity in matters of faith and contesting the privileges of the Catholic Church.[11] The main targets of the *lumières'* attacks were institutions in France, in particular the monarchy. However, they also turned their attention to European practices overseas, producing a strong current of thought opposed to the activities of the trading companies in the Americas and Indies. Scrutiny of the companies, coupled with an awareness of alternative institutions and ideas in the non-European world, fed a growing sense that existing orthodoxies in Europe—political, religious, economic, and social—stood in need of major reform.

The Americas and Indies had entered the thought of a growing number of philosophers and writers as European trade and influence in the Atlantic and Indian oceans expanded. Francis Bacon wrote of a utopian world in North America where complete freedom of religion existed and all men were equal before the law. The idea of the noble savage emerged in the European literary imagination—a figure of the non-European world that was naturally good and uncorrupted by the trappings of modern civilisation. The first major French writer to weave ideas about India into a critique of European institutions was the first *lumière* to command significant attention—Charles-Louis de Secondat, better known as Montesquieu. Born into a noble family near Bordeaux, Montesquieu had gained prominence when in 1721 he published a set of fictionalised letters purportedly written to recipients at home by two Persian gentlemen travelling through France. Recording the pair's observations on French society and culture, the letters acted as a device through which religious intolerance in France could be critiqued. Having chastised the French church and government for prosecuting non-Catholics, Montesquieu used the ambiguity of the 'Persian letters' to question royal absolutism in turn.[12]

As his frustrations with the government of Louis XV grew, Montesquieu's critique of French politics and society intensified, culminating in *L'Esprit des Lois* (1748). In this prodigious work, Montesquieu advocated the separation of government into executive, legislative, and judicial branches—laying the foundations of modern political theory—and praised the freedom guaranteed by effective administration of the rule of law. Here a perception of the nature of government and society in India came into play. On account of the heat of the country, Montesquieu argued, the people of India were weak and barbarous and the women licentious; Indian rulers were poor, petty, and despotic. The Hindu religion, he held, sapped physical and mental strength, leaving its adherents to live out their lives uneventfully, awaiting cremation and the scattering of their ashes in the Ganges.[13] To our contemporary sensibilities, Montesquieu's thoughts on the effects of climate on the character of a people appear crude; his ideas about the Hindu religion set a precedent for later European caricatures. The essential object of *L'Esprit des Lois* was not, however, to rank India as inferior to Europe but to attack irrationality, intolerance, and arbitrary government in all its forms.[14] By arguing that no single mode of government was suited to all societies, Montesquieu's cultural relativism provided a philosophical basis for later thinkers to critique the European exercise of power in the rest of the world.

Montesquieu's mantle as the leading French public intellectual and writer was claimed in the middle of the eighteenth century by François-Marie Arouet, a Jesuit-educated Parisian who assumed the name Voltaire. In the early 1730s Voltaire had visited England, where he was struck by the religious tolerance, parliamentary system, and relative freedom of speech that he found. He returned to France a radicalised critic of the ancien régime, using his pen to challenge royal absolutism, the privileges of the nobility, and restrictions on freedom of expression.[15] An occasional guest at the court of Louis XV, Voltaire's increasingly acerbic attacks on French government and society would in later years force him into exile in Geneva. Like Montesquieu, Voltaire brought ideas about India into his work. In a treatise on religious toleration he praised the religion of the Brahmans for its purity and simplicity, contrasting it favourably with priest-ridden and irrational Christian faith. The antiquity of the Brahmanical tradition was evoked to disprove the notion that the Judeo-Christian world was the oldest and highest form of civilisation.

In 1763 Voltaire finished writing his *Précis du siècle de Louis XV*, a work of political and cultural history building upon his understanding of historical progress as the result of clashes of ideas. It was in this text that Voltaire first directed sustained attention to the practices of European trading companies in India, developing an influential anticolonial critique. The French and English companies, he observed, had been founded for the purposes of commerce, which ought to have ensured peace—only in the absence of war could trade with India be profitable. However, in part because of Anglo-French competition in Europe, commerce had been turned into an instrument of war. Some Europeans in India, such as Clive and Dupleix in Bengal, had made fortunes through private trade. However, the militarisation of the companies had meant that their official accounts were consistently in the red. Because France had been the last major European power to arrive in India, Voltaire observed, it commanded only a small portion of trade and the Compagnie was reliant on the financial support of the French crown to keep it afloat. Dupleix's policy in the Carnatic—of major military campaigns followed by the installation of compliant Indian rulers—had proven a financial disaster, further overstretching the Compagnie and antagonising the English. Now, at the end of the Seven Years' War, France was left with nothing to show for its considerable investment in Indian trade.[16]

In the *Precis*, Voltaire left open the possibility of a return to peaceful European trade with India; the militarisation of the European companies, rather than their trade, was his primary object of attack (perhaps unsurprisingly, given that Voltaire himself was a Compagnie shareholder). As time went on, however, he became increasingly sceptical about whether or not commerce could be sustained without war. Almost all European trade with Asia and the Americas from the Portuguese onwards had been accompanied by fighting between the European powers, he wrote: 'In order to keep up this trade ... the Powers made war on each other, in which the first cannon shots fired in our climes sets fire to all the batteries in America and in the heart of Asia.'[17] Voltaire was well aware of events on the Hooghly during and after the Seven Years' War, narrating to his readers the capture of Chandernagore, the deposition of Siraj-ud-Daula, and the establishment of the English Company as a territorial power. Bengal, he wrote, was no doubt 'the most beautiful, the richest, and the most delightful country in the world.'[18] English gains there had 'swelled the riches of the nation' as one person after another returned home 'to spend what he has been able to amass on the banks of the Ganges.'[19] European rivalry had however come at great cost to the people of Bengal: 'We have lain waste their country, we have manured it with our blood. We have shown wickedness, and how inferior we are to them in wisdom. Our European nations have killed themselves in this very land where we went only to get rich, and where the Greeks only travelled for knowledge.'[20]

Paris after the Seven Years' War was a hotbed of intellectual activity. In coffee houses and salons, in books, newspapers, and journals, established ideas and institutions were called into question and discarded. Amid this ferment, opposition to the activities of the European trading companies in India was intensified by the publication of a series of memoirs and tracts written by eyewitnesses of events on the subcontinent, and particularly of English actions on the Hooghly. The most influential of these was Willem Bolts' *Considerations on Indian affairs*, published in London in 1772 and translated into French soon after. A cosmopolitan Dutchman who moved fluidly from one European state and language to the next, Bolts had entered the service of the English East India Company in 1759. Sent to Bengal as a factor, he quickly added Bengali to his arsenal of languages and, taking advantage of the possibilities created by the Company's position after the dethroning of Siraj, acquired a fortune through private trade in wool, saltpetre, and opium. Accused of mistreating Indian traders and disobeying Company orders to curb his private profiteering, he was dismissed from English service in 1766, leaving Bengal the following year. Back in Europe, Bolts became one of the most outspoken critics of the Company's activities on the Hooghly.[21]

From its starting point as one trading party among many, Bolts argued, the Company had monopolised not only the commerce of Bengal but its land, revenues, and justice as well. 'Monopolies of all kinds are in their natures unavoidably pernicious,' he observed, 'but an absolute government of monopolists, such as at present that of Bengal in fact is, must of all be the most dreadful.'[22] Bolts was adamant that the Company was now the sovereign power in Bengal. However, its responsibilities as sovereign, to act for the well-being of the country and peoples under its rule, were diametrically opposed to the pursuit of profit demanded by its shareholders. As such, Bengal had been ruined under Company rule. Bolts devoted a substantial part of *Considerations* to documenting the abuses carried out by the Company and its agents on the Hooghly. To ensure a monopoly on the trade of cotton, he wrote, Company servants regularly flogged and imprisoned weavers, forcing them to sell only to the English. To collect revenue, they harassed and tortured peasants only to pocket a portion of the collections themselves. Clive had accepted the *diwani*, Bolts argued, only so that his and others' private trading fortunes could be protected. Justice was administered arbitrarily without due regard for legal process. Little wonder, he concluded, that the Company had been 'rendered hateful to the natives'—it exercised 'powers of despotic sovereignty' that no former ruler of India, not even the Mughals, had possessed.[23]

A second first-hand writer influential to the *lumières'* developing anti-colonial critique was Alexander Dow, a Scottish officer of the English company serving in Bengal for most of the period 1760–74. A scholar in his spare time, Dow published an acclaimed *History of Hindostan* under the Mughals to which he added a preface on the state of Bengal under Company rule. Dow's key contention in the preface was that the Company's attempts to extract profit from Bengal had been self-defeating, exhausting the province's revenues, crippling its manufacturing, and ruining its agricultural production—an avoidable process of decline culminating in the great famine of 1770. In line with Bolts, he said the enforcement of trading monopolies and the coercive collection of taxes were to blame. War between the armies of the Company and the nawabs, meanwhile, had left behind a desolate landscape, expelling or destroying huge numbers of people while adding unnecessarily to the Company's expenditure. 'We may date the commencement of decline, from the day in which Bengal fell under the dominion of foreigners,' Dow contended, before calculating exactly what he thought the annual financial drain from Bengal to England to be.[24]

Encouraged by the accounts coming out of Bengal, French writers extended and sharpened Voltaire's criticism of the European trading companies—and in particular of the pernicious effects of the English seizure of power on the Hooghly. In 1768, the Abbé Roubaud, an economist and popular writer, published *Le Politique Indien*, a text in which he accused the English company of governing Bengal despotically, abandoning the responsibilities of state for private gain. The playwright Pierre-Augustin Caron de Beaumarchais wrote of the Englishman's propensity to oppress and annihilate in America and the Indies.[25] The *Journal Encylopédique* noted the contrast between English laws and freedoms at home and the oppressions carried out by Englishmen in Bengal: the English, it stated, 'revolt against any imposition of a yoke on them, but suffer no shame in imposing it on others ... and oppress the Hindoos with impunity.'[26]

The culmination of these criticisms was the monumental *Histoire Philosophique et Politique des Établissemens et du Commerce des Européens dans les Deux Indes* (1770). Published—in order to protect its authors—under the name of the Abbé Raynal (a Jesuit priest turned radical Enlightenment critic), this work was in fact a major collaborative effort, bringing together the leading French thinkers and writers opposed to European abuses of power in the non-European world. The *Histoire* was an underground publishing sensation. Banned by the French and other governments, and by the papacy in 1774, it was translated and disseminated through Europe's literary circles all the same. The French original was republished in revised and enlarged form twice in the next decade and was more widely read than almost all other texts of the French Enlightenment that we consider important today.[27] According to one estimate, it was the third-most-read book in later-eighteenth-century France, reproduced in more than seventy authorised and pirated versions.[28]

The *Histoire*'s main argument was that the expansion of European trade and influence across the globe had been founded on a military-backed oppression contrary to the true spirit of commerce—free exchange between peoples—and therefore lacked moral or legal legitimacy. In the Americas and Indies, Europeans had deployed violence in a systematically exploitative way. Philosophically, the authors of the *Histoire* conceived of oppression as a complex social, cultural, and economic phenomenon produced by defective institutions and the supremacy of ignorance and superstition over enlightened rational thought. They appealed to public opinion to protect the rights of humanity and projected a future when men across the globe, informed by Enlightenment ideas of democracy, secularism, and the rule of law, would become equal, contented, and free.[29] Like other anti-colonial texts of the period, the *Histoire* attacked European practices overseas in part to critique institutions and ideas at home. Overthrowing exploitation in India and usurping existing structures in France would be interrelated steps in a global process of change.

The third and final edition of the *Histoire*, published in 1780, was the most radical of all. Produced in ten volumes combining extensive narrative, commentary, and criticism, it included chapters on Spanish, Portuguese, Dutch, French, English, and other European colonialisms in the Americas and the Indian Ocean (the *'deux Indes'*). While this edition, like the others, was a collaborative enterprise, recent research has uncovered that its main author was Denis Diderot, who wrote up to half of it and edited the rest—a herculean task that consumed almost a decade of his life.[30] A native of Champagne in eastern France, Diderot was an Enlightenment polymath whose writings included works on philosophy, science, theology, and history in the form of multi-volume tomes, essays, novels, and plays. Opposed to the privileges of the Catholic Church, he was attracted to Deism but moved gradually towards the rejection of all religion. In the political realm, he argued for representative institutions and the prevention of abuses in taxation and administration. In economics, he advocated the more equal distribution of wealth and lauded the virtues of agricultural production over manufacturing.[31] The collaborative undertaking for which Diderot is best remembered today is the *Encyclopédie*, a seventeen-volume compendium of articles on science and technology, theology and philosophy, politics, history, and the arts—among other subjects. Diderot edited the *Encyclopédie* and wrote many of its entries; the leading figures of the French Enlightenment, including Montesquieu, Voltaire, and Rousseau, also contributed to it, motivated by a belief in the necessary triumph of reason over superstition, knowledge over ignorance. The *Histoire* was an equally impressive achievement, carrying the *Encyclopédie*'s concern to challenge dogmatism and despotism onto the global stage.

In the *Histoire*, Diderot passionately denounced Spanish, Portuguese, and Dutch colonial practices but the oppressions carried out by the English around the globe were his major concern. The activities of the East India Company and its agents on the Hooghly claimed his particular attention. Before the arrival of Europeans, Diderot noted, echoing Voltaire, Bengal was 'the richest and most populous' province in the Mughal Empire, with lucrative inland and overseas trade carried out by Asian merchants.[32] The English, however, had taken advantage of the trading privileges granted to them to monopolise the trade of cloth, saltpetre, and opium before encroaching on inland manufacturing and the trade of other commodities, destroying pre-existent commerce. Diderot, who never travelled further east than St Petersburg, was very knowledgeable about the recent history of Bengal, recounting in detail the break-up of the Mughal Empire, the rise of independent nawabs, the influence of the Jagat Seths, and the English seizure of power. Readers of the *Histoire* were transported to the Hooghly by his description of a journey up the river. Calcutta, he imagined, was fortified and prosperous but possessed of an 'unwholesome air'.[33] Chandernagore, in contrast, had an excellent harbour and air 'as pure as can be found on the banks of the Ganges'.[34] At Hooghly, a Portuguese flag fluttered in the wind, recalling grander times past.

Informed by the reports of Bolts and Dow, Diderot believed that the English Company's monopolisation of trade and control of revenue administration had produced an economic crisis in Bengal: goods and money were sent to Europe but little was brought in return, with exports financed by land revenues. The human costs of trade monopolisation and revenue maximisation had been immense: farmers and peasants were bled dry, tradesmen and merchants impoverished—processes only possible through the exercise of violence by the Company's soldiers and civil agents on an unprecedented scale. The result was the great famine, which 'the very love of humankind, that sentiment innate in all hearts' should have moved the English to do more to prevent.[35] Employing a technique common in the *Histoire*, Diderot adopted the voice of an imaginary Bengali appealing to his English overlords, asking them why they were not trying harder to alleviate the famine:

What have you done for our preservation? What steps have you taken to remove from us the scourge that threatened us? Deprived of all authority, stripped of our property, weighed down by the terrible hand of power, we can only lift our hands to you to implore your assistance. Ye have heard our groans; ye have seen famine making very quick advances upon us; and then ye attended to your own preservation ... Where are the laws and the morals of which ye are so proud?[36]

In Bengal, Diderot answered, in the absence of established laws and motivated solely by profit, Englishmen had abandoned their sense of moral and social responsibility. The pretence of the sovereignty of the nawab facilitated this self-interested neglect of the basic human duty to act justly:

> Strange indignity, to wish to exercise oppression, without appearing unjust; to be desirous of reaping the fruits of one's rapine, and to throw the odium of it upon another. Not to blush at acts of tyranny, and yet to blush at the name of tyrant. How wicked is man, and how much more flagitious would he be, if he could be convinced that his crimes would remain unknown, and that the punishment or ignominy of them, would fall upon an innocent person.[37]

In the salons and coffee houses of Paris, the perception of English abuses in Bengal spread by the rhetoric of the *Histoire* raised the question of what role, if any, France should play in India in the future. Some public figures believed that their country should abstain from contact with the subcontinent altogether. France had no right to colonise India, they argued; to do so would be in contradiction of ideas of freedom and the rights of man. Trade with the subcontinent, it was added, had never been profitable and no advantage could be derived from restarting it; the Indian *comptoirs* had been nothing more than a drain on the nation. Adherents to this school of thought were influenced by a prominent group of economists known as the Physiocrats, who argued that the wealth of nations derived solely from the cultivation of agricultural land. The import of 'luxury' goods, they contended, had proven financially unsustainable and weakened the moral character of the nation.[38]

A second school of thought suggested that while, in light of the ultimately ruinous policy of Dupleix, all territorial ambitions in India should be abandoned, trade with the subcontinent should be resumed. Most of the leading *lumières* interested in the European presence overseas, including Montesquieu and Voltaire, distinguished between trade as mutually beneficial exchange and trade sustained by force, though their faith in European parties maintaining this distinction wavered and varied. As France began rebuilding after its loss in the Seven Years' War, its military capacity crippled, the idea of a peaceful reciprocal Indian trade was revived and claimed widespread support among the educated classes.

Almost imperceptibly, the endorsement of this idea slipped into a third understanding of what the French role in India should be. Bengal, it was widely accepted, was groaning under the yoke of oppressive English rule, its economy ruined and its people impoverished. Here and elsewhere in the subcontinent the legitimate rule of Indian kings and princes had been usurped. Alongside the resumption and growth of its trade, then, France had a responsibility to assist the people of India in resisting English oppression and overthrowing the Company's rule. In *Le Politique Indien*, Abbé Roubaud advocated the renewal of trade with India and the extension of French assistance to the dispossessed rulers of Bengal and southern India, one of the earliest articulations of this view.[39]

For all his opposition to European oppressions in the Americas and Asia, Diderot too would stop short of advocating a prolonged French withdrawal from engagement with the extra-European world. In a section of the *Histoire* on the future of the French in India, he endorsed the continuation of trade, suggesting that peaceful and open commerce could constitute a beneficial link between nations. Noting once again that the English in Bengal governed despotically, he then indicated that the correct role for the French on the Hooghly might in fact be more than commercial. Should the people of Bengal unite to overthrow English oppression, he suggested, it would be right, in the interests of humanity, for the French to assist their cause. Should French merchants, through their support of the rightful Indian rulers of the province, find themselves in a position of influence once again, they must act justly and humanely, faithfully observing treaties, mediating in but not manipulating disputes, and pursuing moderate profits from trade. Should Frenchmen acquire control of land, they must govern it in the interests of the whole population, securing the liberty of the individual and property, fairly administering justice and developing industry and agriculture. They would gain the support of the native inhabitants by exhibiting their justness.[40]

Diderot thought that the people of Bengal would one day rise up 'in favour of their common liberty'.[41] How far he truly believed that it would be possible for the French to assist them in this task by placing the interests of humanity above their self-interested pursuit of gain is unclear. What is evident, however, is that Diderot's critique of the English exercise of power in India after 1757 contained within it the seeds of a new legitimation of empire based on the idea of European benevolence—that India might be administered by a European nation in the interests of its indigenous population. French notions of benevolent imperialism developed in opposition to the perception of British oppressions in India, especially on the Hooghly. The idea of the French as liberators of India from oppressive English rule would exercise a powerful hold on Frenchmen in Bengal as Chandernagore was rebuilt from 1765.

* * *

Under the terms of the Treaty of Paris, signed at the end of the Seven Years' War, France lost most of its possessions in North America. In return for the restoration of those territories that it had seized from Britain, however, its Indian *comptoirs* were restored, along with some of the Caribbean islands that it claimed. Most of the French possessions in India were returned without conditions attached. In the case of Chandernagore, however, France was forced to commit to terms promising that the settlement would not be fortified and that no troops except for a handful necessary for the preservation of internal order would be stationed there.[42] By these stipulations, the centrality of the Hooghly to the Anglo-French struggle for global dominance was confirmed.

The man appointed director of the French territories in India upon their restoration was Jean Law de Lauriston, nephew of the financier John Law whose reforms had been so important to the flourishing of the new Compagnie from 1721. In 1757, Law Junior had been the Compagnie's chief factor at Cossimbazaar. When the English defeated Siraj-ud-Daula at Plassey he escaped Bengal, fleeing to Patna with 300 troops before journeying across northern India to Delhi. At Lucknow, he attempted unsuccessfully to convince the nawab of Awadh, Shuja al-Daulah, to invade Bengal and rescue it from the English. In the Mughal capital, he formed an alliance with the future Shah Alam II. His participation in Shah Alam's campaigns against the Company was brought to an end when he was apprehended and arrested by the English in January 1761.[43] After a three-year absence from Bengal he returned in 1765 to find Chandernagore in ruins. Fort d'Orléans and other large buildings had been reduced to rubble. Commerce was at a standstill. The *comptoir's* population had shrunk to less than half of its total before the English takeover and was in a thoroughly 'languishing state'.[44] Conscious that the trade of Bengal was potentially the most lucrative in India, Law entertained the idea of stationing himself at Chandernagore and making it the administrative centre of the French Indian territories, in spite of the military restrictions imposed by the Paris treaty. When he saw the condition of the town, however, he changed his mind and set up his government at Pondicherry instead.

The governorship of Chandernagore was awarded to Jean-Baptiste Chevalier, an enterprising and patriotic Bengal veteran who in the 1750s had led a series of expeditions to establish trading links with the kingdom of Assam.[45] Under Chevalier's direction, signs of prosperity began to return to Chandernagore. Trade picked up, with three or four ships arriving each year from Europe. Commercial links were re-established with South East Asia and the Persian Gulf. Chevalier played a leading role in the revival of private trade, organising voyages to export Bengali sugar and rice to the Isle de France and the Île Bourbon (Reunion Island). The improvement of French fortunes on the Hooghly was viewed with some concern by Englishmen: Chevalier complained repeatedly to the English authorities in Calcutta about their attempts to disrupt his compatriots' trade.[46] Nevertheless, the prosperity of Chandernagore continued to recover. In 1769, the French crown, prompted by growing domestic criticisms of the principle of monopoly, revoked the Compagnie's right to exclusive trade between India and France, creating new opportunities for merchants with capital to invest. Chevalier and other residents of Chandernagore responded by organising a succession of joint-stock voyages to Europe. The growing wealth of Chevalier and his administration at this juncture was exhibited by the conversion of the governor's country residence at Goretty from a small house dating back to Dupleix's governorship into a large and gracious columned chateau set in a forested estate on the Hooghly's bank. With its elegant staircases, saloons, and painted ceilings, the chateau of Goretty was thought by some to rival the palace of Versailles in splendour.[47]

Chevalier enjoyed warm personal relations with some Englishmen in Bengal, including the head of the Company's council in Calcutta, Harry Verelst, and his successor Warren Hastings. High-ranking Englishmen enjoyed his hospitality at Goretty, a favourite weekend retreat from Calcutta. As the prosperity of Chandernagore revived, however, the governor began to plan the overthrow of English power in Bengal. Behind his 'expressions of civilities and friendships' towards the English, Chevalier believed that the people of Bengal were oppressed and suffering under English rule.[48] In his correspondence, he wrote determinedly about the need to 'raise the standard of liberty' in the country and expressed a conviction that Bengalis were desperate for French assistance to set them free:

> There is not a soul in Bengal who would not contribute with all his heart to facilitate through our channel, the total expulsion of the English nation. All the people from the biggest to the smallest are tired of their yoke and can no longer bear it; they are only waiting for a favourable occasion to give vent to their sentiments, and it is in the French alone that they place all their confidence for their deliverance.[49]

To liberate Bengal, Chevalier thought, it would be necessary to form alliances with Indian sovereigns, the natural rulers of the land. 'If ever we carry the war to this country,' he suggested, 'we shall find here as many allies as there are Princes.'[50] Chevalier was of course aware that overthrowing English power in Bengal would have advantages for the French, changing the European balance of power and allowing Frenchmen to profit more from Indian trade. Once Bengal had been freed from English dominance, he suggested, the rest of India would follow. Chevalier, however, stopped short of advocating the installing of France as a territorial power on the subcontinent in place of the English. Rather, the province's legitimate Indian rulers would be put back on their thrones; France would resume its policy prior to the Carnatic Wars of peaceful and prosperous trade under the protection of sympathetic Indian rulers.

To put his grand plan into effect, Chevalier opened up diplomatic correspondence with key Indian princes in Bengal, Bihar, and northern India and dispatched secret embassies to their courts. His initial idea was to revive the Nasiri dynasty of Murshid Quli Khan. Since Alivardi Khan's seizure of power from Quli Khan's grandson, Sarfaraz Khan, in 1740, relatives of the deposed nawab had resided at Dacca. Chevalier approached the family with a view to restoring it on the throne, drawing upon the history of dynastic rivalry in Bengal as a possible source of future regime change. Concurrently he approached Mir Qasim, a ruler without territory following his deposition by the English, and made overtures to Shuja al-Daulah at Lucknow.[51] The joint ambitions of Shuja and Mir Qasim to wrestle Bengal from English control had been defeated by the Company's armies at Buxar in 1764. Chevalier believed that with French support they could be convinced to have another go. In 1772, after years of fighting for the recognition of his claim to the Mughal throne, Shah Alam II returned to Delhi and was installed as emperor with the backing of the Maratha ruler of Gwalior, Mahadaji Sindhia. Chevalier's focus now shifted to the formation of an alliance with the emperor and his Maratha friends. If French support were offered to Shah Alam to help him consolidate his position, Chevalier reasoned, the protection of French interests in India would follow. Chevalier wrote to the government at Versailles, requesting the dispatch of 5000 troops from France to Delhi to support the new sovereign. His plea was turned down by Louis XV's court, which rightly thought England would interpret the committing of forces as an act of aggression.[52]

This refusal highlighted a problem with Chevalier's plans. In spite of his rhetoric about offering French assistance to liberate Bengal from English rule, the governor of Chandernagore had no significant military or financial resources at his disposal, while requests for assistance from Pondicherry, the French government on the Isle de France, and Versailles were routinely rejected or ignored. One resource that he could potentially mobilise was the French generals and soldiers in the service of various Indian rulers. After the defeat of France in India during the Seven Years' War, a large number of Frenchmen for whom there was no possibility of returning home and no French power to serve had taken employment in Indian courts, where their knowledge of European military techniques made them valuable. They included the Comte de Modave, who served under Shuja al-Daulah and Shah Alam; Jean-Baptiste-Joseph Gentil, who was hired by Mir Kasim and Shuja; and René Madec, who also found employment at Awadh.[53] Chevalier maintained contact with these military adventurers, believing that through their influence the rulers they served could be persuaded to rise up against the English. His efforts increasingly focused on Madec, who entered into the service of the Rohillas and the Jats after the English victory at Buxar. Chevalier convinced Madec, with his band of 200 European and 3000 Indian troops, to abandon the Jats and attach himself to Shah Alam's court at Delhi.[54] He then came up with his most ambitious scheme yet to counter English power: to convince the emperor, through Madec, to cede to France the province of Tatta, on the coast of Sindh near present-day Karachi. The intention was to use this for the maintenance of a large French army that, if called upon, would come to his support and, when the time was right, unite with Mughal forces to retake Bengal.[55] Chevalier thought this plan less likely to antagonise the English than the direct dispatch of French troops to Delhi and begged Versailles to support it.

The English council in Calcutta received regular intelligence about Chevalier's plans. Many of them were dismissed as fanciful: the governor's scheme to encourage Shuja al-Daulah to re-invade Bengal, for example, was regarded as the 'wild project of a visionary and ambitious man that did not carry for the present any probability of success, nor could we persuade ourselves that the Court of France at this time meant to adopt it.'[56] Some of Chevalier's actions did, however, cause the English alarm. In spring 1769, at a time of heightened Anglo-French tensions in Europe and the build-up of French naval forces on the Isle de France, Chevalier ordered the construction of a large ditch, 50 feet wide and 12 feet deep, around Chandernagore. The governor claimed that the ditch was needed for drainage. To the English, however, it looked suspiciously like an attempt to fortify Chandernagore, in contravention of the Treaty of Paris. The Calcutta council demanded that the ditch be filled up. When Chevalier refused, they sent troops and engineers and did it themselves. Aware of Chevalier's plotting, the English policy was to remain vigilant and 'at all times upon guard against a surprise'.[57]

The possibility that the English most feared was an alliance between the French and the Marathas. By the early 1770s, the Maratha Empire stretched through a confederacy of relatively autonomous rulers across much of the Indian subcontinent. In the south, the Marathas had inflicted major defeats on Hyder Ali of Mysore and Nizam Ali of Hyderabad. Expeditions in the north had forced the surrender of Rajput and Jat governors and resulted in Shah Alam being taken under Maratha protection. From his station at Pondicherry, Jean Law surmised that 'this Maratha nation is unquestionably the most powerful in India; the only one in which there is a very steady government and the only one whom the English respect.'[58] Chevalier agreed, recording that the Marathas were the 'most powerful and most warlike' of Indian powers and those with the greatest resources.[59] As the ditch controversy unfolded at Chandernagore, Chevalier initiated communication with Janoji Bhonsle, the Maratha leader of Nagpur, about a possible invasion of Bengal. Soon after, he dispatched an agent to the Maratha capital of Poona to request a loan to fund the transport of troops from France to India. Maratha successes in northern India in late 1769 made an alliance even more crucial to the governor of Chandernagore: only through Maratha influence could an effective partnership with Shah Alam be secured. Chevalier sent an emissary from Chandernagore to Delhi disguised as a Muslim merchant to seal a deal with Mahadaji Sindhia of Gwalior. Under the terms of the agreement reached, the Marathas would side with the French if war commenced between France and England in India; in return, the French would recognise Maratha sovereignty.[60] Formalising the draft treaty, however, required the consent of the Court of France, which never arrived. Louis XV's ministers, ignoring French opinion in India, favoured an alliance with Hyder Ali, to whom a royal embassy was sent in 1769. Once again, Chevalier's efforts were overlooked.

As time wore on, Chevalier grew increasingly frustrated with Versailles, complaining of the French government's 'inertia' to the Indian cause.[61] One influential figure sympathetic to his plans was Louis XV's foreign minister Étienne François, the Duc de Choiseul, who argued for a French naval campaign against English interests in India as the diversion for an attack on England itself. Choiseul accelerated the redevelopment of his nation's military capacity and gathered naval forces on the Isle de France in preparation for 'Operation Hindusthan'. However, his forward policy of *revanche* was at odds with majority opinion at Versailles, which favoured the preservation of peace with England at least until French military and financial strength had fully recovered from the Seven Years' War. For leading France, allied with Spain, to the brink of war with England over the Falkland Islands without the approval of Louis XV, Choiseul was dismissed as foreign minister in 1770. His successor, the Marquis of Boynes, cautioned Chevalier not to provoke war with the English.[62]

Only with the outbreak of the War of American Independence did the position of the French government change. From early 1776, France, sufficiently confident of its military strength, began arming the Patriots and preparing for war with England. Chevalier's plans now received serious attention in Versailles for the first time: the decision was taken to send a royal diplomat to India to investigate the possibility of an alliance with Shah Alam and a combined French–Mughal invasion of Bengal. To Chevalier's great distress, François Emmanuel Dehaies de Montigny arrived too late. By the time he made it to Delhi, Madec had left for Pondicherry, disillusioned by the court of France's prevarication over his negotiations with the Mughal emperor.[63] War had been declared between England and France and the English had occupied Chandernagore once again.

* * *

As soon as it became clear that France would support the cause of American independence, the English East India Company increased the number of troops it had stationed on the Hooghly. When news reached Bengal that England and France were at war, the Calcutta council acted immediately. Troops entered Chandernagore and a company of soldiers was dispatched to arrest Chevalier at Goretty. Despite his advanced age, Chevalier was too quick for the English soldiers. As they entered the outer quarters of the Goretty chateau he escaped through an open window and fled. Three weeks later he was arrested by Company agents at Cuttack in Orissa. Less forgiving members of the Company's administration wanted Chevalier to remain in their custody for the duration of the war. However, the sympathetic Warren Hastings permitted the ex-governor to return to Europe on board a neutral Danish vessel. He left Bengal for the final time with his dream of overthrowing the English in tatters: 'My heart bleeds at all the events that I witness. The moment of our ruin and of our expulsion from India is approaching everyday.'[64]

The Company's occupation of Chandernagore was heavy-handed. Though the *comptoir*'s residents offered no opposition to the English, merchants' property was seized, boats were embargoed, and seals were affixed to warehouses to prevent the movement of goods. All influential Frenchmen and those in official positions were declared prisoners of war and placed under house arrest. French river pilots, whose knowledge of the navigation of the Hooghly made them very valuable, were imprisoned in Fort William. A flood of protests from the residents of Chandernagore followed. Their settlement, they argued, was purely commercial in character; devoid of a military presence, it posed no threat and ought to have remained unaffected by the declaration of war. Moreover, the confiscation of private property from a people who had shown no antagonism was 'contrary to the laws of war'.[65] Without trade, Chandernagore's population faced ruin.

The Calcutta council was unmoved. Two months into the occupation it resolved that all prisoners of war would have to leave Bengal. They were given a stay of execution to sell their property and arrange their affairs before being deported to the Isle de France. Women, children, the elderly and infirm, along with non-French residents of Chandernagore and Frenchmen of insignificant rank or station, were permitted to remain on taking an oath of allegiance to Britain. For their subsistence they were granted a stipend commensurate with their social standing. To transport the prisoners of war to the Isle de France, the Company chartered a ship named the *Warren*. After the prisoners had been deposited on the island, the government of the Isle de France refused to let the *Warren* leave. Its English captain and crew were arrested and the vessel was claimed for France's war effort. For Chandernagore's residents, the consequences of this breach of trust were grave. All stipends were stopped and the remaining men of French descent were ordered to vacate Bengal. Those who lacked the will or means to quit Chandernagore were interned in a makeshift prison constructed by the conversion of the old arsenal at the Fort d'Orléans. Seventy prisoners, ranging from once-wealthy merchants to the gardener at Goretty, were housed in two small rooms where leaky windows and inadequate sanitation meant that damp and disease quickly set in. The prison's English supervisor resigned in protest at the conditions.[66]

While this spectacle of human suffering was unfolding, English society in Calcutta was preoccupied with Anglo-French relations of a different kind. In December 1778 Philip Francis, Warren Hastings' deputy in council, was caught having an affair with Catherine Grand, reputedly 'the most beautiful woman in Calcutta'.[67] Tall and elegant, with a delicate complexion, auburn hair, and striking blue eyes, Grand (née Worlée) had been born on the Coromandel coast to an Indian mother and a French military officer. She was raised at Chandernagore, where aged fifteen she met and married George Francis Grand, an English civil officer of Huguenot descent. Just a few months later her affair with Philip Francis began. After the pair were discovered by servants at the Grands' home, George Francis Grand brought a lawsuit against Francis for trespass. Details of the affair were scrutinised in the Calcutta High Court for weeks, to gossipmongers' delight. At the end of a long-drawn-out case, Philip Francis was sentenced to pay fifty thousand rupees as damages. Catherine and George Francis Grand separated; Catherine lived with Philip Francis before returning to Europe in 1780. Departure from the Hooghly was not the end of Catherine Grand's notoriety. In Paris she would gain a reputation as the most handsome courtesan of her day. After the revolution, she became the mistress and eventually the wife of Charles Maurice de Talleyrand-Périgord, the former bishop who served as France's chief diplomat under Napoleon.

* * *

No French attempt was made to attack the English in Bengal and relieve Chandernagore during the course of Anglo-French hostilities in the American war. While Chevalier, Law, and other Frenchmen on the subcontinent hoped that the conflict would be used to strike at the English in India, the bulk of French military and financial resources went to the Americas instead. Pondicherry was surrendered to the English in early 1779, after a 77-day siege; the fall of Mahé soon after meant that once again France had none of its *comptoirs* left. Through

1779 and 1780 the English were at war with both the Marathas and Hyder Ali in the south. A French attack on the Company would have stood an unprecedented chance of success. However, the court of Versailles, preoccupied with events in America and the Caribbean, once again failed to seize the moment. A French naval force was dispatched to India only in March 1781 and a land force in December that year. By the time of their arrival, hostilities between the English and the Marathas were at an end. The English war with Hyder Ali continued, but no effective military alliance between France and the Mysore ruler was achieved. Hyder Ali was unimpressed by the size of the French army and its delay in coming to his aid. The news of a fresh peace accord between England and France in Europe reached India in June 1783, bringing an end to hostilities on the subcontinent before a serious blow could be inflicted on the military and political dominance of the English.

The financial costs of the American War of Independence were one of the final nails in the coffin of the ancien régime in France. The French monarchy was insolvent. Louis XVI's attempts to impose a new land tax on the nobility and clergy provoked the meeting of the Estates General in May 1789 that brought the revolution about. Of the fact that the revolution was informed by the Enlightenment ideas of the *lumières*, there is no doubt. The transformation of the Third Estate of the Estates General—representative of the interests of the clergy, nobility, and people to the monarchy—into a National Assembly was guided by notions of freedom and equality that made representative government imperative. The abolition of feudal rights and the Declaration of the Rights of Man and of the Citizen were attacks on absolutist government and aristocratic privilege inspired by the ideas of the *lumières*. Concepts of equality, democracy, and freedom of expression originally expounded in France by the *lumières* dominated in the revolutionary leadership at least until the first national constitution was adopted in 1791.[68] These ideas were shaped by the *lumières'* perception of the inadequacy of existing political, economic, and social structures not just in Europe but across the world, including on the banks of the Hooghly.

European colonialism in India was in the minds of leaders of the revolution as it gathered momentum. The Declaration of the Rights of

Man and of the Citizen—which enshrined the great principle that 'Men are born and remain free and equal in rights'—was proclaimed universally applicable; English oppressions in India were mentioned explicitly in the debate surrounding it.[69] Willem Bolts was heralded a revolutionary hero for his exposure of the despotic nature of English power on the Hooghly during the transformation of the Company from a trading body into a territorial power. Revolutionary leaders attempting to educate French peasants about the ideas of freedom, equality, and democracy delivered lessons on world politics in which the oppressions carried out by the English in Bengal were described.[70]

In 1783, Chandernagore had been restored to France once again, on the same terms as twenty years earlier: French trading rights were to be protected but no fortifications or significant military presence would be permitted. The years of English occupation had taken their toll: little commerce existed and buildings had been taken over by rot and white ants. The population received a boost after the release of the prisoners of war and the return of some of the Isle de France exiles, but opportunities for trade were limited in the face of English competition. The disaffected population of the *comptoir* was ripe for revolution. Political unrest began when Chandernagore's new governor, the naval officer Benoît Mottet de La Fontaine, was dismissed in 1788 for failing to engineer a revival of trade. His replacement was Dehaies de Montigny, who arrived fresh from a lengthy spell as royal ambassador at the Maratha court at Poona after the failure of his embassy to Delhi in the previous decade. The early signs of Dehaies de Montigny's administration were encouraging. To encourage a commercial revival, he established state monopolies on the French trade of salt and opium and granted permits to Chandernagore residents to trade on the state's behalf, with profits split equally. However, Dehaies de Montigny proved a deeply unpopular leader. Since Chevalier's time, power at Chandernagore had been shared between the governor and a committee composed of influential officials and merchants. Though the governor's decision was final, it was expected that the views of other leading figures would be taken into account. Dehaies de Montigny dissolved the committee. When Jean-Baptiste Richemont, prosecutor of the Chandernagore court, objected to this arbitrary act he was accused by Dehaies de Montigny of corruption and suspended from office.[71]

Early in 1790, Richemont travelled to Pondicherry to seek the overturn of Dehaies de Montigny's decision. He arrived within days of the *Bienvenue*'s appearance on the Coromandel coast carrying news of the revolution in France. Richemont's case was heard by the newly established Pondicherry General Assembly, which thought it a classic example of the despotic exercise of power contrary to enlightened democratic government. Richemont was championed as 'a martyr to the cause of liberty' and reinstated as prosecutor.[72] Dehaies de Montigny, it was suggested, had spent so long at the Maratha court that he had turned into a 'despot' himself.[73] Richemont now returned to Bengal to spread word of the revolution in France and challenge Dehaies de Montigny's rule. He played the leading role in the establishment of Chandernagore's General Assembly in May 1790 and populated its executive council with disaffected members of the governing committee that Dehaies de Montigny had dissolved.

A spirit of revolution was in the air. Dehaies de Montigny was summoned to appear before the assembly and swear an oath recognising its authority over his own—just as Louis XVI had been forced to accept the validity of the National Assembly in Paris. Fearing for his safety, the governor swore the oath but had no intention of observing it. The following week, he crept away from Chandernagore and took up exile in neighbouring Chinsurah. His supporters followed him, creating a small colony of Frenchmen in the Dutch settlement. Encouraged by the defection to his side of the commander of Chandernagore's small contingent of troops, Dehaies de Montigny then installed himself at the Goretty chateau and through the summer of 1790 presented his government as the only legitimate administration of the French in Bengal. The climax of the standoff between the General Assembly and the governor came on 2 September 1790 when the assembly armed the citizens of Chandernagore and marched out to surround the chateau. To the revolutionary brigade, Goretty was a symbol of the absolutist government of the French in Bengal; its besieging was the Hooghly's equivalent of the storming of the Bastille. As Dehaies de Montigny and his supporters prepared for the defence of the chateau, news reached him that he had been dismissed as governor by the administration of the Isle de France, which had overarching authority for French colonial possessions in the Indian Ocean. He surrendered without a fight and was imprisoned, with his supporters, at Chandernagore.

The French Revolution in Europe was ultimately undermined by internal divisions and the intervention of external powers, above all England, during the Napoleonic Wars. On the Hooghly, events would follow a remarkably similar course. In November 1791, two months after Louis XVI had been forced to accept the idea of popular sovereignty in France, committing to a written constitution, Chandernagore declared a constitution too: governmental power would be exercised by an assembly composed of all male citizens over the age of twenty-five; justice would be administered by two tribunals, one for Europeans and one for Indians, that the assembly elected.[74] All was not well in the *comptoir*, however. A group of citizens concerned at the growing power of Richemont in the assembly were accused of conspiring to overthrow the revolutionary government and cast into jail. Members of the assembly bickered over how to divide up profits from the opium trade.

The Calcutta council followed Chandernagore's revolution closely. When Dehaies de Montigny was arrested in September 1790 it expressed its alarm. The governor was a figure on whom Hastings' successor, Lord Cornwallis, believed he could rely to stop the revolution getting out of hand. To prevent Dehaies de Montigny's deportation to France, where a trial by the National Assembly awaited him, Cornwallis used the pretext that the citizens' militia that had surrounded Goretty had violated English sovereignty by crossing, while armed, a small stretch of land under English control that lay between Chandernagore and the chateau. Cornwallis moved 2000 troops to the outskirts of the *comptoir* and demanded the handing over of Dehaies de Montigny and his allies. The General Assembly refused, but when Dehaies de Montigny and the other prisoners were put on board a ship for transportation back to Europe, the English caught the revolutionary government by surprise. As it attempted to pass Calcutta, the boat was surrounded and seized. Dehaies de Montigny and his followers were granted asylum in the English capital.

From this point onward, the Calcutta council did all it could to destabilise the revolutionary government without compromising the stance of non-aggression dictated by peace in Europe. Opponents of Richemont were granted security and tacit support. The finances of the Chandernagore administration were undermined by the English refusal to recognise the General Assembly as a legitimate trading partner for the purchase of opium and salt. The report that France and England were once again at war in Europe reached the Hooghly in June 1793. Chandernagore was occupied and its government dissolved for the third time in thirty-seven years.

* * *

The relationship between Enlightenment thought and European imperialism defies easy categorisation. In the second half of the eighteenth century, ideas such as representative government and the rights of man provided the ideological foundation for the emergence of European anti-colonial discourse. In part shaped by European colonial practices overseas, Enlightenment thought also challenged political, religious, social, and economic orthodoxies at home, producing the intellectual basis for the revolution in France. However, the *lumières'* challenge to European violence and exploitation in the Americas and Indies also paved the way for the emergence of a new conception of empire as a benevolent force: that parts of the extra-European world might be administered by Europeans in the interests of their native populations. Evident in the thought of Denis Diderot and other authors of the *Histoire*, as well as in the writing of colonial practitioners such as Willem Bolts and Alexander Dow, this idea would be revived, popularised, and carried to new heights in the aftermath of the French Revolution.

From 1792, French armies attempted to export their country's revolution to other parts of Europe, beginning with assaults on the ancien régimes of Austria and Prussia. Buoyed by their successes, the leaders of revolution then looked further afield and in July 1798 an increasingly prominent revolutionary general, Napoleon Bonaparte, led the French invasion of Egypt. Napoleon's Egyptian campaign provides the most striking illustration of French Enlightenment thought in the service of imperialism. Napoleon and his supporters were convinced of their mission to bring enlightenment and emancipation to a people deemed ignorant and oppressed. Ideas of freedom and the rights of man were deployed in support of the French Egyptian occupation rather than in opposition to it.[75] Many European observers, and perhaps Napoleon himself, believed that India would follow Egypt—that the subcontinent would finally be liberated from despotic and oppressive English rule. In the articulation of Napoleonic-era conceptions of benevolent French imperialism, Chandernagore and the other *comptoirs* in India played an important symbolic role. In rhetoric, they were championed as islands of liberty, equality, and fraternity in an English-dominated sea of despotism and despair.[76]

It would perhaps have been a consolation to the *lumières* had they known that French Enlightenment thought would not disappear from Bengal with the English victory in the Napoleonic wars. Enlightenment thinkers had unleashed intellectual forces that transcended global geopolitics. In the early decades of the nineteenth century, a new class of the Bengali intelligentsia well versed in European and Indian philosophical traditions began to challenge established social and religious practices and ideas. The intellectual ferment that they generated, with its emphasis on rationalism, positivism, and social improvement, became known as the Bengal Renaissance. Later, in the twentieth century, ideas of representative government and human rights rooted in Enlightenment philosophy would be mobilised by Indian nationalists in Bengal in their efforts to consign European imperialism to history once and for all.

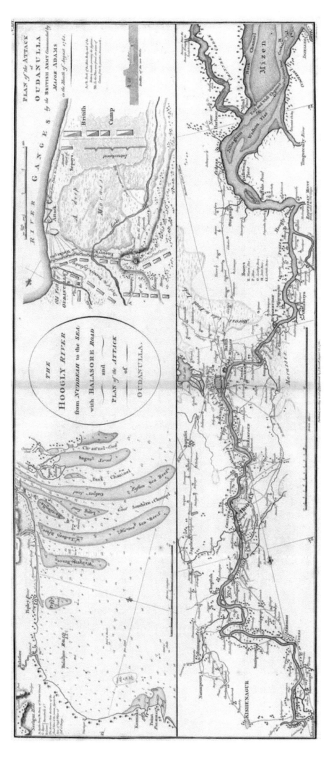

1. An early attempt to map the Hooghly upriver and downriver from Calcutta, with (top left) an inset detailing the dangerous sandbanks at the river mouth. James Rennell was the English East India Company's first surveyor general of Bengal. J. Rennell. *A Bengal atlas: containing maps of the theatre of war and commerce on that side of Hindostan.* [London] 1781. Public domain. Image credit: Harvard Map Collection, Harvard Library.

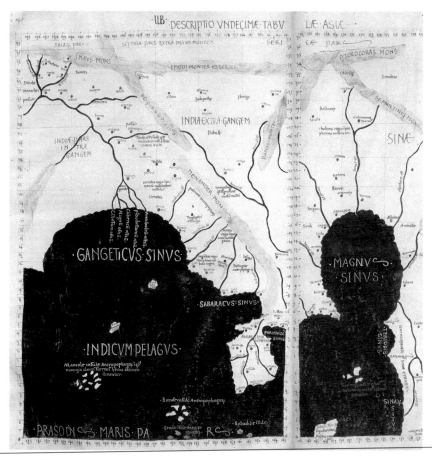

2. A fifteenth century reproduction of a map from Ptolemy's *Geographia* (c. 150 AD), depicting (on the left) the Ganges, with five distributaries arriving in the Bay of Bengal. British Library Harley MS 7182. Public domain. Image credit: Wikimedia Commons.

3. The trading post of the Dutch East India Company (VOC) on the Hooghly. Between the 1630s and the 1680s the Dutch commanded the greatest volume of European trade on the river. Hendrik van Schuylenburgh, 1665, Rijksmuseum Amsterdam. Public domain. Image credit: Wikimedia Commons.

4. Nawab Alivardi Khan with a courtier at Murshidabad. During Alivardi's reign in Bengal (1740–56), Murshidabad developed into a renowned literary and artistic centre. Unknown artist, c. 1745. Public domain. Image credit: Wikimedia Commons.

5. Rabindranath Tagore, whose poetry extolled the Hooghly and other rivers of the Bengal delta as manifestations of the divine. Unknown photographer, 1909. Public domain. Image credit: Wikimedia Commons.

6. A bathing ghat on the Hooghly at Calcutta. For devotees, bathing in the river has long been a spiritual as well as a temporal activity. Bourne and Shepherd, 1890. Public domain. Image credit: Wikimedia Commons.

7. Sagar Island and the mouth of the Hooghly river, photographed from NASA's Terra satellite. Since the photograph was taken in March 2000, rising sea levels caused by global heating have shrunken Sagar Island and submerged some of the smaller islands around it. Public domain. Image credit: Nasa Earth Observatory.

8. The Howrah bridge, connecting Calcutta, on the left bank of the Hooghly, with the industrial suburb and train station of Howrah on the other side. More than 700 metres in length and 80 metres high, the bridge was an engineering marvel when it was opened in 1943. Public domain. Image credit: Wikimedia Commons.

9. The Hooghly at Dakshineswar. Photographer: Michael Dwyer.

5

SERAMPORE

BAPTIST MISSIONARIES AND THE POWER OF PRINT

The town of Serampore lies twenty kilometres downstream from Chandernagore, on the right bank of the Hooghly as it sweeps around to the left before continuing on to Calcutta. The area surrounding the town has long been important as a religious centre, its proliferation of temples, mosques, and shrines indicating prosperity as well as piety through the ages. Of the many pilgrimage sites collected around Serampore, the most significant is the Jagannath temple in the village of Mahesh, founded by a fourteenth-century devotee inspired by his visit to the great Jagannath temple at Puri on the coast of Orissa. The name Jagannath (Lord of the Universe) denotes Krishna in his divine form. As Vaishnavism, centred on the cult of Krishna, spread in west Bengal in the fifteenth century, the temple grew in popularity. Rebuilt in its present incarnation in 1755, it is the site of an annual enactment of a procession of chariots belonging to Jagannath and other deities.

The Danish East India Company settled at Serampore with the permission of Alivardi Khan in the same year that the temple was reconstructed. This was not the company's first attempt to establish a trading post on the Hooghly. Danish merchants had traded in the Bay of Bengal from the early seventeenth century; in 1698 they established a factory next to the French at Chandernagore, abandoned for lack of profitability in 1714. Settlement at Serampore was a sign of the growing confidence of the new Danish company chartered with substantial backing from the crown of Denmark in 1732. At first the growth of Danish Serampore was slow. One Dutch visitor in the 1760s described it as 'the most inconsiderable European establishment' on the Hooghly, with just 'a few houses inhabited by Europeans'.[1] Most trade was local and in Bengali hands: weaving, carpentry, tailoring, and farming were predominant, along with the sale of betel, tobacco, toddy, ganja, and spirits. However, as the commerce of other European companies suffered during the Seven Years' War and the American War of Independence, trade at Serampore grew. In the 1770s, the Danish company's commercial monopoly was ended and its property transferred to the crown. Exports of cotton, silk, saltpetre, and sugar increased, with up to twenty ships arriving from Europe each year. German, French, Portuguese, Armenian, and Greek merchants accompanied the Danes, adding to an already heterogeneous population in the town. Those benefitting the greatest from Serampore's boom were elite Danish businessmen and a class of wealthy Bengali middlemen with whom they dealt. By the end of the century, the population of Serampore exceeded 10,000.[2]

Serampore's growing prosperity was evidenced in the buildings constructed. In the western part of the town, separated from the Danish quarter by a newly dug canal designed to provide irrigation for the surrounding paddy fields, stood the palatial houses of the wealthiest Bengalis. The most impressive of these was the Goswami Rajbari, a mansion on the Hooghly belonging to the trader and landlord Raghuram Goswami, whose father had earned a fortune as the collector of customs in the town. East of the canal lay a high street of neo-classical villas with plastered whitewashed façades inhabited by European traders. A Catholic church had been erected in 1761, when French refugees first arrived from English-occupied Chandernagore. The Protestant church of St Olav was added at the turn of the century, its sturdy nave decorated by an impressive bell tower. A waterfront tavern and hotel welcomed the respectable traveller disembarking at the adjacent Nisan Ghat. In the centre of the Danish quarter was the governor's house, enlarged and improved several times during the three-decade-long administration of Colonel Ole Bie from 1774.[3]

In the opening months of 1800, the main focus of attention in Serampore was not, however, the governor's house nor the Goswami Rajbari but a much more modest property south-east of the Danish quarter. In a small outbuilding in the grounds of a simple porticoed house a group of Baptist missionaries from the English midlands pored over a machine that would revolutionise Bengal: a wooden flatbed hand-operated printing press with mechanical movable types. The press was not the earliest of its kind in Bengal: a modern Gutenberg-style press had been imported to Calcutta as early as 1777. It would, however, prove one of the most influential in the history of Indian printing: over the course of the next four decades, its output would be prodigious, amounting to more than 200,000 volumes in over forty languages, many of which would have their fonts prepared and types cut for the first time at Serampore.[4] Crowds flocked to see the press at work. The missionaries responsible for the machine spent so much time with it that locals christened it a European 'idol'.[5]

The earliest publications emanating from the press were Bibles and religious tracts which would, the Baptists hoped, evangelise the peoples around them. In time, however, the outputs diversified to include grammars and dictionaries, poetry and prose, textbooks, newspapers, journals, collections of laws and regulations, maps, and other texts. The Serampore Mission and its press would leave a profound, irreversible impact on Bengal, in spheres including education, literature, journalism, political engagement, and social and religious reform. The mission played a vital role in the transformation of the English East India Company's government in Bengal into a regime legitimised by notions of the improvement of Indian society. It also provided a template for those who wished to contest and defy colonial rule.

* * *

The story of the Serampore Mission began in rural Northamptonshire with the birth of William Carey, the son of a humble schoolmaster, in August 1761.[6] From an early age, Carey showed a talent for languages, studying Latin, Greek, and Hebrew as he served an apprenticeship as a shoemaker. His growing religiosity made the life of a minister attractive; aged twenty-two, he entered the Baptist fold, working as a preacher and schoolteacher in the village of Moulton. The central theological tenet of the Baptist faith is the saving of repenting individuals from their sins through immersion in water. When Carey read the popular account of the voyages of James Cook, he was shocked to realise the great number of degraded people around the world in need of repentance and salvation. Soon after, he composed a pamphlet entitled *An enquiry into the obligations of Christians to use means for the conversion of the heathens* (1792) in which he briefly surveyed the planet, dividing up its population into Christians, Jews, Muslims, and Pagans and calculating the total number of each. The vast majority of people globally, he concluded, 'remain in the most deplorable state of heathen darkness, without any means of knowing the true God, except what are afforded them by the works of nature ... Pity, humanity, and much more Christianity, call loudly for every possible exertion to introduce the gospel amongst them.'[7] At a meeting of Baptist ministers in Kettering, Northamptonshire, Carey proposed as a subject of discussion 'The duty of Christians to attempt the spread of the Gospel among heathen nations.'[8] Opposition was encountered from those who thought the evangelisation of far-flung peoples impossible, or considered it better that Baptist efforts be concentrated on spreading the word of God at home, but in the end Carey's arguments carried the day. The Baptist Missionary Society was formed, its aim 'to evangelise the poor dark idolatrous heathen by sending missionaries into different parts of the world where the light of the glorious Gospel is not at present published.'[9]

Carey and other members of the society raised funds by knocking on doors in the streets of English towns where Baptists and their sympathisers, mostly self-made middle-class men, resided. His initial intention, following Cook's example, was to undertake a mission to Tahiti or West Africa, but later in 1792 he was introduced to John Thomas, a surgeon of the East India Company who had twice travelled to Bengal and attempted mission work in the preceding decade. Thomas convinced Carey that Bengal was ripe for the spread of the Word, its indigenous population 'the most mild and inoffensive people in all the world, but enveloped in the greatest superstition, and in the grossest ignorance.'[10] Together with Carey's wife and sister, the two found passage on a Danish commercial vessel and set out for India.

Carey left England on the eve of what in retrospect would be identified as the great age of British overseas missions. In the final decade of the eighteenth century, evangelical fervour fuelled a growing campaign against slavery and the slave trade and a rising sense that the British abroad should act for the salvation of backward non-Christian peoples. The renewal of the East India Company's charter was debated in Parliament in 1793. William Wilberforce, the anti-slavery campaigner, epitomised the new evangelical mood with his attempt to insert into the charter a clause stating that the Company must 'promote, by all just and prudent means, the interests and happiness of the inhabitants of the British dominions in the East' and act for their 'religious and moral improvement', not least by supporting missionaries.[11] The London Missionary Society, composed of Anglicans and Nonconformists, was founded in 1795 and dispatched a mission to Tahiti the following year. The Anglican Society for Missions to Africa and the East, later the Church Missionary Society, followed in its wake.

Among the English in Bengal, as Carey would soon discover, the mood was very different. Of course, some were affected by the growing metropolitan interest in propagating Christianity and converting Indian peoples. Charles Grant, a Company servant and indigo planter, had earlier supported Thomas' efforts to establish a Bengal mission, while appealing to Company authorities for permission to set up a network of local schools imparting Christian instruction. After returning to England, Grant joined Wilberforce as one of the leading advocates of 'the communication of Christianity to the natives of our possessions in the East'—and in particular to the 'exceedingly depraved' and idolatrous people of Bengal whose absurd and ignorant beliefs included the veneration of a river.[12] However, members of the late-eighteenth-century English community in Bengal interested in evangelisation were a small minority.

As we have seen, faith and commerce were closely entwined elements of Portuguese imperialism in the Indian Ocean; the Estado's ecclesiastical establishment dispatched Jesuits and Augustinians to Portuguese trading posts to propagate the faith among Europeans and Indians alike. Until the Revolution, the Catholic Church had been a consistent presence in French territories in the Indies as well; at Chandernagore, spiritual responsibilities were divided between Jesuits and Capuchins, the latter catering for the European population and the former responsible for evangelising indigenous peoples.[13] The approach of the Dutch and English companies—the dominant Protestant trading nations in India—was different. Except for a brief aborted mission in Ceylon in the 1640s, the Dutch had kept commerce and Christianity separate, preferring secular profits to the salvation of souls. The English Company concurred: its shareholders and employees were largely unconcerned with propagation of the faith. From the middle of the seventeenth century, a small number of ministers were sent out to look after the spiritual needs of Englishmen in Company factories. After Plassey, however, as the Company became a territorial power, a conscious attempt was made to distance it from proselytising activities. English authorities widely believed that an Indian perception of a link between the Company and Christianity would jeopardise its rule. Proposals for the introduction of an extensive ecclesiastical establishment into Bengal were therefore ignored and, in London, Company directors pressured Parliament into rejecting Wilberforce's mission clause, arguing that to permit missionaries in the Company's territories would endanger peace and security. The Company was suspicious of all attempts by non-official Europeans to enter Bengal; licences were rarely granted and often revoked. Troublemakers with Bibles were the last thing it wanted.

It was probably because they came on a Danish ship that the arrival of Carey and his party on the Hooghly passed unnoticed by Company authorities. Carey rented rooms in Calcutta and began preaching in the commercial streets around Bowbazaar. For a group of outcasts without a source of income, however, living in Calcutta was expensive. When a sympathetic English official, George Udny, offered the party lodgings and employment on an indigo plantation in the northern district of Malda, where the Hooghly and Padma go their separate ways, Carey jumped at the chance. (Thomas, who always had several irons in the fire, left the mission party to pursue business ventures.) In Mudnabati, a small village half Muslim and half Hindu, Carey spent five years managing an indigo factory with ninety local employees. He learnt to speak and write Bengali with fluency, studied Sanskrit, preached to the villagers, and translated large parts of the New and Old Testaments. Carey's plan at this time was to form a self-sustaining rural mission community. The Malda district suited perfectly his scheme. In the autumn of 1799, however, four new Baptist missionaries arrived in

Bengal from England on an American ship captained by a sympathetic Presbyterian. On landing, they made the mistake of declaring to Company authorities their occupation as missionaries and were denied entry to Calcutta.

That the final destination of the ship's voyage was Serampore was fortunate. Unlike their Dutch and English counterparts, the Danish company had always been sympathetic to missionaries. A Protestant mission had flourished on the Tranquebar coast of southern India from 1705 with the support of the Danish crown and spread to Bengal in the 1750s under the direction of a Swedish minister, Johann Kiernander.[14] At Serampore, Governor Bie was personally sympathetic to mission activity. When the new Baptist party arrived, he granted them asylum, refusing English demands that they be deported. On hearing of Bie's sympathetic stance, Carey was convinced to abandon Malda and join the others in the Danish town, and the Serampore Mission began.

* * *

Finding suitable premises was the missionaries' first task. In January 1800, a house and garden were bought in Serampore using funds brought over from England. The house included rooms for the missionaries and their families and a hall for worship. A small outbuilding in the garden was designated the printing house. Of the four new arrivals from England, two died soon after reaching Serampore. The other two, Joshua Marshman and William Ward, joined Carey as the mission's leaders. A set of rules was formulated for the mission community. Its members would live, eat, work, and pray together, making decisions collectively by vote. All were to give themselves up unreservedly to the mission cause, working tirelessly 'for the universal spread of the Gospel'.[15] Resources were to be pooled: no individual profit-making activities would be permitted. In his *Enquiry*, Carey had described the characteristics required of missionaries: they must, he suggested,

> be men of great piety, prudence, courage, and forbearance; of undoubted orthodoxy in their sentiments, and must enter with all their hearts into the spirit of their mission; they must be willing to leave all the comforts of life behind them, and to encounter all the hardships of a torrid, or a frigid climate, an uncomfortable manner of living, and every other inconvenience that can attend this undertaking.[16]

At Serampore, the party prided itself on its simple frugal living.

The missionaries decided their tactics early on. Following Carey's example, they would learn Bengali and other languages until they could converse and write in them freely, and acquire knowledge of local faiths, traditions, and history. 'It is very important,' they concurred, 'that we should gain all the information we can of the snares and delusions in which these heathens are held. By this means we shall be able to converse with them in an intelligible manner … and gain their attention to our discourse.'[17] The errors of Indian beliefs and practices would not be criticised directly; rather, the advantages of Christianity would be extolled and believers in false religion led gradually towards its light. Accurate scientific and practical knowledge would be disseminated, and habits of industry encouraged: conversion to Christianity would go hand in hand with improvements to the condition of the people.

A set of mission methods was agreed. The missionaries took to the streets, conversing with local peoples and preaching in Serampore and surrounding villages; Carey targeted the crowds assembled at markets and temples. Schools were established to deliver basic lessons that would encourage rational thought: a school for boys was opened at the mission house in May 1800 and a girls' school followed. The most important mission method of all would be the translation and dissemination of the Bible in Indian languages, along with tracts explaining the Christian faith. Before leaving England, Carey had noted that the people of India possessed a number of highly developed languages that might become vehicles carrying Christian truth.[18] At Serampore, he and his companions made their intentions clear: 'We consider the publication of the divine Word throughout India as an object which we ought never to give up till accomplished.'[19] Ward added: 'With a Bible and a press, posterity will see that a missionary will not labour in vain, even in India.'[20]

The art of printing—which of course originated in China, where the first movable types were devised in the ninth or tenth century—had arrived in early modern India with the Portuguese. Handwritten texts on tree bark, palm leaf, and paper were produced on the subcontinent long before this; calligraphy and bookbinding were highly valued skills in the Mughal Empire, which conducted large parts of its administration through paper records.[21] The first printing presses, however, belonged to the Estado; they printed government regulations and short theological works. By the end of the seventeenth century, presses had appeared at other places on the south-west coast of India, including Cochin, and the earliest types of South Asian languages had been cut.[22] The watershed moment for Bengali came in 1778 when a first complete set of types was produced by a lower-caste blacksmith, Panchanan Karmakar, under the supervision of English Company servant Charles Wilkins. With the Company's patronage, the types were used to produce *A Grammar of the Bengal Language* (1778), the first book to be printed in the Bengali script. After 1780, a number of presses were established in Calcutta, publishing journals, newspapers, and books, as well as government regulations and laws.[23] The development of print technology facilitated the consolidation of colonial rule, standardising administrative procedures and the training of Company servants.

Carey had begun to put his plan of printing the Bible in Bengali into effect while at Malda, purchasing a second-hand press advertised in a Calcutta newspaper. At this stage, however, commissioning the cutting of a set of Bengali types was prohibitively expensive. It was fortunate for the Serampore Mission that William Ward was an experienced printer. In England, he had worked as editor of the *Derby Mercury* and *Hull Advertiser*, newspapers that provided an outlet for his radical pro-French Revolution views. At Serampore, he was installed as the manager of all printing activities. Type-cutter Panchanan Karmakar and his son-in-law Monohar were recruited to work alongside Ward, producing types in Bengali and other Indian scripts. It was with a 'feeling of exultation' that the missionaries witnessed the first sheets of a Bengali Bible printed in March 1800.[24] Thereafter, printing activities gathered momentum. The complete Bengali New Testament was finished within a year; 2000 copies were printed and work on the Old Testament was begun.[25] Translations into Sanskrit, Oriya, Marathi, and Hindi followed, each printed at Serampore. A mill was established in the mission's grounds to manufacture the paper that the press demanded.

Panchanan and Monohar were not the only Indians attracted to the mission community. To keep the printing house functioning, a host of assistants were needed to work machinery, maintain stores, prepare sheets, and produce the paper and ink. During the first year of the mission, however, Carey and his colleagues despaired that not a single

Indian had been converted. Ramram Basu had served as Carey's *munshi* (teacher) ever since his arrival in Bengal in 1793, instructing him in Bengali and Sanskrit. Though critical of aspects of Brahmanist religion, not even he had been convinced to turn Christian. When a carpenter from a village near Serampore, Krishna Pal, arrived at the mission house expressing a desire to convert, the missionaries rejoiced. Krishna had read one of the mission's printed tracts in circulation. On 28 December 1800, he was led down to the ghat bordering the mission grounds and baptised in the Hooghly, in front of a small crowd that included Governor Bie. Carey was concerned that baptism in the Hooghly would give Serampore's locals the impression that Christians too venerated the river. What should have alarmed him more was the possibility that Hindus would consider the baptism in their sacred water an act of provocation. After news of the ceremony had spread, a crowd of protestors gathered in the town. Krishna was dragged out of his home and jeered at in the street and the mission schools were deserted.[26]

These developments could not go unnoticed in Calcutta. Among members of the English community in the town, support for the Baptists was expressed: a sum of 1500 rupees was raised by private donation to support the mission's work.[27] Needless to say, though, Company authorities were concerned. If one location best summarised the priorities of the Company government in Bengal at this juncture, it was the military station of Barrackpore, which stood facing Serampore on the opposite bank of the Hooghly, some 800 yards away. Barrackpore was the site of the first purpose-built English military cantonment in India, housing five or six Indian regiments of the Company's army. It stood for security and the preservation of order in Bengal, which the Serampore Mission now threatened. Of particular concern to the Company's Calcutta council was the mission's press. Ever since Willem Bolts had attempted to establish printing in Calcutta to publicise his criticisms of Company rule, English authorities had been wary of the dangers of the new technology falling into the wrong hands. The growth of private presses in late-eighteenth-century Calcutta had been carefully monitored; editors who published material critical of government faced the threat of prosecution, deportation, and having their presses shut down. The governor general of Bengal, Lord Wellesley, imposed severe restrictions on press freedom in

English territories in 1799: there would be no printing outside of Calcutta, no anonymous printing, and no printing of newspapers without the prior approval of government. Wellesley viewed the establishment of the press at Serampore with great anxiety but was powerless to intervene in the Danish territory.

In one significant way, however, the Company government did indirectly support the mission during its early years. In the decades after Plassey, as Company rule was entrenched, English administrators had begun the extensive study of Indian history, traditions, cultures, religions, and languages. Their efforts were institutionalised with the foundation of the Asiatic Society of Bengal, a scholarly club dedicated to the European study of Indian antiquity, in 1784. English orientalist scholarship derived in part from intellectual curiosity and a desire to know the unfamiliar country over which the Company now ruled; it was informed by the same Enlightenment universalism that inspired the *lumières* to advance the cause of secular rational knowledge. In no small way, however, orientalism also served the Company, contributing to the institutionalisation of its rule in Bengal. Knowledge of Indian languages was essential to effective administration by English officials, as governor general Warren Hastings knew; an awareness of Indian traditions and practices was helpful too. The study of Hindu and Muslim laws provided a foundation for Company government, during a period in which the English sought to present the appearance of continuity with Mughal forms of rule, even while rewriting Indian history to critique Mughal despotic excesses.[28]

To professionalise the instruction of English officials in the laws, regulations, and languages of India, the College of Fort William was founded in Calcutta in the summer of 1800. Wellesley intended it to become 'the Oxford of the East', training civil officers for the Madras and Bombay presidencies as well as Bengal.[29] Its extensive curriculum included Greek, Latin, and the modern languages of Europe, Arabic, Persian, Sanskrit, and a host of Indian vernaculars. The history and geography of India were taught alongside what were considered modern Western sciences. European professors were appointed, to be assisted by Indian teachers plucked from reputed madrasas and Sanskrit schools. To teach Bengali, Carey was appointed to the college's staff; among Englishmen in Bengal he was by far the best qualified for the task. Because of his outsider status—he was neither an Anglican nor a Company employee—he was denied a professorship and paid just half the salary of his colleagues. Nevertheless, he accepted the position gratefully. It provided a vital source of income for the mission and opened up new opportunities for Carey in his scholarly activities.

Every Tuesday evening, Carey rowed downriver from Serampore to Calcutta, a journey of eighteen miles on the winding river, returning to the mission on the Friday afternoon. He was integrated into the college community, collaborating with Bengali pandits to produce new texts for printing at Serampore, with the encouragement of English colleagues and the Asiatic Society. Carey completed a new grammar of the Bengali language and a collection of Bengali dialogues composed in idiomatic everyday speech to assist students of the tongue. The dialogues offer a glimpse into the life of an English civil officer on the Hooghly. Scenes scripted included the hiring of a *munshi*, negotiations between a moneylender and a debtor, and an enquiry into the river's unpredictable tides.[30] Carey recognised that the learning of Bengali would be made easier if prose writing was available in print. He there-fore encouraged the *munshi*s and pandits with whom he worked to translate Sanskrit stories into Bengali or attempt original compositions. Ramram Basu composed a history of King Pratapaditya, the fabled ruler of Jessore, which is widely considered the first modern work of Bengali prose. Mrtyunjay Vidyalankar, a Brahman from Midnapore who served as Carey's chief pandit in the Bengali department, translated a collection of Sanskrit fables about an ancient Hindu king, Vikramaditya, and later composed an historical account titled *Rajaboli* (Story of Kings).[31] These works constituted a new sort of Bengali literary pro-duction, markedly different from the epic poems recounting the lives of deities that had dominated Bengali written and oral literature from the fifteenth century.

At the college, Carey's interest in Sanskrit language and literature also intensified. He began teaching Sanskrit alongside Bengali in 1806 and was elevated to the rank of professor that year. Company authori-ties commissioned him to produce a Sanskrit grammar and he became a fellow of the Asiatic Society. He oversaw the translation of the Vedas and Ramayana into Bengali and, at the Society's request, into English. Carey's motivations for learning Sanskrit and studying classical Sanskrit texts differed from those of most Europeans in Calcutta engaging in orientalist scholarship: they wished to unlock the secrets of India's past, arrest the decay of Indian learning, or serve colonial rule. His primary concern remained evangelisation, but unlike many later missionaries he saw no contradiction between studying Indian traditions, cultures, and religions and propagating Christianity. Rather, he thought them complementary: learning the Sanskrit language facilitated the acquisition of Bengali, the main medium through which proselytism would take place; reading the Hindu scriptures in their original language was necessary so that their errors could be exposed.[32] Enthused by the favourable reception afforded to his Sanskrit grammar, Carey unveiled a plan to compose A Universal Dictionary of Oriental Languages detailing every one of the languages derived from Sanskrit. The scriptures, he envisaged, would be translated into each of these.

Beyond the College of Fort William, other developments suggest that the presence of the Serampore missionaries was increasingly accepted by the Company government. In April 1801, with the Napoleonic Wars ongoing in Europe, Britain declared war on Denmark. Serampore was occupied without resistance the following month, the Company's forces simply crossing the river from Barrackpore and taking over the town for a year. Deprived of Danish protection, the Baptists were nevertheless left unmolested by the Company; they assumed responsibility for the church of St Olav and organised services that English officers attended. In 1805, four more Baptists arrived from England with their families. Company authorities raised no protest over their arrival. The position of the mission remained precarious, however. When Carey attempted to establish a mission chapel in Calcutta, he encountered government opposition. Further censure followed when he organised a debate at the College of Fort William on the question of whether or not 'the natives of India would embrace the Gospel as soon as they were able to compare the Christian precepts with those of their own books.'[33] The debate had provoked Hindu and Muslim protests outside Government House.

At the end of 1805, Lord Wellesley, who after initial concern had been largely tolerant of the mission, retired. He was replaced by successive governor generals—Cornwallis (very briefly), Barlow, Minto, Hastings—more hostile to the mission enterprise and convinced that it jeopardised the security of English rule. The following summer, Indian troops in the British garrison at Vellore in southern India mutinied, killing some two hundred British soldiers. In a pre-run of the Indian Rebellion of 1857–8, the main cause of the mutiny was widely believed by Company officials to be religious: an act of 'opposition to the innovations in the customs and religious institutions of the sepoys, fanned to heat by general rumours of their forced conversion to Christianity.'[34] The fallout from Vellore quickly reached the Hooghly. Unable to remove the missionaries from Danish jurisdiction, the British authorities considered regulations preventing them from preaching or distributing printed material beyond the boundaries of Serampore. Two new mission recruits landing in Bengal in August 1806 were threatened with deportation. Carey attempted to assure the government that 'it has nothing to fear from the progress of missions, since ... converted heathens, being brought over to the religion of their Christian governors, if duly instructed, are much more likely to love them and be united to them than subjects of a different religion.'[35] For the missionaries, it was unfortunate that a controversy at this moment broke out over pamphlets issuing from the Serampore press attacking the Hindu and Muslim religions.

The Baptists' early resolution to avoid directly condemning Indian religions in their proselytising activities was not in practice adhered to. From the beginning, tracts had been written and published on the errors of Brahmanist and Muslim faith. Ward collected accounts of indigenous beliefs and practices that were later published as *A view of the history, literature and mythology of the Hindoos* (1818). The text included chapters on 'the baneful effects of caste' and the depraved 'moral condition and character of the Hindoos'.[36] The natives of Bengal, Ward suggested, lacked such 'solid virtues, as integrity, humanity, truth, or generosity'.[37] Instead, they were litigious, quarrelsome, untruthful, ostentatious, licentious, and cruel. In addition to caste, the main social and religious practices criticised by Ward and his fellow missionaries included polygamy, early marriage, infanticide, and 'ghat murders'—the exposure of those believed to be dying on the banks of the Hooghly, where they succumbed to malnourishment or drowned. Even more reprehensible was the practice of sati—the cremation of widows on the funeral pyre of their husbands. Carey first witnessed an instance of sati while returning to Malda from a visit to Calcutta in 1799. He described to a friend how the widow ascended the pyre voluntarily but was then held down with bamboo poles to prevent escape as the fire devoured her. 'We could not bear to see more,' he reported, 'but left, exclaiming loudly against the murder, and the full horror at what we had seen.'[38] Fuelled by a sense of moral outrage, Carey arranged for a survey of the number of cases of sati in and around Serampore during a six-month period in 1803: 275 cases were recorded and reported to government with an appeal that the practice be outlawed.[39] For Ward, sati confirmed that women were systematically degraded in the Hindu scriptures.

The intention of the Baptists' condemnations of indigenous practices and beliefs was to reaffirm the necessity of spreading Christianity in India, but in a series of pamphlets assailing Hinduism and Islam they went further than the government was willing to permit. A Bengali pamphlet produced at Serampore described Krishna and other Hindu deities as 'hateful' and 'disgusting' before asking: 'Why do you worship one who has not compassion, mercy, the power to save nor holiness?'[40] Even more dangerous, in the government's view, were a set of Bengali and Persian pamphlets attacking the Prophet Muhammad as a 'tyrant' who 'practised evil', plundering cities and converting people by the sword, while claiming that 'the same lustful gratifications which arise in this world from an intercourse with women will constitute the reward of good men in heaven.'[41] The pamphlets produced a backlash against the missionaries among Europeans in Calcutta wishing to see their activities reined in. Carey was summoned before the Calcutta council to explain how the anti-Muslim texts had come about. He offered the dubious excuse that their inflammatory sections had been added without consent by an overzealous Arab Muslim convert to Christianity, Jawad Sabat, who had spent some time at Serampore.[42]

In the early months of 1807, the survival of the Baptist mission appeared to be in very serious doubt. The council had concluded that its publications were 'evidently calculated to produce consequences in the highest degree detrimental to the tranquillity of the British dominions in India.'[43] Rumours abounded that the Danish authorities would be forced into giving up the missionaries for deportation—or at the very least consenting to the removal of the Serampore press to

Calcutta, where it could be strictly regulated. Once again, however, the Danes protected the mission, refusing to bow to English pressure. A compromise was negotiated, whereby Serampore publications would be scrutinised by English Company censors. For the Baptists, it had been a lucky escape. The mission lived to fight another day.

* * *

In the years between the Vellore Mutiny of 1806 and the renewal of the East India Company's charter in 1813, the pros and cons of permitting missionaries to enter the Company's dominions were debated vigorously in England. Opponents of the measure were either against proselytism on principle—rejecting the idea that indigenous peoples required Christianity to raise them to civilisation—or more commonly believed that missions would destabilise empire. Thomas Twining, who served in the Bengal civil service between 1792 and 1805, conjectured that if the Company sanctioned mission activity, 'indignation will spread from one end of Hindoostan to the other; and the arms of fifty millions of people will drive us from that portion of the globe with as much ease as the sand of the desert is scattered by the wind.'[44] Among the most audible supporters of missionary activity in England were Baptists, who cited the successes of the Serampore Mission as proof of what evangelisation could achieve. The Serampore brethren waded into the debate: Joshua Marshman published an essay on the *Advantages of Christianity in promoting the establishment and prosperity of the British government in India* (1813), in which he claimed that 'one of the most effectual means of perpetuating the British dominion in India will be the calm and silent, but steady and constant, diffusion of Christian light among the natives' because of the understanding and fellow-feeling between rulers and subjects that it would create.[45] A memoir of the lives of Krishna Pal and other Bengali converts was published at Serampore 'to show that the real conversion of all castes of the Hindoos is practicable, as well as, upon every principle of true benevolence, highly desirable.'[46]

Ultimately, when the renewal of the Company's charter was put before parliament, the pro-mission party won the day. With the abolition of the slave trade in the British Empire in 1807, a new sense of British moral superiority had entered metropolitan thought. Nine hundred petitions were submitted to parliament in favour of the admission of missionaries to Company territories, in no small way because awareness of the activities of the Serampore Baptists had spread.[47] William Wilberforce alluded to William Carey in the charter debate in the House of Commons when he declared that 'a sublimer thought cannot be conceived than when a poor cobbler formed the resolution to give to the millions of Hindoos the Bible in their own language.'[48] The charter's key clause stated that it was 'the duty of this country to promote the introduction of useful knowledge, and of religious and moral improvement in India, and that facilities be afforded by law to persons desirous of going to India, to accomplish these benevolent designs.'[49] As a result of the clause, a sum of Company money was allocated to public education for the first time and missionaries were licensed to reside and operate in Company territories. A second clause instituted a small Anglican ecclesiastical establishment in Bengal and the other presidencies.

On the banks of the Hooghly, the new charter had a major impact. The Church Missionary Society and London Mission Society installed themselves in Calcutta. They founded schools and established presses, emulating the Baptists' example. Serampore had been occupied by the English for a second time in 1808, with the Napoleonic Wars showing no sign of letting up. By the time that it was returned to Denmark in 1815, its status as a prosperous trading centre was at an end. The 1813 charter, however, injected the Serampore Mission with a new lease of life. Missionary reinforcements arrived from England for the first time in six years. Indian converts trained as itinerant preachers were sent to establish subsidiary mission stations in other parts of Bengal, including Chittagong, Dacca, and Katwa. Their satellite missions were the earliest sign of an organised Bengali Baptist church. The wives of Carey and Marshman began proselytising among the women of Serampore. Longer-distance missions were attempted to Orissa, Upper India, Bhutan, Burma, Ceylon, and Dutch Amboyna under the supervision of Carey's son Felix and others.[50]

In March 1812, the Serampore printing house had been reduced to ashes by fire. Along with stores of paper and types, many printed volumes and several unprinted translations were lost, including Carey's incomplete Universal Dictionary, the Kanarese New Testament, and a

Telugu grammar. It was a monumental blow. With the support of subscriptions from England, however, the press recovered and was housed
in a new, enlarged building. *Munshis* and pandits were recruited from
across India to meet the mission's needs and the Bible was printed in a
host of new languages, among them Assamese, Punjabi, Pashto, Telugu,
Kashmiri, Gujarati, and Nepali. By the end of the decade, five hand-
operated printing presses were in operation at the mission site. The
craftsmen of the type foundry were renowned for their expertise.

Concurrently, the mission's provision of schooling developed, an
area in which Marshman played the leading role. Before joining the
Baptist Missionary Society, Marshman had worked as a schoolmaster in
Bristol. In Bengal, he considered schooling an essential foundation for
the spread of Christianity: education in scientific and practical knowledge would prepare pupils for the receipt of Christian lessons, which
would be introduced when children reached a suitable age. India,
Marshman thought, had been placed 'under the fostering care of
Britain' by divine providence. Its people were in a 'lamentable state of
ignorance' which only education could cure.[51] A network of village
schools was therefore established to impart basic lessons in the Bengali
language. Just as the European Reformation had removed the control
of knowledge from Catholic priests, vernacular education in Bengal
would liberate it from the sole possession of Brahmans, resulting in
'intellectual, spiritual and moral regeneration'.[52] By 1817, forty-five
schools had been established in a twenty-mile area around Serampore,
funded in part by subscriptions from England.[53]

At the apex of this rapidly growing network of schools, the
Serampore missionaries resolved to establish a college. Its aim was to
foster a class of educated Christian elites who could serve as missionaries and schoolteachers. In design, the curriculum of the college combined Marshman's belief in the dissemination of Western scientific and
literary knowledge with Carey's conviction that Hindu and Muslim
scriptures should be read and understood in order that they might be
countered. As such, the range of subjects taught was extensive: it
included science, philosophy, literature, and history, taught primarily
in Bengali, along with the Sanskrit and Arabic languages and Christian
theology. English-language instruction was provided only to those
pupils who had first mastered Bengali and Sanskrit. The college opened

its doors with thirty-seven students in 1819. Two years later, it moved into a grand new two-storey building with an Ionic porticoed façade facing imposingly out onto the Hooghly, in extensive grounds next to the mission headquarters. The building's Greek style was considered most suitable for the climate of Bengal but also betrayed the missionaries' ambition to create something as lofty and long-lasting as the ancients. Marshman later visited Copenhagen and secured from the Danish crown a royal charter granting the college the power to confer University of Denmark degrees.[54]

While extending the scope of their educational activities, the Serampore missionaries also lobbied the Company government to influence the way in which its post-1813 charter educational funding was spent. Within the English community, the early signs of a division had begun to emerge. Some favoured the gradual introduction of European subjects and languages to institutions predominantly teaching in Persian and Sanskrit—the traditional languages of Indian learning. Others wished to prioritise the teaching of Western scholarly disciplines through the English language, citing the 1817 foundation of the Hindu College, Calcutta, a collaboration between European and Hindu elites, as proof that Bengali parties sought the acquisition of new languages and knowledge.[55] The vital contribution of the Serampore missionaries to this debate was to argue that in any public education efforts the importance of the Bengali language should not be overlooked.[56] In 1815, Lord Moira travelled to Serampore, the first governor general to pay the missionaries a visit. Carey urged on him the need for mass elementary education in Bengali. Carey and his colleagues then played a leading part in the Calcutta School Book Society, an organisation arranging the translation and publication of British school textbooks in Bengali. Naturally, the books were printed at the Serampore press.

A further innovation introduced by the missionaries in this period was the first production and printing of a Bengali periodical and newspaper. English-language newspapers and journals had been published in Calcutta from the 1770s, with James Augustus Hicky's *Gazette* the earliest. In spite of Carey's objection that journalistic activity would provoke government opposition, Marshman oversaw the production of a monthly periodical entitled *Dig Darsan* (The Signpost), first published in early 1818. It was followed by *Samachar Darpan* (Mirror of the

News), a weekly Bengali newspaper, and the *Friend of India*, an English-language monthly issuing from the Serampore press. Each of these publications was political: they included articles and opinion pieces on public questions and government policy in Bengal, India more widely, Britain, and other parts of the world, inspired by the idea that journalism and press freedom were essential to the development of public opinion to act as a check on government—a necessary bulwark against despotism. In tone and content they were also consciously pedagogical: the first edition of *Dig Darsan*, for example, featured articles on history, geography, science, and literature, including an account of Christopher Columbus' discovery of America, written in a simple colloquial style.[57] Subsequent editions included pieces on the importance of vernacular languages and printing to the spread of learning; botany, the compass, and the steamboat; and descriptions of ancient and modern nations. The declared aim of the *Friend of India* was to promote 'the welfare of the people of India'.[58] *Samachar Darpan* included short morality tales with a Christian flavour.[59]

The production of weekly and monthly journalistic series was also a means through which the missionaries' campaigns against sati and other practices deemed abhorrent could gather momentum. In *Samachar Darpan* and the *Friend of India* instances of sati were documented and described in detail and further appeals to government to prohibit the practice were made. 'All such outrages upon the principles of society are unnatural and inhuman, and, when said to be from religious motives, a species of insanity; and hence may properly be suppressed by the powerful voice of reason and authority,' the *Friend of India* declared, before asking: 'When shall these murders cease?'[60] The missionaries argued that the Company government could outlaw sati 'without creating any alarm among the Hindoos'.[61] Sent to England, Serampore publications on the subject were utilised in growing metropolitan campaigns for decisive government intervention.

* * *

Some of the ways in which Bengali parties responded to the Serampore missionaries have already been noted. A number became Christians, joining the mission community at Serampore or setting out to work as itinerant preachers. Though many were no doubt indifferent or untouched by the missionaries' labours, others consciously rejected the mission and engaged in acts of resistance. On occasion the missionaries were heckled in the streets. Their theological claims were disputed or ignored: Carey complained that while most Hindus accepted the myths and miracles of their faith without question, they contested aspects of the Christian scriptures. Muslims were even harder to win over, he added: 'They cannot bear a single syllable of Mahometanism to be disputed.'[62] The protests accompanying the baptism of Krishna Pal in the Hooghly suggest anger and anxiety towards the mission among some at Serampore; converts faced persecution in their communities and Ward suspected that the print house fire might have been caused by arson. When floods struck Serampore, severely damaging several of the mission buildings, some locals considered it an act of divine revenge on the part of their Hindu deities.[63]

The response of others to the mission involved a more complex combination of acceptance and rejection, with ideas and practices introduced by the missionaries selectively adopted and adapted. Many studied at Serampore College or in the mission's schools and benefitted from the instruction without being persuaded to become Christians; others read Serampore publications without abandoning their faith. Despite serving as one of Carey's pandits for many years, Mrtyunjay Vidyalankar was never convinced by Christian theology, penning a number of defences of polytheism and the worship of idols.[64] The missionaries' campaign against sati and other practices met both agreement and defiant opposition.

To articulate and circulate their ideas, Bengali parties resorted to the print technology and production of newspapers that the mission had pioneered. The first Indian-owned English-language newspaper, the *Bengal Gazette*, was launched in Calcutta in 1816. Bengali newspapers followed, inspired by *Dig Darsan* and *Samachar Darpan*, along with several in Persian. These publications reflected the social positions of their editors and patrons. They were produced by Bengali literati, mostly members of the *bhadralok* class of lawyers, moneylenders, teachers, writers, and traders, who had come into some degree of contact with Europeans. In their columns, the major political issues of the day were discussed: press freedom, free trade, the admission of Indians into Company service, trial by jury, and the land settlement of Bengal, to mention just a few of the most significant. Religious questions were also examined, among them the authoritative sources of Hindu faith, monotheism and polytheism, sati and the rights of women in Hindu law. Some deliberated on the relative advantages of different faiths and the abandonment of religion entirely.[65] Before the introduction of print technology to Bengal, political and religious questions were examined in indigenous public spaces through oral discussion and the cheap reproduction of widely circulated manuscripts; communication across an extensive geographical area and the collective expression of opinion were already possible.[66] The effect of printing, however, was to give rise to a new economy of information involving the rapid circulation of knowledge and ideas to new audiences, extending the potential of public opinion to influence government actions. Many of the earliest Bengali newspapers had a circulation of just a few hundred and survived for months rather than years. Nonetheless, they were landmarks in the emergence of a modern Bengali public sphere.

The most high-profile Bengali to engage with the Serampore missionaries was Raja Rammohun Roy, a native of Radhanagar in the district of Burdwan, west of Calcutta. Born in 1772 into a family of wealthy Brahmins, Rammohun acquired a remarkably diverse education even by the cosmopolitan standards of the time. On the request of his father, a Mughal officer and zamindar, he studied Persian and Arabic at Patna, becoming acquainted with the Qur'an, Sufi philosophy, and Arabic science. Later he resided in Benares under the tutelage of renowned Sanskrit scholars before journeying to Tibet and making enquiries about Buddhism. In his early twenties he settled in Calcutta, growing rich as a moneylender and acquiring several landed estates; he learnt English, acting for a time as the *munshi* of an English official, John Digby, and developed an interest in European literature and science. It wasn't long before Rammohun began acting politically. In 1809, he submitted a petition to government protesting against the ill treatment of Indians by English officials, provoked by a personal insult suffered at the hands of a Company district collector in Bihar. Rammohun didn't challenge the fact of Company rule over Bengal. However, he urged the guaranteeing of Indian social and political rights through campaigns for the codification of civil and criminal law, the admittance of Indians into government service, the right of Indians to act as jury members, and the freedom of the press. Rammohun contrasted the rights and freedoms found in England with illiberal elements of the Company's rule and followed with great interest the struggles of liberals in other European countries to establish independence and constitutional government. He supported liberal movements in Italy, Spain, France, Greece, and Portugal, and appealed for the systematic introduction of education in Western subjects to Bengal.[67]

Simultaneously, he developed a public profile as a writer on religious and philosophical subjects. In 1804, Rammohun composed a Persian treatise entitled *Tuhfat-ul-Muwahhdin*, translated into English as *A Gift to Deists* (1889). The text argued for the exercise of reason in religious matters as a defence against dogmatism and reliance on religious leaders. It suggested that polytheism was error—that there was only one God. As time went on, monotheism became the central immovable element of Rammohun's theological thinking. Inspired by the example of the Serampore missionaries, he began translating parts of the Vedanta and Upanishads from Sanskrit into Bengali. His motivation for doing so was very different to that of the missionaries, however: rather than leading people away from the Hindu faith, he sought to encourage a rational monotheistic interpretation of the Hindu texts. Rammohun found in the Vedanta and Upanishads—which he argued were the most authoritative Hindu scriptures—a transcendent formless God who could be worshipped not through ritual and idolatry but individual meditation and the reading of the scriptures. Sacred knowledge, he argued, was accessible to all through the use of reason; morality was about doing right by others.[68] Rammohun's religious ideas were not entirely new within the large tent of Bengali Hindu belief: during the eighteenth century, sects on the fringes of the Hindu mainstream had questioned polytheism, idolatry, and caste.[69] His ideas owed most, however, to his understanding of Muslim and Christian thought. Study of the Qur'an and Islamic philosophy had led Rammohun towards a conception of the oneness of God; the Serampore Baptists and other Christians reinforced his ideas on monotheism, shaped his criticism of idolatry, and steered him towards an emphasis on the authority of scriptures. Rammohun followed his Bengali translations of the Vedanta and Upanishads with English ones to prove to a European audience that

Hinduism was monotheistic rather than polytheistic, rational not superstitious—an argument made explicitly in his English tract *A defence of Hindu Theism* (1817).

Like the Serampore brethren, Rammohun combined a theological attack on idolatry and ritual with the condemnation of specific Hindu practices. Polygamy was an 'evil' Rammohun had experienced first-hand; among his Kulin Brahmin caste group it was the norm and by the age of nine he had been married three times. He began to campaign for monogamy, arguing that polygamous social relations were at odds with Hinduism's moral precepts. Rammohun also sought to overturn the common Hindu practice by which widows were denied the right to inherit property from their husbands, adamant that this was a latter-day addition to a pristine ancient faith. Consistent with the missionaries, Rammohun reserved his strongest criticisms for the practice of sati. The approach of government to the sati question since the Baptists drew attention to it had been one of caution; Company authorities feared interfering with a traditional religious practice, lest Indian opposition be incited. Carey's 1805 appeal that sati be outlawed had therefore been ignored. Responding to metropolitan pressure at the time of charter renewal, problems regarding sati were then acknowledged by government for the first time in 1813. Regulations were issued which dictated that sati would be permitted 'in those cases in which it is countenanced by the Hindoo religion and law' but prohibited in others: when it was involuntary, involved very young or pregnant women, or those who were not the husband of the deceased.[70] Company officers were instructed to prevent cases of sati where Hindu law was contravened. Critics of these regulations, including the Serampore missionaries, argued that far from reducing instances of sati they had encouraged it by appearing to lend the practice government sanction in particular circumstances. Mrtyunjay Vidyalankar, in other respects a defender of Brahmin orthodoxy, was moved to publish a tract in 1817 arguing that, according to the Hindu shastras, a life of chastity was more pious for a widow than death on the funeral pyre.[71]

Rammohun's campaign against sati began in earnest in 1815 when he began collecting statistics on the number of sati cases in districts around Calcutta, copying efforts at Serampore in the previous decade. In August 1818 he submitted a petition to government, signed by hundreds of Indians in Calcutta, arguing that the majority of acts of sati in Bengal were being carried out in a manner contrary to the 1813 regulations and were rarely voluntary. Rammohun then built on Vidyalankar's intervention to suggest that the Company had got it wrong: sati was not countenanced in the Hindu scriptures at all. He published a volume of imaginary dialogues between a supporter and an opponent of sati, followed by more petitions and letters. To propagate his ideas, Rammohun emulated the Serampore missionaries by founding a Bengali newspaper, *Sambad Kaumudi* (Mirror of the News), dedicated to the improvement of Bengali society and the representation of Indian interests; and a bilingual monthly journal, *The Brahmanical Magazine*. He also submitted regular items to newspapers and journals in European hands.[72]

Rammohun's conception of a monotheistic Hindu faith was welcomed enthusiastically by a small section of the Bengali *bhadralok*. In 1815 he founded the Atmiya Sabha, an organisation for the worship of a single supreme Hindu God through hymns, prayer, and scriptural readings. Meetings of the Sabha were held in Rammohun's Calcutta home and attracted upwards of fifty attendees. For many others, however, including most Brahmin scholars, Rammohun's thought was a threat. As early as 1814, a group of Brahmins in Rangpur challenged his elevation of the Vedanta and Upanishads above other sources of Hindu belief. In a widely circulated pamphlet, *An apology for the present system of Hindoo worship*, Vidyalankar elaborated on this point, arguing that no contradiction existed between the single God of the Vedas and the contemporary Hindu veneration of multiple deities: the worship of each was ultimately the worship of one.[73] In response to Rammohun's foundation of *Sambad Kaumudi*, a rival newspaper, *Samachar Chandrika* (Moonlight of the News), was instituted to represent the views of those intent on defending Hindu beliefs and practices from criticism, along with a rival association to the Atmiya Sabha, the Gauriya Samaj. The editors of *Samachar Chandrika* reproduced the views of orthodox Brahmin scholars in defence of sati. Rammohun was forced to deny the charge that because he ate meat and drank wine, he was no longer a Hindu: the individual pursuit of the knowledge of God, he argued, was more important than social expectation and specific observances.[74]

In early 1816, Rammohun visited the Serampore Mission. He conversed with Carey and Marshman on theological and political questions and maintained correspondence with the missionaries thereafter. A significant effect of this connection was Rammohun's increasing recourse to Christian vocabulary: from this point onwards, his theological writings contained references to salvation, forgiveness, and an infinite 'Supreme Being'.[75] Rammohun decided that Christian morality was second to none: 'I have found the doctrines of Christ more conducive to moral principles and better adapted for the use of rational beings than others which have come to my knowledge.'[76] The missionaries, in turn, found much to admire in Rammohun: his renouncing of polytheism and idolatry was admirable; his campaign against sati was invaluable; and his political views on issues such as press freedom and the employment of Indians in Company service were in accord with their own. Rammohun's first tract against sati was paraphrased in the *Friend of India*. One of his anti-idolatry pamphlets was described as 'a masterly exposure, by a Native, of the absurdities of the present Hindoo system.'[77]

On one key point, however, Rammohun did not agree with the missionaries: for all his admiration for aspects of Christianity, he refused to accept the idea of the Trinity and the divinity of Christ. On this theological issue, the two parties would have a major falling out. In 1820, Rammohun published a tract entitled *The precepts of Jesus, the guide to peace and happiness*. The text was an attempt to summarise for non-Christian peoples the moral precepts of Christianity as contained in the New Testament; precepts which, he wrote, were conducive to peace and harmony, 'beyond the reach of metaphysical perversion, and intelligible alike to the learned and the unlearned.'[78] By distinguishing between Christian moral teachings and the literal truth of the Bible and emphasising the former, however, Rammohun implied that parts of the scriptures, such as the accounts of Christ's miracles, should be dismissed—or at least could be, without any great loss. There is no reason to think that Rammohun intended his tract to be provocative, but the Baptists were greatly distressed. A review in the *Friend of India* lamented that the tract might 'greatly injure the cause of truth'.[79] Joshua Marshman described Rammohun as a 'heathen, whose mind is as yet completely opposed to the grand design of the Saviour's becoming incarnate.'[80]

It was perhaps because he felt slighted by being called a heathen that Rammohun went on the offensive rather than turning the other cheek.

The moral precepts of Christianity, he responded in a follow-up pamphlet, were far more valuable than its stories of miracles and petty dogmas which had divided the Christian church into so many conflicting denominations and 'caused continual wars and frequent bloodshed to range amongst them, more dreadfully than between Christians and infidels.'[81] If all they cared about was dogma it was no wonder that the Serampore brethren had made so few converts in their two decades in Bengal. Now it was Marshman's turn to rise to the provocation. (The relatively small number of converts that the mission had secured was a sore point often noted disappointedly by members of the Baptist Mission Society hierarchy in England.) If Jesus wasn't the Son of God, he argued, and his miracles not real, he was a liar: how then could his moral example be championed? The Christian message must be taken in its entirety: the Old and New Testaments, the moral principles and the doctrine.[82] Rammohun's response made explicit a point that had been implicit in his arguments all along: that belief in the Trinity amounted to polytheism and was incompatible with the fundamental oneness of God. Christianity had arrived at the Trinity only in the fourth century A.D., he claimed, corrupting monotheism in just the way that Brahmanist faith had corrupted the monotheism of Vedic religion. The Baptists were as much polytheists as the Bengali Hindus they sought to convert![83]

Further fuel for this ferocious theological fire was hardly required but in the summer of 1821 it was provided. Rammohun was collaborating with William Adam, a Baptist missionary in Calcutta, on a new translation of the Gospels into Bengali. Under Rammohun's influence, Adam began to have doubts about the divinity of Christ. To the despair of Carey, Marshman, and Ward, he renounced the Trinity, abandoned the Baptists, and joined the small but growing community of Unitarian Christians in Calcutta. For the Serampore brethren this was a major affront: one of their own, in Bengal to propagate Christianity, had instead been influenced by a Bengali to doubt and renounce his faith. He was labelled, surely not without a hint of dry humour, a 'second fallen Adam'.[84] Though Rammohun never dropped Vedantic Hinduism in favour of Unitarian Christianity, he supported Adam and others in starting a Unitarian committee and press in Calcutta, which began establishing schools and printing books, mirroring Serampore. The press provided Rammohun with an additional medium for criticising what he considered polytheism in both its Hindu and Christian incarnations. Among its publications was the satirical text *A dialogue between a missionary and three Chinese converts* that revolved around the confusion of the Chinese men having the Trinity explained to them: was there one God who was three—or was it three gods who were one? And how many of them died on the cross?[85] Rammohun concluded that Trinitarian Christians should be approached 'in the same manner as we act towards those of our countrymen who, without forming any external image meditate upon Ram, and other supposed incarnations and believe in their unity.' They should be shown 'compassion on account of their blindness to the errors into which they themselves have fallen.'[86]

The debate between Rammohun and the Baptists was followed with interest by Unitarians and Trinitarians in England—where it became known simply as the 'Serampore Controversy'—before it petered out, naturally unresolved, in 1823. Rammohun continued thereafter with his efforts to extol and promote the monotheistic credentials of the Hindu faith. In 1828 he founded the Brahmo Samaj, an organisation for the worship of a single Hindu Supreme Being, Brahman, reviving many of the earlier activities of the Atmiya Sabha. The trust deeds of the Samaj's hall of worship stated that it was 'for the worship and adoration of the Eternal Unsearchable and Immutable being who is the Author and Preserver of the Universe' but not for the veneration of 'any particular Being or Beings'.[87] To prevent idolatry, it would admit no 'graven image, statue or sculpture, painting, picture or portrait or the likeness of anything.'[88] The Samaj's congregation numbers fluctuated significantly in its early years and were at a low ebb when Rammohun died in 1833. After his death, however, Brahmo organisations sprang up across Bengal, and further afield in Bihar, Orissa, and elsewhere, celebrating a monotheistic and rational Hinduism. Different factions emphasised different theological tenets and ideas, but most shared Rammohun's openness towards new scientific ideas, literary creativity, Western education, and social reform. The Samaj encouraged cross-cultural exchange and innovation, contributing profoundly to processes of learning and encounter later christened the 'Bengal Renaissance'.[89]

Rammohun had taken on board many of the religious ideas of the Serampore missionaries, including their criticism of popular Hindu practices and beliefs and emphasis on scriptural authority, moral improvement, and individual relationships with God. He adopted many of their methods, not least the formation of a religious society, schooling, vernacular translation, and printing. However, he challenged the fundamental basis of the missionaries' belief: the Trinity of God the Father, the Son, and the Holy Ghost. Instead of embracing Christianity, he deployed the mission's practices and ideas to discover or devise a new kind of Hindu faith. His arguments that Hinduism was ultimately rational and monotheistic undermined the Serampore Mission's attempts to spread Christianity in Bengal, yet Rammohun was unapologetic: 'If a body of men attempt to upset a system of doctrines generally established in a country, and to introduce another system, they are, in my humble opinion, in duty bound to prove the truth, or at least, the superiority of their own.'[90]

* * *

The end of the Serampore Mission was a drama in several acts. In May 1830, the College of Fort William was closed, depriving the mission of a much needed source of revenue. The new governor general, William Bentinck, considered it surplus to requirements: in future, Company servants would be trained in England before setting sail for India. Almost simultaneously, Calcutta suffered a financial crash when one of its largest merchant and banking houses, Palmer & Co., collapsed, triggering the ruin of other smaller banks. Most of the mission's savings were lost. Carey was getting on in years, his mobility and eyesight declining. He died in June 1834 at the age of seventy-two, just after completing revised translations of his Bengali and Sanskrit Bibles. The mission's most illustrious figure had outlived his first and second wives, his son Felix, his co-missionary William Ward, and their first convert Krishna Pal. Joshua Marshman lived on until December 1837 but, in his final years, suffered mental health problems, 'sinking under a morbid depression'.[91] When he died, the mission was transferred into the hands of English Baptists in Calcutta and its activities wound down, though Serampore College remained open. The town of Serampore had ceased to be profitable to the Danish after the Napoleonic Wars. By the 1830s, more than half of the grandiose European villas built during its heyday were unoccupied, the total population of Europeans no more than 500.[92] The town was finally sold to the English Company in 1845.

Judged by the number of converts it secured, the mission was a failure: conversion figures rarely topped a hundred each year, and during the mission's first decade were only a fraction of this, a meagre return on such an investment of time, resources, and lives. This, however, is not really the point: the mission's significance extended well beyond conversions. At Serampore, parts or all of the Bible had been translated and printed in thirty-four different languages; grammars and dictionaries were produced in a number of these languages, many for the first time.[93] Bengali prose writing had been cultivated: works of history and literature, collections of stories, newspapers, journals, and pamphlets spilled out of the mission press. A network of schools was created at a time when few Europeans on the Hooghly showed much concern for Bengali education, and a college was founded that flourishes to this day. Word of the achievements of the mission and its press spread extensively in Britain, Continental Europe, and America.

The most significant impact of the mission, however, is fully evident only in retrospect: its influence on the nature of English colonialism in Bengal. In 1833, the Company's charter was once again renewed. The role of the Company on the Indian subcontinent was dramatically revised: rather than conducting trade, the Company would in future be a purely administrative body, concerned with government; Europeans would be permitted to travel and settle in India, manufacturing, trading, and proselytising as they pleased. The new charter marked the culmination of the gradual transformation of the Company from a commercial into a governmental body that had begun in the late seventeenth century and accelerated with the assumption of administrative responsibilities after Plassey. The Serampore missionaries expedited this change, showing how non-official Europeans could prosper in Bengal without destabilising Company rule. Advocates of the reform of the Company's role once more championed the Serampore example in parliamentary debates on charter renewal.

In the years either side of the new charter, Company authorities introduced a series of reforms that bear the imprint of Serampore demands. In 1833, it was decreed that no person be disqualified from Company service by reason of caste, colour, creed, or place of birth: Indian parties were granted the right to serve in the colonial administration and sit on juries.[94] The Baptists had argued repeatedly for the

Company to adopt this course. The relationship of the Company to Indian religious traditions was also revised. Under Bentinck's leadership, an attempt was made to sever the connection between Company administration and indigenous religion through the relinquishing of control over religious endowments, the management of temples, and the regulation of pilgrimages. Legislation was passed to ensure that Hindu converts to Christianity would not be deprived of their property rights, an adjustment of Hindu law campaigned for by Carey from which Company authorities had for a long time shied away.[95]

The strongest indication of a new government approach towards Indian beliefs and practices came with the December 1829 prohibition of sati, as a result of which, supporters rejoiced, the Hooghly for the first time in history 'flowed unblooded to the sea'.[96] At the end of the 1820s, public moral outrage over the practice of sati was at a peak in Britain, fuelled by texts such as Baptist James Peggs' *India's cries to British humanity* that drew heavily on the Serampore Mission's publications. Bentinck decided to act, outlawing sati in all circumstances. His regulation—translated into Bengali by Carey and printed at Serampore—met with protest: a new organisation, the Dharma Sabha, was founded in Calcutta to protest against sati abolition. A petition signed by eight hundred Bengali gentlemen questioned the right of the Company to interfere with a long-standing Hindu religious practice.[97] However, the regulation stood. To ensure that it wasn't overturned, Rammohun Roy travelled to England, where he was feted by English Unitarians and celebrated as the founder of a 'Hindoo Reformation' before contracting meningitis and dying in Bristol in September 1833.[98]

By the mid-1830s, the idea that the Company had a moral responsibility to rule over India and act for its improvement had gained widespread English acceptance. Alongside sati prohibition, this was nowhere more manifest than in the Company's assumption of responsibility for Indian education. Under Bentinck, public instruction was placed at the top of the Bengal administration's agenda. In Calcutta, official opinion was divided between on the one hand those who sought the continued teaching of Sanskrit, Persian, and Arabic subjects in colonial schools and colleges, accompanied by the steady introduction of European subjects ('orientalists'), and on the other hand those who urged the sweeping away of older systems of learning in favour of the teaching of Western science and literature and the English language ('anglicists'). The ascendancy of the 'anglicist' party in this debate meant that the educational philosophies espoused by the Serampore missionaries, with their emphasis on vernacular language instruction and the study of Indian classical subjects alongside the introduction of new knowledge, were overlooked. Before long, the study of English formed an important part of the course of studies at Serampore College, as in other colonial educational institutions, and the time devoted to the study of Sanskrit was reduced. Strikingly, however, both 'orientalists' and 'anglicists' in the prolonged debates over colonial education in the 1830s accepted that the Company should be committed to the moral and intellectual improvement of India and considered public instruction an important means towards that end. The Serampore missionaries had been influential in the development and adoption of the idea that the English role in India should be fundamentally pedagogical. Once so suspicious of the Baptists' efforts to change, improve, and educate the people of Bengal, the Company government had committed itself precisely to this course.[99]

The response of Bentinck's administration to the question of press freedom provides further illustration of the Company's new approach. Concurrent with its acceptance of a pedagogical role, the Bengal authorities overcame their long-held fears that an unregulated press would imperil government by allowing radical and subversive ideas to be expressed. Instead, the press was increasingly looked upon as an important means for the dissemination of knowledge and ideas, contributing to education and useful to government in so far as it allowed public opinion to be expressed and taken on board. Restrictions on press freedom dating to the time of Governor General Wellesley were removed, encouraging a rapid growth in the number of newspapers and periodicals in circulation. By 1833, there were more than twenty English-language newspapers produced in Calcutta and a similar number in Bengali—dailies, weeklies, and monthlies—plus several in Persian.[100] The influence of the Serampore missionaries on these developments, through their pioneering of print journalism, was second to none. The *Friend of India* remained in print after the mission's end as a weekly newspaper dedicated to the discussion of moral, social, and material questions related to Indian 'improvement'.

The new Company commitment to improve India and its people would not, however, be straightforwardly successful: colonial subjects argued against and resisted aspects of the English administration's approach. Here too the influence of the Serampore missionaries was felt. For almost four decades they had conducted their activities— social organisation, printing, and education—at a distance from government and often in defiance against it, providing examples of negotiation and resistance for subjects of the Company to follow. Bengali parties took to print technology in large numbers: by the mid-1850s, the widespread adoption of lithography meant that there were half a million books for sale in Calcutta, in addition to newspapers and journals printed by presses under the control of the *bhadralok* and lower-class parties.[101] A Bengali print culture was firmly established on the banks of the Hooghly; through the medium of print, Bengalis propagated diverse religious, social, and political ideas, arguing with each other and vying for the attention of government.

Often in acrimonious disagreement were members of the Dharma Sabha seeking to protect traditional Hindu practices and beliefs and those Bengali elites educated in Western ideas who had come to reject religious faith altogether. After 1830, a younger generation of the Bengali intelligentsia, many of whom had studied at the Hindu College in Calcutta under the instruction of the radical thinker and poet Henry Louis Vivian Derozio, adopted the rationalist approach to religion championed by Rammohun Roy and arrived at even bolder, more radical conclusions: while supporting Rammohun's campaign against sati and other practices, they rejected his monotheism, instead embracing scepticism, positivism, and atheism. They were christened either 'Derozians', after their inspirational teacher, or 'Young Bengal'. The publication of their ideas in print provoked conflict with the Dharma Sabha and other subscribers to Hindu orthodoxy. In the ideological tussle that ensued, both sides appealed to government for the protection and promotion of their interests. The Derozians argued that their right to freedom of speech permitted them to pour scorn on the false beliefs and superstitions that surrounded them. Orthodox opponents countered that they should be allowed to practice and propagate their religion without criticism.[102] Debates about freedom of speech and the right to criticise Indian religions which had earlier been played out between Serampore missionaries and Company authorities were now enacted between radical and conservative Bengali parties in a print-dominated public sphere. They bear a remarkable resemblance to recent controversies in both Europe and India in which arguments for the protection of the sacred from criticism and abuse have been countered by claims to freedom of speech and the right to offend.[103]

While appealing to government to protect their interests, parties with widely differing social and religious views challenged some of the actions of the Company-state: the Dharma Sabha contested the right of English authorities to outlaw the practice of sati, for example, while members of the Young Bengal movement protested against the suppression of the more radical and democratic elements of their political thought. Colonial rulers attempting to realise their new-found commitment to remould and improve Indian society would not have it all their own way.

6

CALCUTTA

THE UNFINISHED CONQUEST OF NATURE

At the end of the nineteenth century, the Hooghly was the busiest it had ever been. On the water, simple wooden boats competed with barges and ferries for the transport of people and goods upriver and down, from one bank to the other. Where once nature had held full sway, producing a dense thicket of mango trees, tamarinds, banyans, neems, and palm groves, human life had staked its claim. The banks of the river were studded with villages and towns, temples and ghats. From Murshidabad to Serampore, handsome stone villas and luxuriant gardens claimed much of the riverside terrain. The esplanades of Hooghly, Chinsurah, and Chandernagore evoked faded glory and wealth, while acting as the focal point of bustling industrious towns. The view from the river was enhanced by lofty new constructions—most strikingly the Hooghly Imambara, a grand two-storey mosque and ceremony hall bequeathed by a local Shia landowner, Muhammad Mohsin.

The volume of people and activity on the Hooghly increased with proximity to Calcutta. Below Serampore and Barrackpore, both banks of the river were lined with mills, factories, warehouses, and docks, presenting a scene of industrial activity which, in the view of one contemporary observer, 'rivalled that of the largest cities of Europe'.[1] Calcutta had long outgrown Fort William and the European quarters surrounding the open ground—the Maidan—on which it stood, with Chowringhee to the east, Ballygunge and Alipore to the south, and northwards to the great tank in what would become Dalhousie Square. Bowbazaar and Barabazaar developed as commercial and residential centres to the north; the outlying industrial areas of Cossipore, Chitpur, Maniktola, and Garden Reach were integrated into the city as it grew. In 1900, the city stretched six miles along the Hooghly's left bank, covering some 20,000 acres of land.[2] Opposite, on the right bank of the river, lay the ever growing suburb of Howrah.

By reputation, Calcutta was a 'City of Palaces', defined by its attractive European architecture combining elements of the classical and neoclassical, the Gothic and the Baroque. The most palatial residence of all was Government House, opened in 1803 with a porticoed central core and four radiating wings. It was situated just a stone's throw from other architectural landmarks: St John's Church, the Town Hall, the Writers' Building, and the General Post Office among them. The skyline of European Calcutta consisted of 'innumerable towers, spires and pinnacles'.[3] To focus on the city's landmarks, however, obscures the fact that Calcutta was home to a population of staggering size and diversity. In contrast to the wide avenues and open spaces of the colonial 'White Town', most residents lived in narrow lanes in one-storey brick homes or tiled mud huts. Through the course of the nineteenth century the city's population grew rapidly: in 1830 it was estimated at 200,000; forty years later, when the first municipal census was taken, it had more than doubled; and in 1901 it was officially recorded as 847,796.[4] When suburbs such as Howrah, beyond the city's official limits, were added, the total exceeded a million. Calcutta was undeniably a megacity by the standards of the time.

The principal force behind this population explosion was migration. Calcutta attracted migrants from across India, ranging from prosperous Marwari merchants seeking commercial opportunities to impoverished Bihari labourers attracted by the promise of better pay than at home. Moreover, it was a truly global city. In addition to its European residents, immigrants arrived from China and South East Asia, traversing the Bay of Bengal; and also from Africa, Australia, and the United States. Just a third of the city's population in 1901 was estimated to have been born there; of the remainder, half were from other parts of Bengal and the rest from further afield. In this melting pot of ethnicities and religions, a remarkable fifty-seven different languages were recorded as spoken.[5]

The development of Calcutta into the second city of the British Empire is customarily explained as the triumph of free trade. With the curtailing of the East India Company's commercial role and the opening up of Company territories to private investors, European capital flooded into Bengal, where a small but growing number of Indian parties had the means and opportunity to invest, and large-scale industrialisation began. In place of silk and cotton goods, the chief exports from Bengal became coal, indigo, tea, rice, and raw and manufactured jute; European piece-goods, yarns and textile fabrics, metals, machinery, oil, and sugar were imported. The epicentre of this industrial revolution was the Hooghly at Calcutta: by the end of the nineteenth century, thirty-six mills for the manufacture of jute crowded its banks, employing more than 120,000 people.[6] They jostled for space with cotton mills, silk factories, paper mills, oil mills, flour mills, sugar refineries, lime works, iron and brass foundries, potteries, rope works, cement works, brick kilns, as well as shipbuilding yards, railway workshops, and arms and ammunition factories. The main port of maritime trade in the eastern Indian Ocean, Calcutta was also the centre of the domestic economy: raw materials extracted from the Bengali countryside—coal, iron, mica, gold, silver, tin, saltpetre, slate, lac, and limestone—were carried to the metropolis along with other commodities for consumption, manufacturing, or export overseas. Foreign imports arrived at Calcutta before being distributed across Bengal and Upper India.[7]

Little noticed in existing accounts is that Calcutta's remarkable growth during the age of free-trade imperialism was dependent on human control of the Hooghly: the river was indispensable for the transport of people and goods, the provision of food and water, the health and hygiene of inhabitants. Mastering the Hooghly was of great symbolic importance too, representing to Victorian colonial administrators the progress of man, the advance of civilisation, the triumph of capital, and the superiority of the West. As the nineteenth century wore on, however, British authorities would come to realise that their mastery of the river would never be complete.

* * *

During the nineteenth century, as a new scientificity entered colonial practice and thought, British attempts to understand and control the natural environment of India took many forms. Grand trigonometrical surveys mapped the Indian landscape and geological surveys uncovered mineral resources for extraction and productive use. The science of botany focused on the collection and study of plants indigenous to the subcontinent and experimented with the introduction and acclimatisation of foreign species. The botanical gardens of Calcutta were the most impressive of all. Stretched over 270 acres on the right bank of the Hooghly at Shibpur, below Howrah, they were home to over ten thousand varieties of flower, fruit, and vegetable, cultivated for food and medicinal purposes.[8] The later zoological gardens at Alipore spoke of a similar desire to research and govern the animal world.

Efforts to study the Hooghly had a long history. In the final third of the seventeenth century, the first navigational and topographical charts of the river had been produced.[9] Once the rule of the East India Company had been established, renewed attempts were made. Major James Rennell was appointed the first surveyor general of Bengal in 1763. Collating information collected by English armies during their campaigns on the subcontinent, he produced great atlases of Bengal and the rest of India that included information on the winds and currents of the Hooghly and other rivers.[10] Alexander Dalrymple, the Company's first dedicated hydrographer, soon after supervised the publication of charts of all major Indian coasts and rivers. The Government of Bengal understood that knowledge of the Hooghly was of vital commercial and strategic importance—the river was the most effective and, particularly during the rainy season, often the only traversable route from the Bay of Bengal to Calcutta and further north. In the 1830s the official post of Hooghly Surveyor was created. Captain Richard Lloyd produced new charts of the river from Calcutta to Sagar Island, and then higher up, re-measuring its currents and depths.[11]

Lloyd's charts confirmed what many already knew: that for those attempting to navigate it, the Hooghly was one of the most challenging and dangerous rivers on record. Close to the river mouth, where the Damodar and Rupnarayan rivers entered it from the west, were a series of sandbanks and shoals collectively referred to as the James and Mary Sands, in memory of an English ship, the *Royal James and Mary*, lost in 1694. Vessels that struck the sands were liable to become stuck and then pushed onto their side by the force of the current. The bed of the river shifted so much from one year to the next, with sandbanks forming and moving, that following navigation charts was no guarantee of safe passage. The currents of the river were liable to sudden and unexpected changes, contributing to the rapid creation and erosion of channels. In addition, tides were usually fast. The hemming of tidal flows into narrow channels of the estuary produced alluvial phenomena known as 'bores'—head waves of up to ten feet that could break smaller boats in half. Violent winds completed what both figuratively and literally came close to a perfect storm, particularly in the hot season before the rains. Tornadoes arriving from the Bay whipped up whirlpools on the river, which 'assume[d] the appearance of a mighty ocean lashed into fury by the winds of a thousand caves.'[12] Boats stationed up and down the river were lifted from their moorings and 'driven at random into the whirlpool'.[13]

Accompanying these challenges was a strong concern that over time the Hooghly was silting up, its median depth on the wane. Colonial officers understood that the Hooghly's fresh water was supplied from three major sources: the Ganges, via three main distributaries, the Bhagirathi, the Jalangi, and the Matabhanga (known collectively as the Nadia Rivers); the rivers of the Chota Nagpur plateau, principally the Damodar and the Rupnarayan; and through underground filtration.[14] Historically, the removal of silt occurred through these freshwater sources and the tidal inflow of salt water, which travelled as high upstream as Nabadwip. A major change occurred in the late eighteenth century, however, when the Damodar altered direction: rather than entering the Hooghly at Naya Sarai, thirty-nine miles north of Calcutta, it cut a course southwards to reach the Hooghly near its junction with the Rupnarayan, thirty-five miles below Calcutta. The result was doubly disastrous. Not only did the James and Mary Sands become more treacherous, silt deposited from the Damodar meeting estuary inflows to form new, larger shoals. The Damodar no longer scoured the Hooghly higher up; the river shallowed and began to dry up entirely in places.

In 1854 the Government of Bengal was sufficiently alarmed to appoint a commission on the state of the river. It heard the opinion of engineers, naval captains, and other interested parties and determined a course of action: the shoals of the riverbed would be stirred using a specially designed rake dragged by a tugboat, with the expectation that disturbed silt would be carried by the river towards the sea. Concurrently, efforts would be made to increase the supply of fresh water into the Hooghly from the Ganges: the Hooghly's strong currents, it was believed, would ensure that its channels were deepened in spite of the larger volumes of silt that would be deposited. Bamboo and timber spurs were inserted into the bed of the Bhagirathi and Jalangi rivers at strategically significant points to direct the flow through particular channels, shutting off minor distributaries so that a greater volume of water entered the Hooghly. The chief government engineer, Hugh Leonard, was meanwhile considering how best to keep in the Hooghly what water it had. After studying river improvements along the Danube and Rhine in Central Europe, he proposed the construction of embankments to narrow and deepen the river in certain places, and prevent water spilling out. In 1865 construction began on an embankment all the way down the left bank of the Hooghly from Akra, a few miles south of Calcutta, to the coast, with drainage through designated sluices.[15]

In the records of these engineering endeavours, examples of success are found: specific channels were deepened and navigability improved. Largely, however, the successes were short-lived: changes in the current and direction of the Hooghly meant that channels navigable in one season could be found too shallow or entirely dried up in the next; embankments collapsed, sometimes with disastrous consequences for surrounding villages. Raking shoals had proven successful on English rivers such as the Tees. On the Hooghly, however, they had a limited effect, the build-up of silt too great and the currents too unpredictable for consistent results. Authorities accepted that maintaining deep channels through the James and Mary Sands was all but impossible for as long as the Rupnarayan deposited large quantities of silt. Instead, a team of specialists was retained to pilot ships between Calcutta and the mouth of the river; every ship entering or leaving the Hooghly was steered by a member of the Calcutta Pilot Service. Above Calcutta, larger ships could navigate the Hooghly only during the rainy season. In spite of British efforts, the Bhagirathi and Jalangi were reduced during the rest of the year 'into a string of pools connected by shoals which are seldom navigable'.[16] The Nadia and Murshidabad districts were described in one official report as 'a land of dead and dying rivers, whose beds are out of reach of the scour of the tides; and of great rice swamps, which will never now be filled, because the rivers which should perform this office are locked within their channels by the high banks of silt which they have deposited.'[17]

It was on account of their failure to arrest the Hooghly's deterioration that colonial officials turned to the development of a network of canals. Where once the overflowing of riverbanks, in addition to rainfall, had been sufficient for irrigation, canals were dug. The Eden Canal, for example, took water from the Damodar and distributed it over the Burdwan and Hooghly districts. An even more significant motivation for canal construction was navigation. The impossibility of traversing the Nadia Rivers for nine months of the year meant that parties seeking to reach the Ganges from the Hooghly had no choice but to find alternative routes. In the 1770s, Major William Tolly, spotting a commercial opportunity, had canalised a dried-up riverbed in southern Calcutta known locally as Adi Ganga and revered as the Hooghly's original course to the sea. Linking the latter-day Hooghly with the Bidyadhari River to the east, it completed a direct, navigable route between Calcutta, the Sunderbans, and eastern Bengal.[18] Other canals followed—from Chitpur, for example, a circular canal was dug around the eastern perimeter of Calcutta—and in time an extensive network of waterways connected the Hooghly with rivers and natural channels further east. The canals were crucial arteries for the movement of people and goods between Calcutta, eastern Bengal, and Assam. When the Nadia Rivers were unnavigable, boats heading for Upper India took advantage of them to reach Khulna, before following the Padma upstream to the Ganges proper.

* * *

Since time immemorial, boats on the Hooghly, from the simplest canoe made from the hollowed-out trunk of a tree to stately gold-decorated barges, had been propelled by wind, rowed, or dragged along from the riverbank. During the rainy season, favourable winds made it possible to sail upriver, as long as the downward current wasn't too strong; when the winds failed, or the current became too much, little choice existed but to moor and wait. The dangers of navigation made it foolhardy to travel at night. As such, progress upriver was very slow: at the start of the nineteenth century, the journey from Calcutta to Allahabad on the Hooghly and Ganges averaged from three to four months. Travelling downriver was much quicker—the return trip could be as short as twenty days—but also more dangerous: 'Boats are absolutely whirled along,' wrote one English traveller,

> and if, while forced at an almost inconceivable rate by the impetuosity of the current, they should strike against the keel of a former wreck, or come in contact with some of the numerous trees and other huge fragments, victims of the devouring wave, destruction is inevitable. The boat sinks at once, and the crew and passengers have little chance of escaping with their lives, unless at the moment of the concussion they jump into the river, and are able to swim to shore.[19]

Collisions were a common occurrence when boats were forced together by the strength of tides and currents.

The arrival of steam technology in Bengal promised to change radically the nature of transport on the river. In Britain and America, experiments with the use of steam to propel boats had begun in the late 1700s and by the second decade of the nineteenth century steam navigation was becoming commonplace. An initial scheme to introduce steamers to India was formulated in 1812: the American engineer and steam pioneer Robert Fulton argued that steamboats would be of incalculable commercial and military value to the East India Company.[20] At first the Company's directors were sceptical but in time they, along with official and private parties in Bengal, began to extol the advantages of steam. The technology would make river transportation faster and easier, freeing it from the uncertainties of wind, current, and tide—a great advantage to trade and English authority. In British minds, steam became synonymous with civilisation: steam technology symbolised the progress of man and his mastery of nature; steam navigation would deliver this progress to India, exposing new parts of the country to the civilising influence of British rule.[21] Thomas Prinsep, captain of one of the first steamships in Bengal, was convinced that steam power would 'promote the convenience and increase the powers of mankind ... diffusing over the world an activity, the effect of which, in extending the power of civilization, the most sanguine would not venture to prophecy.'[22]

In 1823, a new steam navigation company was formed in Britain with the support of European capital from Calcutta. It financed the construction of the *Enterprise*, a 60-horsepower vessel that made the inaugural steam journey around the Cape of Good Hope to India, arriving at Calcutta in late 1825. The length of the journey disappointed investors at 114 days but a breakthrough had been made: over the next couple of years two further steamboats, the *Emulous* and the *Telica*, were built in Britain and sent out to Bengal. Simultaneously, the construction of steam vessels on the Hooghly, at the shipyards of Kidderpore and Howrah, got under way. The *Diana* was a modest 32-horsepower vessel sent on trial voyages in the waterways of east Bengal before being sold to government for use in the first Burmese War in 1824. The *Forbes* was employed as a tug from Calcutta to Diamond Harbour; the *Irrawaddy* and *Ganges* were used for transporting troops and supplies from Calcutta to Chittagong and Rangoon. The design of these early vessels was far from satisfactory—the engines of the *Irrawaddy* and *Ganges*, for example, drew too much water and were ineffective against headwinds and strong currents—but for the advocates of steam there were successes too, not least when the *Forbes* completed a voyage to China. The royal charter for a regular steamer service between Britain and India was awarded to the Peninsular and Oriental Steam Navigation Company.[23]

Within a few years, the attention of the Bengal government turned to the use of steam for inland river navigation. With its patronage, two new vessels were assembled for the purpose: the *Burhampootur* and the *Hooghly*. Built by the Howrah Docks Company, the *Hooghly* was a teak wood vessel 102 feet long and 18 feet broad, with two 50-horsepower engines. Its flat bottom was specifically designed with the shallowness of the Hooghly in mind. In September 1828 the *Hooghly* departed for Allahabad, the first steamship expedition on the river above Calcutta. The challenges faced were immense. The use of steamers for river navigation had proven successful in America where the rivers were broad and deep and fuel available in abundance. The Hooghly and Ganges were the opposite: coal had to be sent on in advance to the main stations on the route, Murshidabad, Rajmahal, Patna, Ghazipur, and Benares; local parties knowledgeable about the rivers' currents and depths were sourced to help with navigation. Twice the *Hooghly* got stuck on sandbanks, most seriously near Allahabad, but ultimately the voyage was a success, the 800 miles negotiated in 240 hours under steam on the outbound leg and 120 on the return, with the rivers surveyed en route.[24]

An indication of the growing British confidence in steam navigation on the Hooghly is provided by the launch of a regular government steamer service between Calcutta and Allahabad in 1834. By this point the average journey time on the outbound leg had been cut to about three weeks; in the next decade it would fall as low as ten days. Each steamer service consisted of a steamboat towing a second vessel known as a 'flat'. The steamboat housed the engines and carried fuel, as well as providing quarters for officers; the flat accommodated passengers and freight. The demand for freight carriage was high, particularly when roads were impassable during the rains: the government shipped its own arms, money, and supplies and auctioned the space that remained. The volume of shipping and tonnage of goods transported by the river steam service rose steadily, though the role of cheaper and more numerous country boats in the transport of goods and people was not eclipsed; by 1840 the government had ten river-going steam vessels on its books.[25] The sight of steamships—referred to in Bengali as *agkee jehazee* (fire-ships)—going up and down the Hooghly drew crowds of spectators to its banks: 'every employment is suspended while the fire-ship shoots rapidly along.'[26]

From the outset it was not just Western parties that recognised the potential of steam technology and engaged in steam-navigation ventures. During the 1830s, most large-scale business in Calcutta was funded and organised by joint-stock companies, many of which brought together British and Indian business interests and capital. Among the wealthiest and most high profile of Bengalis to enter into business with the British was Dwarkanath Tagore, described in contemporary accounts as a 'remarkable man' of uncommon ability.[27] Born in 1794 into a family of Brahmins who had grown rich as commercial agents to the English Company, Dwarkanath was educated in English as well as Bengali. In his twenties he had become acquainted with Rammohun Roy, siding with him in his campaign against sati and developing an interest in Unitarian thought that would result in his leadership of the Brahmo Samaj. After the death of his uncle, Dwarkanath inherited land and became de facto leader of the branch of the Tagore family stationed at Jorasanko, near Barabazaar. He worked for the English as an officer in the government salt department and acted as a legal adviser and accountant to Bengali zamindars. Moneylending and commerce were added to his sources of revenue as he began investing in the export of indigo and silk and participated in the coalition of business interests coming together to form a new joint-stock banking house, the Union Bank.

As Calcutta recovered from a succession of commercial crises in the early 1830s, Dwarkanath emerged as its pre-eminent businessman, a status cemented by the legendary parties hosted at his newly constructed villa at Belgachia, on the city's northern fringe. In 1834, he entered into partnership with William Carr, a long-term English resident of Calcutta, and other British partners to form Carr, Tagore & Company. The firm's initial interests lay in the export of raw silk and silk piece goods, indigo, rum, sugar, and rice but swiftly diversified to investment in ocean shipping: Dwarkanath would part-finance the construction of several large ships built at Howrah and Kidderpore and owned one, the *Waterwitch*, himself. The company's next venture was in coal. In 1836 a mine was purchased at Raniganj, in the district of Burdwan, home to Bengal's largest coalfields. Carr, Tagore & Company was contracted to supply coal for the government steamer service and other industries. It was extracted all year round and shipped during the rainy season via the Damodar and Hooghly to Calcutta and the steamer refuelling stations higher up.[28]

With its capital in shipbuilding and coal, the firm was well placed to invest in steam technology. In 1836 Dwarkanath played a leading role in the foundation of the Calcutta Steam Tug Association, a joint-stock company set up to institute a regular tug service between Calcutta and the mouth of the Hooghly, thereby ensuring the safe passage of vessels to open sea. Carr, Tagore & Company was appointed the association's managing agent and oversaw the purchase of the *Forbes* and construction of a second tug vessel. The association operated with a monopoly on tugging on the Hooghly until 1844. That year, following a voyage on the government steamer to Allahabad, Dwarkanath founded the India General Steam Navigation Company to challenge the Company's monopoly on steam navigation upriver from Calcutta. Five vessels were acquired and the first private inland steamer service began.[29]

Dwarkanath's vision, which he shared with a large number of non-official Europeans in Calcutta—merchants, lawyers, artisans, and planters—derived from Enlightenment universalism and early-nineteenth-century liberal thought: under British tutelage, India would be industrialised and raised to the standards of Europe; Indians should be permitted to live under British rule without discrimination, as partners in a truly inter-racial society. A number of political arguments stemmed from this starting point: within the Company's territories there should be freedom of trade and press and Britons should be allowed to settle freely. Dwarkanath's participation in Anglo-Indian ventures like Carr, Tagore & Company was about more than business opportunity: it reflected a deeply held belief that Indians and Britons should be social, cultural, and political as well as mercantile partners, with a view to the development of a commercially successful and politicised Indian middle class. Dwarkanath invested a substantial portion of his personal profits in civic projects in Calcutta, often with the encouragement of government. In his view, commercial success should be allied with the inculcation of progress.[30]

Making a profit out of steam navigation on the Hooghly was not, however, straightforward. In a country where labour for rowing and sailing was cheap, steam technology was expensive; the initial investment was high, with engines and other parts usually shipped out from England and swiftly depreciating in value. Fuel was also expensive: the low-pressure engines on which early navigation depended consumed far more coal than steamers could store; the need to maintain a large number of refuelling depots en route meant that coal accounted for more than 40 per cent of running costs.[31] Only the very wealthy could afford to travel on steamships at the outset. Official vacillation between a desire to develop steam technology, a commitment to its own steam services, and growing faith in the doctrine of laissez faire meant that government support for private steam enterprises was sporadic at best. Little surprise then that the India General ran at a loss for its first six years of operation; when its prospects improved it was challenged by a succession of new competitors, most notably the Ganges Steam Navigation Company, which removed the flat from its steamers in an attempt to beat the India General and government services for speed.[32]

Particularly problematic for each of the steamer companies were the challenges of nature. In spite of official efforts, the Hooghly was silting up; changes in the direction and depth of the river made navigation risky. One of the earliest vessels of the India General, the *Sir Herbert Maddock*, was grounded on the riverbed near Allahabad and broke its hull on just its second voyage, a huge blow for the infant company. In the rainy season, when water levels were highest, even steamers with a high engine capacity struggled against the current. To assist in navigation, the captains of steamboats continued to rely on local knowledge over more modern scientific methods such as charts and depth measurements; at least until the 1860s, Indian boatmen were employed to 'read' the movement of the water, detecting channels by the patterns and colours on the surface and spotting hidden shoals, a method meaning that, as in the pre-steam age, there was no travel at night.[33] Over time the design of vessels improved: engineers realised that the Hooghly and Ganges demanded shorter and smaller vessels with shallow drafts and stronger reinforced bottoms to mitigate against the effects of running aground.[34] The loss of speed that resulted meant that journey times were very long in comparison with the similar distances covered by steamers on other rivers around the world. Even then the Nadia Rivers were traversable by steamers only from mid-June to mid-October. During the rest of the year ships were forced to take the Sunderbans–Padma route, which added almost 400 miles to the Calcutta to Allahabad trip. Allahabad was as far along the Ganges as the steamers went: in 1845 an exploratory voyage to survey the river higher up was declared a 'complete failure' after the steamboat *Megna* repeatedly ran aground.[35]

That negotiating the Hooghly by steam remained a perilous exercise is revealed in an account left by a German military officer, Leopold von Orlich, who boarded the 100-horsepower *Pluto* at Calcutta in April 1843. The *Pluto* was led downriver towards the Bay of Bengal by a steam tug. When it arrived at the river mouth, a storm broke and its engines failed. For three days it pushed out towards open sea, advancing at a speed of just two knots per hour, before admitting defeat and returning to Calcutta. A few days later von Orlich tried to leave Bengal again, on the *Hindostan* steamer of the Peninsular and Oriental Steam Navigation Company, headed for Aden. The *Hindostan* was the grandest steamship of its day, a 250-foot long, 550-horsepower vessel fitted with stately cabins, a library, and an exercise deck. Before its scheduled departure it was torn from its anchor at Calcutta by the force of the Hooghly's current and carried a mile downstream. When the *Hindostan* finally did set off, the voyage from Calcutta to open sea was hair-raising: proceeding cautiously at only half-power it was caught in a bore and almost dashed on the rocks, before scrapping its hull on the James and Mary Sands. Orlich concluded that it would have been better had the steamer been boarded at Diamond Harbour, near the river mouth, rather than at Calcutta, adding that the Hooghly was beyond doubt 'one of the most dangerous rivers of the world'.[36]

* * *

Alongside shipping, the other great transport revolution utilising the power of steam in 1840s Britain and America was the railways. In England, private investors laid lines in a frenzy of speculation with the encouragement of government; it was only a matter of time before railway 'mania' found its way to Bengal. Initially, Company administrators were unconvinced. Was railway construction realistic on the subcontinent, in light of its climate and size? Would Indians be willing to travel on trains? Before long, however, this scepticism gave way to an appreciation of the commercial and governmental advantages of railways. Railways would be comfortable, reliable, and fast; for the movement of troops and civil officers, goods, and private individuals, they were second to none. In economic terms, it was suggested, this meant the reduction of commodity price variations, the opening up of new markets, and the alleviation of famine. Strategically, it meant the consolidation and extension of British power.[37] To these arguments was added a conviction that the railways would civilise India, acting as an agent of science and education that would raise the country morally as well as materially. No shortage of ink was spilt in conjectures on 'the civilising influence of steam'.[38] Many of these arguments had of course been made in relation to steam shipping in the previous decade. Trains extended the promise of steamboats to 'annihilate distance' and transform the subcontinent while freeing the transport of people and goods from the vicissitudes of the river.[39]

Supported by a powerful lobby in London, railway investors secured a good deal in their negotiations with the Company. The investors would raise the initial capital for railway construction on land that the

Company provided; the two parties would agree on the route and train service, with the Company acting effectively as a regulatory body. Profits would be split equally between the two parties, with the Company guaranteeing 5 per cent interest on investments in years when no profit was made. In return, mail would be carried on trains for free, and troops and government goods at a reduced rate. Among those interested in investing in the railways was Dwarkanath Tagore. In 1842 he visited England, where he was treated like a visiting prince, meeting Queen Victoria and the prime minister, Robert Peel. He travelled by rail to Scotland, observed the manufacture of steam engines in Liverpool, and took in the sight of coal mining near Newcastle, returning to Calcutta convinced that railways were the future.[40] Dwarkanath founded the Great Western of Bengal railway company and began negotiating with Company authorities for a line northwards from Calcutta. In August 1846, however, he died. The contract for Bengal's first line was awarded six months later to a rival group of investors forming the East India Railway group.

Deciding on the route that the line should take involved lengthy deliberations. Because of lingering doubts about passenger demand, discussions focused on how best to capture the traffic of goods. The initial East India Railway plan advanced by engineer Rowland Macdonald Stephenson was for a line from Howrah up the right bank of the Hooghly to just north of Hooghly and then north-westwards through Burdwan to Mirzapur.[41] This was the quickest and most direct route from Calcutta to the central Gangetic plain, linking Bengal with the North Western Provinces and, in future, even the Punjab. It was favoured by those prioritising the extension of British commercial and strategic interests further into Upper India and had the advantage of running directly through the Burdwan coalfields.[42] As critics pointed out, however, most trade between Bengal and Upper India took place in the Gangetic valley, which was far more densely populated than the hills and plains: for commercial reasons, and if the railways were to act as a civilising influence on the indigenous population, would not a line following as closely as possible the course of the Hooghly and Ganges make more sense?[43] In favour of this alternative plan, the deterioration of the Nadia Rivers was noted: the railway would provide an important new link between the Hooghly and the Ganges, given that movement between the two was impossible for large boats over nine months of the year.

This second scheme was eventually chosen: the East India Railway was to run up the right bank of the Hooghly from Howrah, turn briefly away from the river to cross Burdwan, and arrive at the Ganges near Rajmahal, thereafter skirting the right bank of the river through Bihar to Mughal Serai, opposite Benares. A branch line would collect coal from the Burdwan coalfields. Construction began in 1851 and the first stretch of track, from Howrah to Hooghly via Serampore, Chandernagore, and Chinsurah, opened with great fanfare in August 1854. Six years later the route to Rajmahal was complete and a contract was signed to continue the railway to Delhi, where it arrived in 1864. Two chord lines traversing the hills and plains of Bihar were built soon after, one following Stephenson's original route, and by 1868 some 1350 miles of the East India Railway network had been laid.[44] The Eastern Bengal Railway company was meanwhile responsible for the first tracks on the left bank of the Hooghly. They ran from the Calcutta suburb of Sealdah to Naihiti, opposite Hooghly, and onwards away from the river to the port of Kushtia on the Padma, where they linked with steamer services to Dacca and Assam.

The building of the Indian railways is often recounted as a battle against hostile natural forces.[45] British engineers and officials fretted over the heat, winds, rivers, flooding, animals, insects, and germs that they encountered in sourcing materials and laying lines. On the route from Calcutta to Rajmahal, a never-ending succession of culverts, flood arches, and bridges was required. The land was mercifully flat but so inundated with water—'treacherous, sinking and shifting'—that constructing embankments and foundations was difficult.[46] A huge number of streams and minor rivers feeding into the Hooghly had to be crossed; between Calcutta and Raniganj, a stretch of line approximately 150 miles in length, 460 bridges were required.[47] The construction of sections of the line was outsourced to contractors responsible for organising equipment, material, and labour. Bricks and timber for sleepers were sourced locally where possible, while ironworks, including bridges and rails, were imported from Britain and transported by river to their final destination. 'Not a day passes,' wrote one observer of the Hooghly, 'without the cheerful sight of boats laden with rails and sleepers ... passing the river.'[48]

For every success, however, there was a failure. Attempting to prevent the flooding of the East India Railway in the low-lying areas between the Hooghly and the Damodar, which were regularly submerged during the rains, British engineers removed large sections of the Damodar's right bank and reinforced the left bank, hoping that the river would drain away from the train line rather than spill over it. The attempt succeeded only in flooding the surrounding villages while the railway remained submerged.[49] Flooding affected the construction of the Eastern Bengal Railway; the collapse of embankments and build-up of pestilential water were common occurrences. Railway construction was taking place in an age when little was known about the prevention of disease: cholera, pneumonia, typhoid, and smallpox all affected construction workers—4000 labourers were killed in a cholera epidemic in the district of Rajmahal in late 1859.[50] Difficulties transporting supplies on the Nadia Rivers delayed the construction of the Allahabad to Agra section of the East India Railway for more than a year.

In reality, the construction of the railways was more about compromise with than overcoming nature, and in Bengal with the Hooghly in particular, as the case of bridge-building reveals. At one stage, in deliberations over the East India Railway's route, engineers had proposed that the line should avoid the flood plains between the Hooghly and the Damodar by starting at Calcutta, rather than Howrah, and travelling up the left bank of the Hooghly to cross the river just below Chandernagore. An alternative suggestion was that the line should carry on up the left bank of the Hooghly as far the Nadia district, only then crossing to arrive on the south side of the Ganges. Both were rejected because they involved bridging the Hooghly, which was not considered possible in the 1850s. The alluvial soil of Bengal provoked regular concern that roads and buildings were shifting and sinking into the ground. Engineers had little confidence that bridge foundations dug into the bed and banks of the Hooghly would stay fixed, given the strong currents and shifting course of the river.[51] Through the remainder of the century and beyond, as the volume of trade passing through the port of Calcutta increased, the proposal was regularly made that the Hooghly should be bridged at Calcutta to allow the East India Railway to terminate in the city, perhaps with a new station at Bowbazaar. Each time, however, it was rejected on grounds of feasibility and cost.

Until 1874 railway passengers and others crossing between Calcutta and Howrah had no choice but to take a ferry; the ferries were slow and dangerous, with hundreds drowning each year when they capsized. Goods arriving at Calcutta docks were unloaded and put on smaller vessels to cross the river before being loaded onto trains—a laborious and time-consuming process which handicapped the city in its competition with Bombay for maritime trade. One of the earliest to propose the bridging of the Hooghly was Dwarkanath Tagore, who raised capital and purchased equipment to install a floating iron bridge pulled across the river on chains. His plan was aborted when the equipment proved defective and the body responsible for managing Calcutta docks complained that the river would be blocked.[52] In 1874 a floating pontoon bridge was finally installed across the river on the site that Dwarkanath had in mind: 1530 feet long and wide enough for carriages and pedestrians to cross, it was opened three times each week for ships to pass.[53] In the following decade, the Hooghly was bridged with a permanent structure for the first time: a cantilever bridge joined the East India and Eastern Bengal railways just above Hooghly, and a selection of East India trains began arriving at Sealdah. There would be no permanent bridge across the river at Calcutta, however, until 1943. The opening of a grand new East India Railway terminus at Howrah in 1905 was an admission of defeat on the part of engineers: that the Hooghly would not be bridged at Calcutta any time soon.

In economic terms, the railways of Bengal were a success. The later nineteenth century witnessed an explosion in the number of passengers on the network and a steady growth in freight traffic: the East India Railway carried six million passengers annually by 1875 and received the highest freight receipts of any Indian line.[54] Railways were the principal means of transporting goods from Upper India and facilitated the further extraction of natural resources, not least coal. The promise of railways to reduce commodity price fluctuations and alleviate famine was in part fulfilled: grain surpluses were carried from as far as the Indus valley when scarcity struck northern parts of Bengal and Bihar in 1873.[55] Once the East India Railway was operational, steamer services no longer progressed up the Hooghly further than Kalna; the grand landing places at towns on the Ganges like Allahabad fell out of use. It would be wrong to conclude, however, that with the advent of rail, river transport was eclipsed. Just as steamships operated on the Hooghly alongside older forms of river traffic, the railways coexisted with pre-existent riverine networks of trade and people flow. The rivers and railways were not so much competitors as feeders of each other, with goods unloaded from trains into boats for dissemination locally and from boats onto trains for longer-distance transport. Steam navigation companies like the India General increasingly looked eastwards, tapping into trade routes across the Sunderbans to Assam; the shipping of tea became a major revenue source. The Eastern Bengal Railway launched a flotilla of steamships to integrate trade along rail and river networks. The waterways of Bengal remained the primary means of transporting such vital commodities as jute, rice, grain, indigo, opium, and oilseeds within the province. The Calcutta canal network carried a million tonnes of traffic annually by 1900 and the Hooghly remained 'one of the most-frequented waterways in the world'.[56]

It is significant that the one major attempt to bypass the Hooghly in colonial infrastructure development failed. During the 1850s, concerns about the silting up of the river led a group of speculative investors to buy up land on the Matla River, fifty kilometres south-east of Calcutta, and propose the establishment of a new port linked to Calcutta by rail. Port Canning, as it was named, opened in 1862 and began attracting maritime trade. Within five years, however, it became clear that the site of the new port had been chosen badly—the water supply was irregular and malaria widespread—while there was little appetite among most Calcutta merchants and businessmen to relocate.[57] Calcutta was the heartbeat of the north-east Indian economy and of major importance on the imperial and global stage. The Hooghly, despite its challenges and the development of the railways, was indispensable.

* * *

Calcutta's economic boom and the migration to the city that followed created health and sanitation challenges that could only be met with the assistance of the Hooghly. The river had been vital to the establishment of Calcutta as a global industrial and commercial centre; now it would be utilised to ensure the health and well-being of its burgeoning population.

British concerns about the dirtiness and unhealthiness of Calcutta were as old as the city itself. 'It is the truth,' wrote one apparently very well-travelled eighteenth-century critic,

> that, from the western extremity of California to the eastern coast of Japan, there is not a spot where judgement, taste, decency, and convenience are so grossly insulted as in that scattered and confused chaos of houses, huts, sheds, streets, lanes, alleys, windings, gullies, sinks, and tanks, which, jumbled into an undistinguished mass of filth and corruption, equally offensive to human sense and health, compose the capital of the English Company's Government in India. The very small portion of cleanliness which it enjoys is owing to the familiar intercourse of hungry jackals by night, and ravenous vultures, kites, and crows by day. In like manner it is indebted to the smoke raised on public streets, in temporary huts and sheds, for any respite it enjoys from mosquitoes, the natural productions of stagnated and putrid waters.[58]

The parts of Calcutta inhabited by non-European residents came in for particular criticism: 'the lanes are narrow, tortuous, and badly lit; the dwellings are overcrowded and insanitary,' a government report lamented.[59] Official statistics on the population density of different quarters of the city appear to confirm that overcrowding was a problem: in the most densely populated areas, more than 25,000 people were crammed into each square mile by 1901; in Barabazaar, 10,000 people lived in rooms of four or more.[60] Health epidemics were common, with cholera, fever, malaria, dysentery, diahorrea, smallpox, and plague especially prevalent.

Under the direction of the municipal government, a wide variety of initiatives were introduced to improve the health and sanitation of the city. Streets were widened, cleaned, and watered; slums, referred to as *bustees*, cleared; and the regular collection and disposal of rubbish was instituted. Hospitals and medical dispensaries were set up; vaccination schemes were introduced; markets, slaughterhouses, and other food distributors were subject to inspection. Tighter regulations governed the burial and cremation of bodies; the sight of partially cremated bodies cast into the Hooghly from one of Calcutta's sacred ghats, or left on the riverbank for the vultures, became less frequent. The city's first public toilets opened in 1854.[61]

Perhaps more important than any of these other innovations to Calcutta's cleanliness and the health of its residents were its systems of water supply and drainage—concerns with which the Hooghly was intimately connected. During the eighteenth century, as a functioning city developed around Fort William, open drains and sewers had been dug, usually along the sides of streets. They led into the Hooghly but carried no consistent flow of water and were often blocked, a cause of concern for the British governor general, Lord Wellesley: 'The construction of the Publick Drains and Water-Courses of the Town is extremely defective,' he wrote in 1803: 'The stagnate water ... endangers the lives of all Europeans residing in the Town, and greatly affects our Native Subjects.'[62] Wellesley must have given the subject some thought because he arrived at an insight that would be crucial to the development of a more effective system of drainage thereafter: Calcutta lay on land that naturally declined away from the Hooghly towards the Saltwater Lake in the east, at a rate of almost three feet per mile; the attempt of early engineers to drain the city into the river had been a mistake, rendering the drains inefficient at the best of times and useless when the river level was high.

From Wellesley's time onwards, the drainage schemes developed by British engineers were focused on emptying the city's effluents away from the Hooghly. In 1821 plans were unveiled for a series of parallel sewers running west to east from the Hooghly to the circular canal, to be flushed through the regulated inflow of river water. Funds were raised through the institution of a lottery and the accusation that the city, because of its location, was 'beyond the powers of sanitary science' was rebuffed: 'there is no natural obstruction whatsoever,' concluded the municipal authority, 'to the establishment in the City of Calcutta of a system of Drainage and Cleansing, adequate to the rendering [of] it dry and free from soil and impurities.'[63] On account of the high cost, however, no definite course of action was taken until the appointment of a municipal engineer, William Clark, in 1857. As British control of the subcontinent was shaken by the Indian Rebellion that year, Clark's focus remained firmly on sewage. New plans were drawn up for three main sewers running eastwards under Calcutta from the Hooghly to converge on the eastern edge of the city where Durumtollah (now Dharamtolla) Street met the Circular Road. Intersecting these would be two further main sewers converging in the same place as the other three, one beginning at the Hooghly in the north of the city and running south-eastwards and the other at Tolly's Nullah running north-east. At the junction of Durumtollah Street and the Circular Road a steam-powered pumping station would lift the city's sewage into a tank from which declining pipes would carry it to Tangra Creek, a natural stream flowing into the Saltwater Lake.[64]

Clark estimated that his plans would require thirty miles of brick sewerage and eighty miles of pipe and cost the government almost three and a half million rupees. Construction began in 1862 with the sewer from Tolly's Nullah amid significant scepticism, particularly regarding the water that the system required. Clark believed that inflows from the discharge of homes, from the annual rains, and periodically from the Hooghly would be sufficient to prevent the build-up of waste. Critics predicted that natural changes in the volume of rain-water and the movement of the Hooghly's tides would result in either too little water or too much, and asked: would refuse collect indefinitely in the Saltwater Lake or be naturally flushed? To this was added the charge that excavating the sewers would disturb the foundations of buildings, particularly in more congested neighbourhoods.[65] Through Clark's assurances and the success of the early part of his scheme, these fears were largely allayed. By 1868, the sewerage network was in operation south of Park Street, with the homes of wealthy Europeans connected to the sewers by stone tubes. Six years later, when Clark left Calcutta, all five of his main sewers had been built.

Clark considered himself a saviour rescuing Calcutta from itself. At 36.4 per 1000, he claimed, mortality rates in the city were 50 per cent higher than in the average English town. He acknowledged that the climate of Bengal, with its cycles of heat and moisture, was partly responsible for this fact, creating conditions favourable for fever, dysentery, cholera, malaria, and other infectious diseases. All the more reason, he contended, why filth and impure water should be efficiently carried out of the city, removing the 'organic poisons, or ultimate germs of disease' and the means by which they were conveyed. In England, Clark held, 'science and civilization have reached their highest stages of development, in the history of the world', resulting among other things in the introduction of modern systems of drainage to most cities and towns. A large proportion of health problems in Calcutta could be prevented through the similar application of science—effective drainage was 'the most important measure for preventing disease'.[66] After Clark's departure, the scheme that he had inaugurated was extended into suburban and industrial areas, beginning with the construction of a new main sewer from the Kidderpore docks to the district of Ballygunge, where a second pumping station was built. By the mid-1880s roughly half of Calcutta's buildings, some 20,000 premises, were connected to the sewerage network.[67] Clark became renowned and later oversaw the construction of drainage systems in Madras and a host of Australian cities.

The introduction of a regular supply of water for drinking and other purposes was also occupying British authorities. Until the nineteenth century, water for Calcutta was drawn directly from the Hooghly or from earthen wells dug on land adjoining its banks. Tanks were excavated to store rain and river water, with channels connecting to the river. Among the Hindu population, a hereditary caste of carriers drew water from the river at auspicious times of the month and distributed it among their clients. In large part, Europeans mistrusted Hooghly water, considering it drinkable only during the winter months, if at all; during the rest of the year it was either too dirty or too saline for consumption. Many preferred collecting rainwater in jars during the annual wet season and making it last the year. Early British authorities attempted to improve matters by enlarging existing tanks, excavating new ones, and filling in those that were unhealthy. As the city grew, however, more systematic measures for the supply of water were demanded.

As early as 1820, the technology of steam was enlisted. A steam-powered pumping plant was built on Chandpal Ghat, near Barabazaar, to lift water for distribution through a set of gradually sloping stone aqueducts across a small section of the city: Durumtollah, Chowringhee, Park Street, and Bowbazaar. It operated throughout the year, except during the rainy season, and was extended in the 1850s as far as College Street and Wellington Square. Aqueducts had a couple of major advantages over pipes: because they were open, they could be regularly cleaned to prevent silt deposits building up; water could be drawn from them by coolies watering the streets. These were outweighed by the disadvantages, however: aqueducts took up much needed space in the streets and regularly leaked; water was far too easily stolen and contaminated. It was this final consideration that convinced the municipal government to invest in purification technology and underground cast iron pipes—a commitment coinciding in the 1860s with the growing acceptance that cholera was transmitted in drinking water.[68]

The water of the Hooghly was tested in several different locations for its purity. Because of pollution in the immediate environs of the city, Calcutta's authorities determined to construct a pumping station at Palta, seventeen miles to the north, adjacent to Barrackpore. Water would be pumped from the Hooghly into settling tanks, filtered and delivered through a large iron pipe to a stone reservoir at Tallah near Chitpur. Here a second pumping station would distribute it through iron pipes around the city. The system became operational in 1865; before long, the three 50-horsepower steam engines at Palta delivered seven million gallons of water per day.[69] Once the population of Calcutta had exceeded half a million, this was no longer sufficient and a new Palta pumping station with more powerful engines was built in the shadow of the old. An extended network of pipes from Tallah across the city was completed in 1891, with more and more houses connected to the grid. Howrah received its supply of water from a pumping station installed opposite Palta at Serampore.

The Hooghly had been tested, manipulated, and put to productive use. This, however, was not a case of the simple uninterrupted application of science in the cause of progress: the introduction of drainage and water-supply systems to the city involved multiple problems and setbacks. Demand for both consistently outstripped supply; a majority of the city's population had no regular access to filtered water well into the twentieth century. Despite filtration, water was not always clean: the bacteria causing cholera remained. Death rates in Calcutta declined steadily in the second half of the nineteenth century but every so often severe epidemics of fever, dysentery, plague, and cholera caused 'violent variations in the statistics'.[70] The city did not entirely escape the annual mortality cycle of cholera and fever in the hot months and dysentery during the rains. In 1900, epidemics of plague and cholera produced a death rate exceeding one in twenty; more than 40,000 people fled the city on trains, spreading the contagion as they went.[71] In teeming, industrial Howrah, mortality actually rose as the century ground to a close.

* * *

By the end of the nineteenth century, Calcutta was an imperial megacity, connected to regional, subcontinental, and global networks of industry and commerce by the technology of steam. A vast railway network linked it with the rest of India, carrying great volumes of people and goods. Steamers served Dacca, Assam, Kalna, and the Orissan coast; Madras, Pondicherry, Colombo, Rangoon, and Bombay; and locations in Europe, Africa, and wider Asia—London, Trieste, Penang, Singapore, Hong Kong, and Durban among them. Steam engines had transformed many of the industries around which the economy of Calcutta revolved and sustained the systems of drainage and water supply that kept the city alive. Reflecting on Calcutta's extraordinary growth, British officials were given to self-congratulation:

> There are probably few cities in the world that, from so humble an origin, and apparently under so unfavourable conditions, have within so short a period attained the position now occupied by the capital of India. Less than two centuries ago the site of the present city of Calcutta presented the ordinary aspect of a rural district in the delta of Lower Bengal—a flat rice-swamp, interspersed with patches of jungle, with a few scattered villages on the riverbank. Few would have ventured to predict that here would shortly arise a 'City of Palaces'; that physical drawbacks would be made to yield to the indomitable energy of a foreign race; that in spite of morasses, malaria, hurricanes, and the difficult navigation of a treacherous river, Calcutta would in the nineteenth century be an emporium of trade of the first magnitude, and the Capital of an Empire in East.[72]

The basic premise of rhetoric of this kind—that British fortitude, industry, and enterprise 'made' India—has been reproduced in many post-independence accounts of the development of Indian infrastructure during the Raj.[73] Even studies critical of the exercise of colonial power have largely accepted that European science and technology mastered the Indian natural environment, rendering it subservient to the interests of capital and empire.[74]

This, however, is only part of the picture: the colonial mastery of nature was precarious and never absolute. Crops failed and scarcity reigned; the recurrence of disease epidemics could not be prevented; railway lines were inundated during the rains and trains were derailed in high winds. The vicissitudes of the Hooghly generated unforeseen and often tragic events: ships ran aground and sank after the river had changed course; fields were flooded when its embankments were breached; malaria spread when waters stagnated and mosquitoes bred. In September 1900, heavy rainfall flooded much of the Howrah district and land between Calcutta and Diamond Harbour: the rice crop was wiped out, cattle were lost, and hundreds of villagers drowned. As such, colonial confidence was punctuated by moments of anxiety and doubt. In 1882 government oceanographers admitted 'large discrepancies' between the Hooghly's predicted and actual tides and conceded that the river's tidal movements could not fully be known.[75] Newspapers lingered on incidences of nature fighting back, like the spectacle of crocodiles entering villages and dragging people away.[76]

Every so often an event would occur that shook British certainty to the core. Cyclones were common in the Bay of Bengal during periods when the monsoon winds were changing, and in particular at the end of the south-west monsoon in October–November each year. On occasion they would strike Calcutta and its environs: the steeple of St Anne's Church in Fort William was blown down in 1737. Nothing, however, had prepared the city for the cyclone that would visit it in October 1864. The stormy wind currents building in the centre of the Bay were registered on Ceylon and the Andaman Islands and gathered momentum as they moved northwards to the mouth of the Hooghly. When they struck land, they left a trail of devastation in their wake: across the districts of Hijli, Midnapore, and Hooghly, on Sagar Island and in Calcutta, buildings were destroyed and trees ripped from their roots, the debris scattered for miles. An estimated half of the trees in Calcutta's botanical gardens were blown away and the others lost all of their leaves. One eyewitness described the terrifying noise made by the cyclone as 'like the letting off of steam from a steamer, but on a gigantic scale.'[77]

More damaging than the cyclone itself was the tidal wave that it whipped up in the Bay. The population of the low-lying areas along the coast had no time to react when the wave arrived: entire families and villages were swept away. As the wave forced itself into the narrow channels of the Hooghly, it grew to a height of twelve feet: Diamond Harbour, on the approach to Calcutta, was submerged. The wave arrived at the port of Calcutta on 5 October 1864, ripping ships from their moorings and surrendering them to the currents of the Hooghly, to be dashed against each other or driven onto the shoals. Of the 195 vessels in the port that day, 97 were damaged severely and 36 were lost, including several large ocean-going steamers.[78] The Peninsular and Oriental's steamer *Bengal* was grounded on Shalimar Point. Most of central Calcutta's buildings escaped the cyclone untouched but outlying areas like Dum Dum and Cossipore were badly hit and the port suffered devastation that would take years to repair. Two steamer companies, the Oriental Steam Navigation Company and the Commercial Navigation Company, never recovered from the loss of their ships and were liquidated soon after. The East India and Eastern Bengal railway networks suffered serious damage to stations and tracks.

The cyclone would have a lasting effect on British colonial thought. While casualty numbers in Calcutta had been relatively small—49 killed and 16 injured—across western Bengal almost 50,000 people were killed.[79] In the hardest hit rural areas, the immediate devastation was followed by famine, cholera, dysentery, and smallpox, more deadly than the cyclone and tidal wave themselves. An initial colonial response to the catastrophe was to rearticulate the need for scientific enquiry to understand and, if possible, control the Indian natural environment: a government meteorological department was established to forecast atmospheric changes and anticipate future disasters. Other British figures began wondering, however, if the manipulation of India's natural environment by human actors had in some way contributed to the production of the cyclone and other extreme weather events. In the years that followed, efforts to conserve and protect Indian nature would attract serious attention for the first time: concerns were expressed about the ecological effects of redirecting the natural flow of rivers and streams; the idea that the Hooghly and other waterways around Calcutta were being over-fished was considered; and official attempts to protect and re-plant forests across Bengal accelerated.[80]

A sense of resignation gained ground: that in spite of progress in science and technology, India's natural environment would remain unpredictable and unruly—that it could never be fully known or controlled. The feeling was strengthened by subsequent events. In June 1897 a devastating earthquake shook Assam. Its tremors were felt across Bengal, with buildings in Calcutta not spared damage. The earthquake stayed long in British minds. In the following decade a huge new steel reservoir elevated ten storeys above ground level was constructed at Tallah to hold nine million gallons of water for Calcutta. The newspapers reporting on it were filled with 'gloomy prophecies of cataclysmic disasters'—most gravely that an earthquake would lead to the reservoir's collapse and a flood of biblical proportions.[81] Increasingly, colonial self-assurance was permeated with feelings of vulnerability.

* * *

By the turn of the twentieth century, it was not just in relation to India's natural environment that doubts had begun to enter British minds: the people of India were also proving less pliant and submissive than their colonial overlords wished.

Earlier generations of British rulers, their worldview informed by Enlightenment universalism, had expected the moral, intellectual, and material improvement of India under British tutelage—an outlook crystallising in the Company government's liberal imperialist agenda of the 1830s, which would inform colonial administration over the following decades. In this period, British authorities celebrated incidences of Indian political mobilisation as evidence of the ongoing transformation and improvement of the subcontinent, even when challenges were offered to aspects of colonial policy. Dwarkanath Tagore's championing of the rights of fellow Bengalis under Company rule may have at times exasperated British officials but was also welcomed as an example of the enlightened native in action. Early Indian political organisations like the Bengal Landholders' Society, in which Dwarkanath participated, were encouraged by colonial administrators as vehicles for the expression and useful gauges of Indian public opinion.[82]

With the Indian Rebellion of 1857–8, this would change. Sparked by the mutiny and subsequent hanging at Barrackpore of sepoy Mangal Pandey, who attempted to kill his commanding officer, the Rebellion consisted of a string of mutinies and uprisings across Upper India that shook the foundations of British rule. With the aid of new technology, including steamships for the movement of soldiers and supplies, the Rebellion was finally supressed, but it left a lasting impact on the ideologies sustaining imperial government. In the Rebellion's aftermath, some colonial administrators affirmed that the principal object of British rule was the improvement of the subcontinent, rearticulating the universalist belief that through benevolent British rule India and its peoples could be elevated to a level of civilisation on par with Britain itself. A growing number of others, however, would question the possibility of transforming the subcontinent upon Western lines and emphasise instead that there were fundamental and irreconcilable differences between Britons and Indians—a departure from universalism towards alternative culturalist and racist justifications for colonial rule.[83] The effect of the Rebellion on British approaches to the government of the population of India was analogous to that of the cyclone of 1864 and other natural disasters on its approaches to Indian nature: both the people of India and its natural environment had proven more difficult to control than anticipated; the confidence of colonial authorities in their ability to fashion a particular kind of Indian subject was dented in just the way that their certainty in managing the natural environment of India had been knocked. British authorities would increasingly view Indian education, political organisation, and economic success not as vindicating their rule but as threats. The cosmopolitan society that Dwarkanath Tagore and his contemporaries had known, in which at least some Bengalis were the equals of Europeans and enjoyed commercial success, was replaced by one in which racial and cultural differences mattered more. In the final four decades of the nineteenth century, a growing proportion of capital, trade, and large-scale industry in Calcutta was concentrated in British hands, while at a local level Bengalis began to lose out economically to migrants from other parts of India.[84]

One response to a declining economic position was to reject commercial activity: among the Bengali *bhadralok* a pronounced anti-commercial attitude developed, according to which 'respectable' people owned land or studied to enter public service—as lawyers, doctors, teachers, engineers, and so forth—but did not participate in trade.[85] A second response took place in the domain of culture: with their economic and political opportunities limited, Bengalis moved to demonstrate the richness of their cultural heritage and produced an extraordinary stream of new output in literature, music, and the arts. Unsurprisingly, the Hooghly, along with other rivers, featured prominently in these productions: as revered waterways, they had been important to Bengali religion and culture for centuries; their centrality to the economy of Bengal and significance as sites of scientific and technological innovation made them an obvious focus for works that were often patriotic, spiritual, or anti-materialist in theme.

The poetry of Michael Madhusudan Dutt and the novels of Bankim Chandra Chatterjee bear out this point. Mid-nineteenth-century Calcutta's most celebrated poet, Dutt was educated at the Hindu College and influenced both by English Romanticism and the rationalist, sceptical movement labelled 'Young Bengal'. His best-known sonnet was a eulogy to the river Kapotaksha, which passed through his home village of Sagardanri, a hundred kilometres east of Calcutta:

Constantly, O River, you come to my remembrance,
Constantly I think of you when I am alone;
As men in slumber dream of magical music,
So I hear spell-bound the rippling sound of your flow.[86]

Bankim Chandra Chatterjee was born into a Brahmin family near Naihiti and studied in the Hooghly College before finding employment as a deputy collector and magistrate. While in colonial service, he would write a set of Bengali novels establishing his literary renown in which the Hooghly was the main stage and also a key actor. In *Kapalakundala* (1866), the male protagonist, Navkumar, becomes lost in a forest when he is abandoned by his party while returning by boat from a pilgrimage to Sagar Island. He meets a forest-dwelling girl, the eponymous Kapalakundala; they fall in love, marry, and move to Navkumar's village but Kapalakundala cannot adjust to life outside of the forest and flees her husband. At the end of the book, she flings herself into the river rather than return with Navkumar; he attempts to save her and both are drowned.

Chatterjee's later novel *Anandamath* (1882) was influential in the development of Bengali cultural and political nationalism. Set during the great famine of 1770, it was loosely based on the failed Sannyasi Rebellion, when a disparate collection of Hindu and Muslim ascetics, some in the vicinity of Murshidabad, rebelled against the English Company. Highly romanticised in style, it opens with the collapse of the starving and exhausted heroine Kalyani on the riverbank, where she is rescued by a Hindu monk, and culminates in a showdown across the river between the rebel and British forces.

The revival of Bengali literature to which Chatterjee's writing was seminal would culminate at the end of the century with Rabindranath Tagore, in whose work the honouring of the Hooghly and other rivers was carried to new heights. Born in 1861 into the influential Jorasanko branch of the Tagore family, Rabindranath was Dwarkanath's grandson. At a young age he began writing, producing Bengali poems, short stories, plays, and novels. Aged twenty-nine, Rabindranath was sent to manage some of his family's estates in the Kushtia district, east of Murshidabad on the bank of the river Padma. From this point onward he identified with the rural over the urban, finding in nature proximity to the divine and the basis for a collective Bengali identity. Privately, Rabindranath wrote of nature as intimately connected to his faith: 'My religion is natural religion and the method of worship I employ is the worship of nature.'[87] In his poetry he admired the power and beauty of nature in 'verdurous' Bengal and 'bowed' to its forests, villages, and rivers.[88] Rivers were an essential element in Rabindranath's evocation of the Bengali motherland. In his poem 'The Golden Boat' (1894) a lonely figure on a riverbank surrenders his paddy harvest to a mysterious woman who glides past in a golden boat.[89] In the darker 'Snatched by the Gods' (1898), a boat full of pilgrims returning from Sagar Island is caught in a whirlpool on the Hooghly at the point where the Rupnarayan enters it; to appease the angry gods an infant is snatched from its mother, thrown overboard, and drowned.[90] Rivers were for Rabindranath signifiers or manifestations of the divine: he confessed to feeling closest to the transcendent when sitting on the edge of 'the rippling river' and used the term 'Gangotri'—the name given to the source of the river Ganges in the Himalayas—as a metaphor for the divine or primary source.[91]

Rabindranath juxtaposed a materialist West and spiritualist East, claiming that Asia was distinctive in character to Europe. In 1901, he founded an ashram and school at Santiniketan in the district of Birbhum for study in communion with nature, romanticising the traditional Indian village. However, Rabindranath was also politically engaged. When British authorities attempted to curb the growth of nationalist opposition through the introduction of a Sedition Bill, he accused them of arrogance, racial discrimination, and the ill treatment of Indians. In his prose writing and public action he sought to raise political consciousness among his compatriots: his call for Bengalis to distance their economic activities and education from the British contributed to the growth of anti-colonial opposition focused on indigenous self-reliance that became known as the Swadeshi movement.[92]

The basis of Swadeshi was the idea of Bengali economic independence, through domestic production and the boycott of foreign, especially British, goods, as a first step towards freedom from colonial rule. Related concerns were the organisation of labour, the cultivation of the Bengali language and Bengali print media, and the development of national education. The main phase of the Swadeshi movement was launched in October 1905 in response to the government decision to divide the province of Bengal into two administrative territories—a Hindu-majority west, including the lands adjacent to the Hooghly, and a Muslim-majority east. Claimed by British officials to be necessary for efficient administration, the partition was widely interpreted as an attempt to stem rising political activity and the growing sense of Bengali nationhood through an act of divide and rule. In their protests against the separation, Swadeshi demonstrators, Hindu and Muslim, built on several decades of proposals for Bengali economic self-sufficiency. From the 1870s, the boycott of British imports in favour of indigenous products had been an important cause among politically engaged Bengalis, alongside efforts to develop consciously nationalist business ventures.

One such initiative was the launch in 1884 of the Inland River Steam Navigation Service, which sought to challenge the British monopoly on steam river transport with a passenger service between Khulna and Barisal and cargo route to Calcutta. Led by one of Rabindranath's older brothers, Jyotirindranath, who was inspired by his grandfather Dwarkanath's steam enterprises, it was enthusiastically supported in the Bengali press but suffered from the same problems as other steam companies in their infancy: the large capital outlay to acquire steamships, the high running costs, and fierce competition. After one of its ships collided with the pontoon bridge across the Hooghly at Calcutta, the company was liquidated.[93] Nevertheless, an important point had been made: steam power symbolised progress; an indigenous steam company, no matter how short-lived, struck at the heart of *fin de siècle* British claims to superiority over India. When the main phase of the

Swadeshi movement got under way, several new Bengali steam shipping companies were founded, along with other indigenous enterprises
ranging from cotton and cloth manufacturing to banking and insurance.[94] The Hooghly and adjoining rivers were vital symbolic and commercial battlegrounds between Bengali nationalists and supporters of
the colonial status quo.

In December 1911 the Swadeshi movement achieved one of its foremost aims: the partition of Bengal was annulled. In that same month,
however, it was announced that the capital of British India would be
transferred from Calcutta to Delhi, where a new imperial city was to
be constructed. Bengal was too politically charged to host comfortably
the imperial government. The economic predominance of Calcutta
among the major Indian cities had been threatened in the later nineteenth century by Bombay, particularly after the opening of the Suez
Canal in 1869 facilitated readier steamship access from Europe to the
western Indian Ocean. Now Calcutta's political pre-eminence was also
coming to an end. Without the connections between the port cities and
Upper India offered by the railways, the transfer of the capital to Delhi
would have been unthinkable. In consequence of the technology of
steam, through which Calcutta had been transformed into one of the
world's first megacities, its political and economic significance was
ultimately undermined.

7

SAGAR ISLAND

THE HOOGHLY'S GLOBAL FUTURE

South of Calcutta, the Hooghly completes its final descent to the sea, following first a meandering, broadly south-westerly course down to Hooghly Point, where the Rupnarayan enters it from the west. En route, after the suburbs of Calcutta have been left behind, are the ruins of the fort of Budge-Budge, seized by English forces from Siraj-ud-Daula in January 1757. Just beyond it, on the river's left bank, is a temple whose symmetrical tiered gateway and Chinese lettering distinguish it from other temples and ghats on the Hooghly. It dates to the late eighteenth century, when a Chinese tea trader, Tong Achew, was granted permission by the English East India Company to settle in Bengal. Here, on a site named after him as Achipur, he established a sugarcane plantation and factory, setting a precedent for later Chinese settlement in Calcutta. The temple serves as a reminder that the integration of the river into global trading networks was about more than Indian–European exchange.

At Hooghly Point the river swings to the east, bolstered by the inflow of the Rupnarayan's waters, before veering south again at Diamond Harbour, touted in the nineteenth century as an alternative port to Calcutta when concerns about the navigability of the Hooghly grew. From here, the river widens to enter the Bay of Bengal and Sagar Island comes into view. About thirty kilometres in length and up to twelve wide, the flat mass of Sagar Island sits at the mouth of the Hooghly, with the river passing it on each side to join the sea. From its northern tip, the village of Kastala, the Hooghly estuary is on display, with the Sunderbans, the world's largest mangrove forest, to the east. From the beach along the island's southern edge, sweeping views are had out into the vast expanse of the Bay of Bengal. The name 'Sagar' denotes the ocean.

Referred to by its sacred name, Gangasagar, Sagar Island occupies an important place in the myth of the Hooghly's origins—the descent of the Ganges from heaven.[1] It was on Sagar Island, according to the story, that the sage Kapila sat deep in meditation when the 60,000 sons of King Sagara falsely accused him of taking the king's horse, and here that Kapila turned the sons to ash. When King Sagara's great-great-grandson, Bhagiratha, convinced Lord Brahma and Lord Shiva to release the Ganges from heaven, he led it across North India to enter the sea next to the island, appeasing Kapila and persuading him to restore the sons to life.

As the site where the sacred Ganges meets the sea, Sagar Island is today one of the most auspicious locations in India's sacred geography. Bathing in the spot where the river and ocean meet is a particularly holy act. Those who manage it, according to the Puranas, go to heaven after death rather than being born again, achieving *moksha*.[2] Sagar Island is therefore the destination of one of the major pilgrimages in the Hindu calendar, a great bathing festival (*mela*) taking place every year from mid-December to mid-January. The basic elements of the festival have remained unchanged through recent centuries. Pilgrims arrive by boat from one of the river ports opposite the island on the mainland, or from more distant ports like Calcutta, and proceed from the landing jetties to the island's southern edge, where bathing takes place along a mile-long stretch of beach. *Puja* to the goddess Ganga is performed, with offerings like flowers or coconut cast into the water. Kapila is honoured in a dedicated temple near the seashore. To reap the promised spiritual rewards, devotees aim to spend three days and nights on the island including, if possible, Makar Sankranti, the first day of spring in the solar calendar, which falls in mid-January.

As we saw in the last chapter, the pilgrimage to Sagar Island has been a recurring theme in Bengali literature. 'I have come here to see the ocean', announces the protagonist Navkumar in Bankim Chandra Chatterjee's *Kapalakundala* on his arrival at Sagar Island, hinting that pilgrims' motivations were not always or only spiritual.[3] At the time of Chatterjee's writing, in the 1860s, the number of annual pilgrims to Sagar Island was estimated at about 100,000, but now exceeds a million.[4] Pilgrims of very different wealth and social status come from across India, with a significant proportion of them peasants and labourers from West Bengal, Bihar, Orissa, and Uttar Pradesh. They arrive carrying food and bundles of clothes to sleep in hostels, out in the open or in makeshift tents. Before dawn, tens of thousands make their way to the beach to stand knee-deep in the water offering prayers and awaiting sunrise. The present temple of Kapil Muni is a modern construction of concrete and corrugated iron about five hundred metres from the beach, previous iterations having repeatedly collapsed in the island's shifting soil or been swallowed by the sea. Inside is a garlanded image of Kapila meditating, his head covered with five giant snakes. On one side is a depiction of King Sagara and on the other a figurine of the goddess Ganga seated on a crocodile (*makara*). Ash-smeared holy men (sadhus) sit in rows along the streets around the temple. Offerings are sold on street stalls along with bottles for the collection of Ganges water to take home.[5]

Guarding the mouth of the Hooghly, Sagar Island has occupied an important position in the global history of the river explored in this book. For voyagers traversing the Bay of Bengal, it was usually the first sight of land: 'With what eager interests you watch the first objects which denote your arrival on new soil, from the moment you see the Island of Sagur like a small cloud in the horizon!' wrote one early-nineteenth-century British visitor. '[T]hen you perceive it thick with mighty forests, you distinguish separate trees, and their luxuriant foliage is so refreshing to your eyes.'[6] For those going in the other direction, Sagar Island represented a farewell to Bengal and the beginning of a sea voyage. The name Gangasagar—literally the meeting of river and ocean—conjured up feelings of uncertainty and dread for many seabound Hindus for whom travel across the 'black water' (*kala pani*) of the oceans was traditionally taboo. Sagar Island symbolised the connection of the Hooghly with the world beyond Bengal, across the Indian Ocean and further afield.

Sebastian Manrique, whose travels we followed in chapter 1, visited Sagar Island shortly before his departure from Bengal for Arakan in 1628. The landscape that he found was a fertile uncultivated jungle rich with areca palm trees. The island was uninhabited except for pilgrims but the extent of ruins near the southern seashore, he surmised, indicated that it had once been densely populated by prosperous Brahmins. Manrique described the practices of the pilgrims he encountered, as they visited the partially ruined temple to Kapila, washing ritually and, in the case of men, shaving their heads and beards before entering. After prostrating themselves in the temple, he observed:

> [T]hey enter the sea up to their breasts and are very soon seized and devoured by certain ferocious male and female sea-monsters which we call Sharks. They have three rows of teeth. And since they are accustomed and thus encouraged by constantly tasting flesh, they become so bloody-thirsty that they rush up fiercely at even a mere shadow. Yet at other times they are either so satiated, or else so far away from the spot, that they reject the offerings of their own bodies, made by these unhappy Idolaters. They then look upon this escape, which they should consider as so much happiness and good fortune, as an event full of ill luck and misfortune, and hence leave the sea weeping and lamenting loudly, believing that owing to their sins and unworthiness they were not considered worthy to have their sacrifice accepted by their false and diabolical gods, and henceforth, they look upon themselves as for ever damned and doomed.[7]

We may be sceptical about how many pilgrims at Gangasagar really wished to be devoured by sharks, but the threat they posed to bathing devotees in Manrique's time is beyond doubt. The sea around Sagar Island was inhabited by several varieties of man-eating shark, including much-feared bull sharks, known in the nineteenth century to venture as far upriver as Calcutta, while the Hooghly was itself home to a species of river shark, the *Glyphis gangeticus*. Most of these species are now critically endangered.

The other main threat to pilgrims during Manrique's years on the Hooghly was the presence of Portuguese outlaws (*arrenegados*) who used Sagar Island as a base for their piratical activities in the Bay of Bengal. Manrique acknowledged that the capture of those found on the island in order to trade them as slaves was a common Portuguese activity and one of the main reasons why, save for pilgrims, the island was now deserted. After Shah Jahan's assault on Hooghly, which, as we have seen, was provoked above all by Portuguese slave trading, survivors of the siege—some 100 Portuguese and 3000 other inhabitants—who escaped downriver from the Mughal forces regrouped on Sagar Island. They attempted to build a fortress from the remains of a ruined temple before plague struck and most died. Those fortunate enough to survive both the siege and the plague fled the island for the coast of Hijli.[8]

Such was the strategic value of Sagar Island's location at the mouth of the Hooghly that, in spite of its inhospitable natural environment, the idea of developing a fortified settlement on the island was revived by the English East India Company as its struggles with the Mughal governors of Bengal intensified at the end of the seventeenth century. In 1681 the Company's Court of Directors, with a view to protecting and enlarging its growing trading interests on the Hooghly, separated the management of its affairs in Bengal from Company authorities in Madras and appointed a new agent, William Hedges, to oversee Bengal operations. Hedges negotiated a stronger legal basis for English trade in Bengal, securing a succession of treaties with the Mughal governor Shaista Khan, but believed that only the development of the Company's military presence on the Hooghly would ensure that the treaties were observed. Hooghly, where the Company's factory was then based, was vulnerable to attack, as the fate of the Portuguese had shown. After conducting research, Hedges determined that Sagar Island was the securest location for a fortified Company settlement on the river and drew up plans for its construction, which were dispatched to London for the directors' approval. They were rejected as too costly and likely to provoke Dutch opposition; Hedges was recalled to England and left Bengal disappointed.[9] Sagar Island was therefore relegated to a footnote in the story of the transformation of the English Company into a militarised territorial power (considered in chapter 3). Within a year of Hedges' recall, the directors had declared war on the Mughal Empire and dispatched troops to Bengal. When the Company reinstalled itself on the Hooghly in the aftermath of its humiliating defeat to the Mughal forces, the site chosen as its base was not Sagar Island or Hooghly but the seemingly insignificant collection of villages that would become Calcutta.

By the end of the eighteenth century, the development of the Company into the de facto government of Bengal, with territorial and revenue-collecting rights underpinned by the exercise of force, was complete. Among Englishmen in India and at home, new understandings of the purposes of Company rule were beginning to emerge, fuelled in part by the evangelical idea that non-European peoples required improvement from their European overlords. Sagar Island was an important testing ground for the evolution of the Company's rule into a regime legitimised by notions of the improvement of Indian society (examined in chapter 5). In their printed writings about the Hindu religion, one of the contemporary practices most strongly condemned by the Baptist missionaries at Serampore was the sacrifice at Gangasagar of humans, particularly children, which they claimed was commonplace.[10] After initially ignoring the missionaries' appeals for intervention, the Company government bowed to English opinion in Calcutta by initiating an enquiry which concluded that in the year 1802 twenty-three children had been cast into the sea and drowned at Sagar Island as a sacrificial offering to the gods. William Carey was commissioned by the government to determine whether or not the practice was sanctioned in the Hindu scriptures. He consulted with several Brahmin colleagues in Serampore and Calcutta before concluding that it was not. Child sacrifice, he contended, was a popular superstition without scriptural basis, often the result of a vow taken by a woman who, fearing she would be childless, sacrificed her first-born on the understanding that she would be guaranteed additional progeny.[11]

The government's response was to outlaw the practice in August 1802, the first example of official English intervention to reform an aspect of Indian society. It was followed, of course, by the prohibition of sati in 1829, by which time English authorities had abandoned their concern for the scriptural basis of religious practice in preference for more decisive intervention. Throughout the nineteenth century, the government would attempt to police the 'frenzy of superstition' that in its view constituted the Gangasagar festival, to make sure that the prohibition of human sacrifice was observed, limit the number of fatal shark attacks, prevent crime, and maintain surveillance over pilgrims.[12] After the Indian Rebellion of 1857–8, colonial authorities remained nervous about the movement of large numbers of people through their territories, even though the intentions of most pilgrims to Sagar Island were wholly apolitical.

In the English imagination, Sagar Island was not just the site of barbaric sacrificial practices and other Hindu superstition. The 'black island', as it was often referred to, was a terrifying illustration of nature at its wildest, thick with jungle and deadly creatures.[13] 'The very appearance of the dark jungle that covers it is terrific,' wrote one observer: 'You see it must be a nest of serpents, and a den of tigers.'[14] The natural response of the authorities, keen to extract value from lands under their control and confident in the early nineteenth century in the progress of civilisation, was to attempt to cultivate the island, 'to change the tiger's den into a dwelling for man, and transfer a noxious wilderness into a seat of plenty.'[15] Efforts began in 1811 under government leadership before a joint-stock company was formed with European and Indian members. The island was leased to the company with a revenue-free period of thirty years to make the land cultivable and plans were drawn up for jungle clearance, the construction of embankments, the digging of tanks, and the settlement of cultivators. On the ground, however, progress was arduous. Jungle cleared rapidly regrew, and rates of mortality among Indian workers and their European supervisors were high, with illness ('jungle fever') and tiger attacks the biggest threats.[16] Writing in 1824 the indigo planter William Huggins noted that the total area of land cleared on the island amounted to no more than seven miles in circumference, 'a poor return for the money and life expended in this undertaking.' He concluded: 'I consider this undertaking to be one of those air bubbles which speculators are so much addicted to forming. The clearing of Saugur appears to be distant, and almost hopeless.'[17]

Adding to the challenges of the cultivation project were the recurring instances of extreme weather events against which the flat island was very poorly protected, particularly in those areas where jungle had been cleared. In 1833 a severe hurricane swept away houses and other buildings and destroyed embankments. Repeat visitations in 1842 and 1848 were dwarfed by the great cyclone and tidal wave of October 1864, which only 1500 of the island's population of 5600 survived.[18] After that disaster, which devastated large parts of lower Bengal, precautions were taken to ensure that future hurricanes and cyclones did not cause such a loss of life on the island: higher and stronger embankments were ordered to provide a break against strong winds and places of refugee were constructed, with the expectation that all homes on the island would be within a mile of a refuge, to protect people and cattle during storms. The process of land reclamation recommenced almost from scratch, with five large estates leased out to private parties and the rest of the land restored to government control. The progress of land cultivation remained so slow, however, that for investors there was little chance of returning a profit. At the turn of the twentieth century, much of the island was still dense jungle and the lease system was abandoned in favour of the direct settlement of peasant cultivators (*ryots*).[19] An earthquake in 1897 destroyed homes and caused the temple of Kapil Muni to collapse into the sea.

In sum, British attempts to cultivate Sagar Island suffered a fate similar to their attempts to control the Hooghly (explored in chapter 6)—limited progress and repeated setbacks—which over time engendered a colonial crisis of confidence. The failure of British efforts to tame and render productive the natural environment of Bengal went hand in hand with growing self-doubt about the capacity of colonial authorities to control and improve the peoples under their rule. A macabre example further illustrates the limits of colonial power in relation to natural forces. In 1887 a cyclone near the Orissan coast caused the steamer *Sir John Lawrence* to sink with 750 passengers on board. Many of the corpses were swept across the Bay of Bengal to wash up on Sagar Island or become lodged on the sandbanks at the mouth of the Hooghly.[20]

In the first part of the twentieth century, the migration of peoples from South East Asia, China, and other locations, through which Calcutta had been transformed into a global megacity, continued. In spite of its eclipse by Bombay as India's largest port, Calcutta remained an important station in imperial networks of trade spanning the Indian, Atlantic, and Pacific oceans. The decades after 1870 witnessed growing outward migration from Bengal too, a response to the increasing demand for Indian migrants in other British imperial sites around the Bay of Bengal, combined with economic slowdown and food shortages at home. Indentured labourers, many of them impoverished Bengalis and Biharis, left Calcutta for the sugar, rubber, coffee, cotton, and tobacco plantations of Mauritius, British Guiana, and Malaya, along with others for eastern and southern Africa. Burma, meanwhile, had been incorporated into the territories of British India in 1885 and required labourers to develop its land, work in industry, and build infrastructure like the railways through which the Burmese economy could be forced into the colonial system. By 1911 more than 100,000 people were arriving in Burma from India each year, many of them peasants and labourers setting sail from Calcutta, down the Hooghly past Sagar Island and into the Bay, their movement encouraged by colonial administrators increasingly of the mind that India was over-populated.[21] Soldiers and civil officers also moved to Burma, while the flood of Indian capital into the Burmese economy financed the cultivation of rice for export on a global scale. Regular steamer services plied the route between Calcutta and Rangoon, which became an overwhelmingly Indian city. Most Indians in Burma retained links with their homeland and periodically returned, often following the patterns of seasonal labour demand.

After the interruption of the First World War, when over a million Indian troops served for Britain overseas, the movement of peoples between the Hooghly and other locations around the Indian Ocean resumed, with overall migrant numbers growing through the 1920s. This, however, was not set to last. As a global economic depression set in after 1929, the sentiments of political and cultural nationalism that in Bengal had first found mass expression during the Swadeshi movement, as well as over the protests against the 1905 partition of the province, intensified in India and elsewhere. Both the push and pull factors that had contributed to migration from Calcutta to other imperial sites were diminished, as anti-colonial elites in India deliberating questions of national development began to view emigration as a drain of the nation's resources, and the inflow of Indian migrants became the focus of nationalist critique elsewhere.[22] In Burma, Indian households and businesses were attacked as nationalists demanded separation from India over and above independence from British rule. The era of the free movement of peoples from the Hooghly across the Bay of Bengal, represented by the voyage out past Sagar Island, came to an end as migration controls were imposed and Burma was cut out from India to become a separate British territory in 1937. A similar line of reasoning provoked demands for migration into India to be curtailed. Among Indian political leaders, the nation-state was almost universally accepted as the natural unit of organisation when independence from

Britain came.[23] In Indian nationalist discourse, immigration increasingly appeared as a problem to be solved.

With the outbreak of World War II, the Hooghly was returned to a central stage in global history: 2.5 million Indian subjects enlisted to fight in the British Indian Army, with hundreds of thousands departing from Calcutta for different theatres of war.[24] The expertise of Hooghly River Survey officers, who were accustomed to the challenges of river navigation and engineering, was utilised as the war progressed to determine landing sites on the African and Mediterranean coasts and construct temporary bridges across rivers.[25] Calcutta's population had expanded to about two million on the eve of the war. The city became vital to the British imperial war effort to stop Japanese advances through South East Asia, with its industries producing an estimated 80 per cent of the armaments, textiles, and heavy machinery used by British forces in Asia during the war.[26] Some 500,000 refugees arrived in the city as the Japanese progressed through Burma after the fall of Singapore in February 1942. Japanese planes bombed Calcutta in December of that year and again in 1943, targeting the heavy industries and dockyards of the Hooghly. Subhas Chandra Bose, a resident of Calcutta, was the most prominent nationalist leader encouraging his compatriots to side with the Axis powers to rid India of Britain for good. Escaping house arrest in Calcutta, he fled to Germany where he spent almost two years before travelling by submarine to Japan in 1943. With Japanese support, he revived the Indian National Army, which had been formed the previous year by Japanese-held Indian prisoners of war who wished to fight against Britain in South East Asia. Numbering 40,000 at its peak, the Indian National Army advanced with Japanese forces through Burma to the borders of British India, penetrating east Bengal when it entered the Chittagong division in 1944.[27]

Over the decades preceding the war, the ecological balance of the Bengal delta, east of the Hooghly, had been eroded by colonial engineering initiatives, including the construction of railway embankments and the diversion of the natural course of rivers and streams.[28] Agricultural productivity had failed to keep pace with population growth, the people of the delta increasingly relying on the import of rice from Burma before the Japanese invasion. During the winter monsoon of 1942, a huge cyclone struck eastern Bengal; a tidal wave followed, flooding fields and destroying crops to produce a massive short-fall in the domestic harvest. The possibility of another famine was all too evident to those in the delta who could remember periods of food scarcity through the 1920s and 1930s.

As with the catastrophic famine that Bengal and surrounding territories had suffered in 1770–1, the situation in early 1943 was exacerbated by a combination of British mismanagement and indifference. After the fall of Burma, the colonial authorities in Calcutta had adopted a policy of confiscating 'surplus' stocks of rice in districts across eastern Bengal, so that the Japanese, in the event of an invasion, would be unable to feed their troops. Rice was moved under military escort to feed the industrial labour force of Calcutta. To prevent the feared Japanese advance through the delta, some 46,000 boats were also sunk, destroyed, or removed to military compounds; transport on the waterways east of the Hooghly was crippled, making it impossible to move rice or people between areas of relative surplus and scarcity in sufficient volume when the crisis worsened.[29] As in 1770, British authorities were slow to recognise the warning signs of famine—rising prices and shortages—and continued to export rice from Bengal, this time to feed troops around the world. When the scale of the famine became clear, Churchill's administration in London refused to divert Allied shipping to provide relief.

The hundreds of thousands who were starving in towns and villages in the delta may have gone unnoticed by many British observers, but it wasn't long before sick and emaciated refugees began pouring into Calcutta. Colonial authorities began rounding up 'sick destitutes' and interring them in camps outside the city, keen to avoid the public spectacle of dead and dying bodies in the streets, about which accounts had been so hauntingly penned in 1770.[30] British and Indian industrialists in Calcutta profited greatly from the dependence of the British war effort in Asia on their factories. Their support of official attempts to ensure the transfer of food from the countryside into the city bears comparison with the activities of English and Indian agents of the East India Company who profited from the requisitioning of grain in 1770–1. By the end of the war, a total of three million had succumbed to the famine, making it the deadliest in Bengal since that time. Most were landless labourers, or fishermen and their families.[31]

With the end of World War II, British rule over India was almost finished. When independence arrived, however, it would be accompanied by a second partition of Bengal, this time with unprecedented tragic consequences. The understanding of religious identities as fixed and mutually exclusive categories in India had its origins in nineteenth-century colonial administration. Religious affiliation appeared in colonial censuses, anthropological and ethnographic studies, and official reports and proceedings as a field requiring definitive, singular identification, a departure from more blurred and heterogeneous conceptions of religious attachment common in earlier periods, not least in Bengal under the nawabs. In Bengal and elsewhere on the subcontinent, many Indian leaders adopted the colonial language of religious identity in their engagement with British authorities, appealing for political, economic, and social concessions from government as representatives of distinct religious groups.[32] As independence from Britain drew near, Muslim leaders across India were faced with a choice. Within the narrow framework of the nation-state, embraced by Indian politicians and statesmen as the primary political and territorial entity to succeed imperial rule, Muslims would be either a minority community in India or a separate nation of their own. In March 1940 the All India Muslim League, which claimed to represent the interests of Muslims across India, adopted a resolution supporting the foundation of a separate Muslim homeland. It was endorsed by the Bengal Provincial Muslim League, the governing party in the province from 1943.

In the summer of 1946, a British plan to keep India united by granting Muslim-majority provinces a large degree of autonomy in the independent Indian state collapsed, amid increasing rancour between leaders of the Indian National Congress and the Muslim League. The League responded by calling for Muslims across India to take 'direct action' to show their support for a separate Muslim state, now referred to as Pakistan. Across most of northern India, Direct Action Day, 16 August 1946, took the form of peaceful protests but in Calcutta fighting broke out between Hindus and Muslims across the city. Between 5000 and 10,000 were killed in violence that prefigured the mass killings accompanying partition in Bengal and, particularly, the Punjab the following year. Explanations of what became known as the

Great Calcutta Killings have usually emphasised the incitement of communal antagonism by Hindu and Muslim political leaders or, conversely, the mass expression of socio-economic grievances by a population impoverished by war and famine, which found an outlet in communal targets.[33] More recent explanations stress the effects of famine and war in not only 'brutalising the consciousness' but also transforming Calcutta in the minds of many into the only place where, given the devastation of the rural economy of the Bengal delta, subsistence was possible.[34] Possession of the city was equated with survival. At the time, the violence came as a great shock. That it took the form of Hindu versus Muslim was antithetical to the spirit of openness and religious pluralism more often characteristic of life on the Hooghly through the centuries.

In Bengal, religion was not the only marker of identity that mattered as independence approached. Peoples on the Hooghly identified variously as Bengalis, Indians, British imperial subjects, and as part of a larger region stretching across the Bay of Bengal, alongside their religious affiliations. In early 1947 a plan gathered pace, with the support of Muslim and Hindu leaders including Huseyn Shaheed Suhrawardy—the new head of the Bengal Provincial Muslim League—for a united Bengali nation independent of India.[35] As in the early twentieth century, when the first partition of Bengal was contested, the idea of a Bengali identity incorporating different religious constituencies had a powerful appeal. The United Bengal scheme was ultimately rejected by Congress and Muslim League negotiators at the national level; however, the League demand for Pakistan was soon after conceded, ensuring that a boundary line would once again be drawn through Bengal.

By August 1947, the question was no longer *if* that line would be drawn, but *where*. The province of Bengal divided with several notable exceptions into Muslim-majority districts in the east and Hindu-majority districts in the west. For the commission appointed to determine the border between India and East Pakistan, however, several key issues required resolution. Foremost was the location of Calcutta: to which state should the city belong, or could it feasibly be shared between the two? A related question concerned the Hooghly more directly: who should take possession of the districts around the upper reaches of the river, thereby controlling the flow of water on which Calcutta, its port, and other locations on the Hooghly, depended? Complication was added to these questions by the fact that the district of Murshidabad, at the top of the river, was a Muslim-majority area, while districts lower down were predominantly Hindu. The geography of the Hooghly defied its straightforward allocation to one state or the other.

The Bengal Boundary Commission held public meetings in Calcutta at which representatives of the Congress, the Muslim League, and other parties presented arguments before reaching a conclusion. Calcutta would be located in India. To guarantee its supply of water, the district of Murshidabad would also be in the Indian state of West Bengal, with Khulna, a Hindu-majority district further east, awarded in compensation to Pakistan. The Hooghly, and the territories immediately either side of it, would therefore be in the Indian nation, with the border of East Pakistan just a few kilometres east of the point where the Hooghly separated from the main branch of the Ganges, which would continue into East Pakistan as the Padma.[36] The movement of refugees across the new border was less immediate and violent than in the Punjab when independence arrived. Nevertheless, by 1951 an estimated 2.6 million people had migrated from East Pakistan into India, with most settling in Calcutta, and 700,000 had travelled in the other direction.[37] On the left bank of the Hooghly, just north of Sagar Island, a small Sufi shrine commemorates this momentous upheaval, while testifying to the survival of syncretic religious practices at odds with the segregating logic of partition.

In the years after independence, some local people, among them fishermen and agricultural workers, continued to make use of the canals and smaller rivers branching eastwards from the Hooghly to connect West Bengal with East Pakistan. Regular movement along the waterways and across the national border did not entirely cease. India, however, had other developmental priorities; many of the smaller waterways of West Bengal decayed and became unnavigable. Meanwhile, the independent Indian state turned its attention to other natural resources within its borders, which were enlisted in the cause of national development. Informed by the experience of the 1930s depression, famine, and World War II, Indian statesmen turned their back on free markets across international borders in favour of state-led agricultural and industrial development aimed at national self-sufficiency. Many of the measures for achieving these ends took after the actions of the state and private parties during the colonial period, among them the extraction of fossil fuels, new irrigation projects, widespread deforestation, and the construction of dams for hydro-electric power. The environmental costs of these initiatives were unknown or ignored as the imperative of national development took centre stage.

On the Hooghly, the growth of heavy industry ensured that the port of Calcutta remained vital. In 1961 an estimated third of the city's population, which had risen to 5.5 million, worked in roles directly or indirectly related to the port.[38] The Hooghly River Survey continued its work, surveying the river and attempting to keep it navigable; a lighthouse on Sagar Island aided the passage of ships around the perilous sandbanks at the river mouth. Fears continued to mount, however, that the Hooghly's water levels were diminishing, with the survival of the port at stake. The governments of India and West Bengal therefore launched one of the new nation's most ambitious infrastructure projects: to dam the Ganges and divert a greater proportion of its water into the Hooghly before it crossed the border into East Pakistan. The construction of a dam and feeder canal linking the Ganges and the Hooghly had first been proposed as a solution to the deterioration of the Hooghly as far back as 1919. When the Bengal Boundary Commission was sitting in 1947, the idea was revived: members of the commission representing the future Indian state noted that 'some means, or other, should be found by which an appreciable portion of the Ganges floods can be induced to pass through the Nadia rivers [where the Hooghly breaks from the Ganges] in preference to the Padma [...] to prevent the Hooghly from languishing altogether and reviv[e] the health and industry of Bengal.'[39] After independence, the advantages of such a scheme were elaborated upon: in assisting the natural flow of water from the Hooghly to the Ganges, a dam and canal would prevent the build-up of silt in the Hooghly, lessening the need for dredging; reduce the salinity of the river in its lower reaches, benefitting agriculture; and maintain a permanently navigable river route between Upper India, Bengal, and the sea, guaranteeing the port of Calcutta's future.

The village of Farakka, just fifteen kilometres from the East Pakistan border, was selected for the dam, which was christened the Farakka Barrage. Plans were drawn up for a dam 2.2 kilometres in length, from one side of the Ganges to the other, with a canal thirty-eight kilometres long entering the Hooghly near the town of Jangipur to the south-east. Construction began in 1961 but would continue through the decade. Like the builders of railway bridges during the previous century, engineers found the embedding of foundations in the alluvial riverbed a huge challenge, while construction was only possible during the drier months of the year from December to May. The basic structure of the dam, which consisted of 109 gated bays, was finally completed in 1969, with a road and rail bridge on top of the structure finished three years later and the canal in 1975.[40]

Among politicians and civil servants and in the domestic media, the completion of the Farakka Barrage was heralded as a triumph, an achievement for which the nation was to be congratulated. Almost immediately, however, problems began to surface. For one, the volume of water reaching the dam from the Ganges was not as great as experts had predicted; authorities in Calcutta began arguing that to keep the port functional during the drier months of the year, a greater proportion of water should be diverted into the Hooghly. This, inevitably, rang alarm bells for Bangladesh, which had established its independence from Pakistan in 1971. Before the completion of the dam, no water-sharing agreement had been reached between India and East Pakistan. Fearful that the Farakka Barrage would critically deprive the Padma of water, Bangladesh now voiced its concerns internationally, taking a case all the way to the United Nations in 1976. A compromise was reached with the signing of a treaty governing the sharing of water between India and Bangladesh from January to May each year in 1977. It was replaced by a series of short-term agreements through the 1980s before the conclusion of a bilateral treaty in 1996, which remains in force today, guaranteeing Bangladesh half of the Ganges' water during the dry season for the next thirty years.[41]

Equally serious have been the ecological problems on both sides of the border caused or accentuated by the dam. It is now clear that the build-up of sediment behind the dam has substantially raised the bed of the Ganges, destabilising the natural flow of water and eroding the river's banks. The river has significantly widened in places and the flooding of surrounding lands has become more common. Water released into the Hooghly below the dam contains significantly less silt than it used to, which has had unanticipated consequences: downstream riverbeds have been eroded, with some channels deepened and others almost drying up, and the river is now unable to replenish the silt of delta—a major reason why large areas of land in West Bengal and Bangladesh are now disappearing below the water level. Contrary to expectations, the river has increased rather than decreased in salinity in its lower reaches, as insufficient volumes of fresh water enter it and sea levels rise; conditions for crop-growing have worsened. Some scientists link the impact of the Farakka Barrage to the rise in waterborne diseases like typhoid, diarrhoea, cholera, and hepatitis among the human population of the delta. The dam has also had a severe impact on fish volumes in the river, affecting the livelihoods of millions. With the movement of fish restricted, some species, like the hilsa, which has traditionally used the upper Ganges to spawn, are fast becoming extinct. The Ganges shark and Gangetic dolphin are both now critically endangered.[42] While these unintended consequences have materialised, the dam has failed in its principal aim of ensuring the sufficient supply of water into the Hooghly: the river receives at best half and in some years no more than a quarter of the estimated 40,000 cubic feet per second required to flush its upper reaches during the dry season.[43]

From the vantage point of Sagar Island, as the Hooghly joins the Indian Ocean, the significance of the river to India's global future can be assessed. In the twenty-first century, India has begun to assert itself—culturally, economically, and geo-politically—on the global stage. The Bay of Bengal has re-emerged as an arena of competition between great powers, but now those powers are Asian—Indian and Chinese—rather than European. China and India compete in the Bay over trade, natural resources, and cultural influence. India's military strategy and diplomatic efforts have been refocused on the Indian Ocean, and South East Asia in particular, with attempts under way to develop the Indian navy into a force with a presence beyond India's coastal waters.[44] Sagar Island may play an important part in these developments. For more than a decade, plans have been under discussion for the construction of a deep-sea port on the island as a base for the assertion of Indian maritime supremacy in the Bay. If implemented, the port would be a major upgrade on the deep-sea dock at Haldia, opposite Diamond Harbour, opened in 1977 to cater for large ocean-going vessels unable to reach Calcutta. Its capacity would be sufficient to accommodate commercial and military shipping—the latest proposals suggest nine berths suitable for huge container ships—with a three-kilometre road and rail bridge linking the port and island with the mainland.[45]

The economy of West Bengal is today recovering from several decades of industrial stagnation and decline under the state's communist-led government (1977–2011). Volumes of trade on the Hooghly have increased, with approximately fifty million tonnes of cargo now passing through Calcutta port each year, a dramatic rise on the fifteen million tonnes recorded in 1991.[46] There are reasons to believe that this figure will continue to grow. In 2014, the central Indian government announced its intention to revive the nation's waterways as arteries for freight transport, integrating them into a comprehensive Inland Water Transport System. Designated 'National Waterway 1', the Hooghly–Ganges has been identified as a priority route, its development supported by the award of US$50 million from the World Bank.[47]

Before the revival of the Hooghly is celebrated, however, several notes of caution should be sounded. Having passed through successive eras of imperial free trade and post-colonial state planning, the West Bengal economy is today shaped by global financial and economic orthodoxies designed in and enforced by institutions of global governance largely produced in Europe and the United States, not least in the countries of former colonial powers on the Hooghly. From the 1980s, as the Indian economy has opened itself up to international financial markets, public-sector debt has become a major concern; austerity policies have been imposed to reduce public deficits.[48] In West Bengal, state funding for public institutions like the Kolkata Port Trust has been cut. Since the turn of the twentieth century, the Port Trust has been responsible for the river and the lands on either side of it from Konnagar, near Serampore, to the sea. Among its tasks are to maintain the river's navigability, regulate traffic, and deliver the river pilot service. As recent research shows, the Port Trust has responded to cuts in its funding by pursuing short-term policies like the selling of assets, speculative planning and investment, and the recourse to rentier income from temporary land use. It has struggled to invest in the longer-term infrastructure, technology, and manpower required to arrest the deterioration of the river, with many of its channels narrower and more dangerous than before, and the frequency and seriousness of accidents on the rise.[49]

As in other economies around the world shaped by neo-liberal dynamics and an overriding concern with public debt, the declining capacity of public institutions on the Hooghly has corresponded with growing private investment and the proliferation of public–private partnerships underpinned by new mechanisms of finance. At its most beneficial, private investment has created jobs and stimulated innovations, like the introduction of more efficient technologies to aid river navigation.[50] All too often, however, it has meant the prioritising of short-term profits over long-term public good, resulting in cheap, ineffective investments and infrastructure decay. Public institutions like the Port Trust and private companies on the river resort to the use of contracted and casual labour; inequality rises as the growth of the private sector provides investment opportunities for a few, while for most, wage levels and job security are eroded.[51] The Sagar Island port project exemplifies many of these trends. Desperate to attract private investment to complement state and international development funds, the government has committed to guaranteeing the profits of private investors in the scheme. After the construction of the port, berths would be rented to private operators who would be free to fix the pay and conditions of workers.[52] In spite of these guarantees, the private sector has been reluctant to offer up the necessary funding. It is now unlikely that the port will be completed before 2035.

A second note of caution concerns the environmental degradation of the river. As it crosses northern India, the Ganges passes through a basin supporting hundreds of millions of people. It receives vast quantities of sewage and household waste, agricultural pesticides and fertilisers, industrial refuse and other pollutants before entering the Bengal delta. On the Hooghly, the situation worsens. Its banks remain home to coal-fired power stations, brick kilns, pharmaceutical manufacturers, and illegal cottage industries that deposit their waste in the river.

Agricultural chemicals run off the fields into streams that flow into the Hooghly. Human remains continue to enter the river from its many cremation ghats. The most serious pollutant of all on the Hooghly is sewage. At present, most households near the river are not connected to sewerage systems; sewage flows into the river without being processed in a treatment plant. As such, the river contains volumes of faecal bacteria greatly in excess of the World Health Organisation safe limit.[53] On the route of the Ganges–Hooghly, only the stretch between Kanpur and Varanasi in Uttar Pradesh contains higher overall pollution levels than the Hooghly. The impact on the human population living around the river is catastrophic, with diarrhoea, dysentery, and parasitic infections common, and rates of cancer, most often of the gall bladder, kidneys, liver, and skin, on the rise. Experts now warn of a new breed of 'superbug' highly resistant to most antibiotics that is spread by sewage-borne waste.

In recent years, new initiatives have been undertaken to counter the river pollution crisis. In 2014 the Indian government launched a 'national mission' to clean up the Ganges under the direction of its renamed Ministry of Water Resources, River Development and Ganga Rejuvenation. Similar schemes have periodically been announced since the 1980s, but this time the resources allocated are significant and detailed action plans have been drawn up.[54] Municipalities along the river, including on the Hooghly, have been instructed to introduce measures for the better treatment of sewerage waste. In March 2017 the high court of the state of Uttarakhand, home to the source of the Ganges, declared that it and the Yamuna River should be treated in law like human beings: to harm the rivers by, for example, disposing of waste in them, would be the legal equivalent of harming a human being.[55] The ruling was overturned by the Indian Supreme Court but is indicative of a growing environmental consciousness among those residing in proximity to the Ganges. In West Bengal, a hundred or so industries heavily polluting the Hooghly have been closed down; new sewage treatment plants and cremation facilities are being installed.[56] The Gangasagar festival has gone 'green', with plastics banned, the discarding of rubbish into the water forbidden, and the use of toilets enforced among pilgrims.[57]

Incidences of pollution at Gangasagar—and indeed along the course of the Ganges–Hooghly—indicate that, historically, the sacredness of the river has not been an impediment to its pollution. Some suggest that it may even have contributed to the problem, in the sense that those believing the river to be a goddess are less likely to accept criticisms of its condition.[58] Certainly, religious devotees and environmental activists use very different vocabularies when speaking about the river. As has been pointed out, effective long-term solutions to the pollution problem require the engagement of people with very different backgrounds and perspectives on the river. The solutions need to be cultural and theological as well as technical and scientific.[59] Recent initiatives offer a degree of encouragement. It is hard to escape the conclusion, however, that current developmental schemes like the Sagar Island port and inland water transport projects risk undermining progress in the protection of the environment, with increases in freight river traffic likely to add to pollution levels. The Hooghly's ecological balance will be further disturbed if the two projects advance. Both the construction of the Sagar Island port and the preparation of the Hooghly for a higher volume of traffic would require major dredging. Outcry followed the government announcement in July 2014 that new barrages would be constructed on the Hooghly–Ganges every hundred kilometres, to facilitate the deepening of the river, along with the installation of floating freight terminals.[60] The proposal has subsequently been shelved, but justifiable fears linger that among Indian policy-makers important lessons about the environmental and social costs of the Farakka Barrage have not been learnt.

The final note of caution to be sounded about the Hooghly's global future concerns the effects of climate change and the global climate emergency. As Sunil Amrith points out, no area of the world is more at risk from the impact of planetary warming than the coastal zone around the Bay of Bengal, home to almost half a billion people.[61] Though the causes of increases in the world's sea and air temperatures are global, its consequence will be distributed unevenly and strongly felt around the Bay. Over recent years the population of Sagar Island has risen to about 160,000, most of whom earn their livelihoods through agriculture or fishing.[62] Along with other islands at the southern edge of the Bengal delta, its survival is now severely under threat. One problem is the increasingly extreme weather conditions that the coastline experiences. Since the 1950s, the intensity of cyclones in the

Bay has increased—a change correlating with rising sea-surface temperatures. Changing monsoon patterns indicate declining overall rainfall coupled with more extreme storms.[63] More serious still are rising sea levels, as a result of which some islands at the mouth of the Hooghly, like Lohachara, previously a few hundred metres above the northern tip of Sagar Island, have disappeared. Nearby, Ghoramara Island has just a few years left if current rates of land loss per annum continue. Sagar Island has accommodated more than 25,000 refugees from other islands that are disappearing below the water level, but it too is shrinking, with one estimate putting the loss in recent decades at thirty square kilometres.[64] Some 10,000 families live on the island's coast. The expectation is that a further 15 per cent of the island's surface area will be lost in the next eight years because of rising average sea levels and the lack of sediment in the Hooghly to replace eroded land.[65] Tidal surges have become more regular, as extreme sea levels also increase. In July 2014 a tidal surge swept through fourteen villages on the eastern side of Sagar Island. More than 4000 houses were destroyed and some 500 hectares of cropland were turned saline.[66]

Responses to the threats posed by climate change on Sagar Island have included the replanting of trees to act as natural wind and flood defences, the construction of new embankments, and the introduction of new salt-resistant varieties of rice. In addition to these local defensive measures, however, more radical and global solutions are required. On the Hooghly today, social and economic inequality is rising and the concept of the public good is under threat. As population levels continue to increase, large areas of inhabited land disappear under water, changes in weather and climate make the delta more inhospitable, and pollution takes its toll. As in every region of the world where similar phenomena are evident, the effects of these processes are most strongly felt by the poorest. The hope must be that new ideas emerge in the twenty-first century that alleviate the river's most pressing problems while signposting solutions of possible global significance. Those solutions should focus on the rights and needs of peoples on the Hooghly as citizens of India and members of wider regional and global communities. Efforts should be directed to reversing current trends towards widening inequality and to investment in the public domain; markets should be reconfigured to serve public ends rather than dictate the limits of the public or social.[67] Climate and environmental goals, not the pursuit of development or growth, should be the focus of policy and thought—a revision of priorities that will necessarily engender cross-border co-operation and may even call the logic of existing borders into question.

In thinking about the Hooghly's future, understanding its global history will be instructive. For one, comprehending past mistakes—the assumption of cultural, religious, or racial superiority over another people, for example—may help to ensure that they are not repeated. The Hooghly's past, moreover, teaches us the errors of treating the natural environment as an unlimited resource at human disposal or an object to be acted upon without consideration of the consequences. It also tells us that private corporations are rarely equipped or disposed to serve the public good. At a more fundamental level, studying the Hooghly's global history reminds us that existing institutions, practices, and prevailing ideas are not inevitable but historically contingent, the product of particular times, events, people, and configurations of power. Just as the eras of monopolistic trade, free exchange, and centralised state planning were usurped, the current ascendancy of neoliberal economics need not last. On the Hooghly, successive powers established themselves and were removed. The institutions through which they governed varied dramatically over time, before the contemporary, constitutionally defined, and territorially precise nation-state came into being. As a political entity, there is no reason to think of the nation-state as any more natural or permanent than its predecessors. Through the Hooghly's history, borders have been traversed; the interaction and exchange of different peoples and cultures has created new identities and rendered others less meaningful.

Above all, the Hooghly's global history prompts us to remember that power is never absolute. Dominant actors and ideas can be challenged, as indeed they were in the nineteenth and twentieth centuries by individuals and groups contesting aspects of the colonial status quo. This dimension of the Hooghly's past should inspire the search for new approaches and ideas to shape its global future.

NOTES

INTRODUCTION: THE HOOGHLY IN GLOBAL HISTORY

1. In some existing literature, the name 'Hooghly' and its variants ('Hoogly', 'Hugli', etc.) refer only to the lower reaches of the river between Nabadwip and the sea, approximately 260 kilometres long, while in other sources they refer to the entire length of the river from the point where it breaks with the Ganges. This book adopts the latter approach. 'Hooghly' is preferred to the other names by which the river is known (the 'Bhagirathi' or the 'Bhagirathi-Hooghly') because it best captures the global dimensions of the river's past. See chapter 1 on the likely origins of the name 'Hooghly'.
2. Bagchi, *The Ganges delta*, pp. 39–71; Eaton, *The rise of Islam*, pp. 3–6; and on the role of rivers in the definition and enactment of place in South Asia, Feldhaus, *Connected places*.
3. On this early history, see Majumdar, *History of ancient Bengal*, pp. 219–40; and Eaton, *The rise of Islam*, pp. 6–13.
4. See Lahiri, *Ashoka in ancient India*.
5. Eaton, *The rise of Islam*, pp. 10–13.
6. Amrith, *Crossing the Bay of Bengal*, pp. 16–17.
7. See the chapter dedicated to the sacred significance of rivers in India in Eck, *India*, pp. 131–88.
8. Ibid., pp. 138–40.
9. Darian, *The Ganges in myth and history*, pp. 48–9.
10. Mukerjee, *The changing face of Bengal*, pp. 110–40.
11. Thomas, *To the mouths of the Ganges*, p. 12.
12. Eck, *India*, p. 140.
13. Darian, *The Ganges in myth and history*, pp. 153–4.
14. See the final chapter for a more detailed description of this festival.
15. Eaton, *The rise of Islam*, pp. 110–12.

16. For an account of the rise and fall of the Delhi Sultanate, see Keay, *India*, pp. 231–61.

17. On the Bengal Sultanate, see Eaton, *The rise of Islam*, pp. 40–70.

18. See chapter 2. Eaton, *The rise of Islam*, remains the authoritative account of this process. See especially pp. 228–67.

19. For a description, see *Ancient India as described by Ptolemy*.

20. See chapter 1.

21. Conrad, *What is global history?*, pp. 67–72.

22. For an overview of these different approaches, ibid., pp. 101–7; and Osterhammel and Petersson, *Globalization*.

23. Subrahmanyam, 'Connected histories'; Conrad, *What is global history?*, pp. 115–40.

24. Amrith, *Crossing the Bay of Bengal*, p. 1.

25. L. Bear, *Navigating austerity*, p. 5.

26. Darian, *The Ganges in myth and history*, p. 143.

27. Amrith, *Crossing the Bay of Bengal*, pp. 49–50.

1. HOOGHLY: THE RISE AND FALL OF THE PORTUGUESE

1. The story of Tavares' journey to the court of Akbar and subsequent founding of Hooghly is recounted in Manrique, *Travels of Fray Sebastien Manrique*, pp. 32–9, first published in Spanish in the 1650s. See also Chaudhury, 'The rise and decline of Hugli', pp. 33–67.

2. Monserrate, *The commentary of Father Monserrate S.J.*, p. 27.

3. Foster (ed.), *Early travels in India*, p. 17.

4. On the Mughal conquest of Bengal, see Richards, *The new Cambridge history of India*, pp. 33–4; Eaton, *The rise of Islam*, pp. 137–58; and Raychaudhuri, *Bengal under Akbar and Jahangir*, pp. 1–93.

5. Pyrard de Laval, *The voyage of François Pyrard of Laval*, vol. 1, p. 332.

6. Ibid., p. 327.

7. Ibid., p. 331.

8. Latif, 'A description of north Bengal in 1609 A.D.', p. 145.

9. Bernier, *Travels in the Mogul Empire*, p. 439.

10. For an excellent overview, see Subrahmanyam, *The Portuguese empire in Asia*.

11. The most detailed account of early Portuguese activity in Bengal is found in Campos, *History of the Portuguese in Bengal*, pp. 100–20. See also Raychaudhuri, *Bengal under Akbar and Jahangir*, pp. 94–118.

12. Subrahmanyam, *Improvising empire*, p. 102.

13. Campos, *History of the Portuguese in Bengal*, p. 65.

14. Federici, *The voyage and travaille*, p. 22.

15. For a contemporary description, see Federici, *The voyage and travaille*, pp. 21–4.

16. Cabral, 'The fall of Hugli', p. 393.

17. Subrahmanyam, *Improvising empire*, p. 102.

18. Chaudhury, 'The rise and decline of Hugli', p. 60.

19. Ibid., p. 45.

20. Manrique, *Travels of Fray Sebastien Manrique*, vol. 1, p. 55.

21. Sharma, 'Introduction', pp. xi–xvii.

22. Pyrard de Laval, *The voyage of François Pyrard of Laval*, vol. 2, pp. 125–31.

23. Huyghen van Linschoten, *The voyage of John Huyghen van Linschoten to the East Indies*, vol. 1, p. 95.

24. Cabral, 'The fall of Hugli', p. 408.

25. Hosten, 'A week at the Bandel convent, Hugli', on p. 43.

26. Manrique, *Travels of Fray Sebastien Manrique*, vol. 1, pp. 40–6.

27. Ibid., p. 54.

28. On the social practices of the Portuguese at Hooghly, see also Raychaudhuri, *Bengal under Akbar and Jahangir*, pp. 247–53.

29. Manrique, *Travels of Fray Sebastien Manrique*, vol. 1, pp. 55–6.

30. Ibid., p. 60. Several decades later a group of Englishmen in Bengal felt compelled to find out if the reported effects of bhang were true. They each bought a pint in the bazaar and returned to their residence to drink it. 'It soon took its operation upon us,' one of them later wrote, 'but merrily, save upon two of our number ... One sat himself down on the floor and wept bitterly all afternoon; the other terrified with fear did run his head into a great Pegu Jar [a large ceramic container with an open top], and continued in that posture four hours or more; 4 or 5 lay upon the carpets (that were spread in the room) highly complementing each other in high terms, each man fancying himself no less than an Emperor. One was quarrelsome and fought with one of the wooden pillars of the porch, until he had left himself little skin upon the knuckles of his fingers. My self and one more sat sweating for the space of three hours in exceeding measure.' Bowrey, *A geographical account*, pp. 80–1.

31. The rumour that Bengali crocodiles were immune to gunshot was later tested by Jean-Baptiste Tavernier, an intrigued French traveller and jewel merchant. See Tavernier, *Les six voyages de Jean-Baptiste Tavernier*, part 2, p. 86.

32. Bernier, *Travels in the Mogul Empire*, p. 446.

33. Subrahmanyam, *Improvising empire*, p. xviii.

34. Manrique, *Travels of Fray Sebastien Manrique*, vol. 1, p. 438.

35. Ibid., p. 64.

36. Ibid., p. 66.

37. Ibid.

38. Ibid., p. 79.
39. Ibid., p. 67.
40. Ibid., vol. 2, p. 183.
41. Ibid., vol. 1, pp. 229, 231.
42. Ibid., p. 77.
43. Ibid., p. 293.
44. Ibid., vol. 2, p. 117.
45. Campos, *History of the Portuguese in Bengal*, pp. 112–20.
46. Bernier, *Travels in the Mogul Empire*, p. 175.
47. The reproduction of this moralising narrative continued into the twentieth century. See for example the explanation of the fall of Hooghly in Campos, *History of the Portuguese in Bengal*, pp. 121–7, in which Portuguese decline is precipitated by their 'decadence'.
48. Richards, *The new Cambridge history of India*, pp. 121–3.
49. Elliot and Dowson (eds), *The history of India*, vol. 7, pp. 31–5.
50. Stewart, *The history of Bengal*, pp. 239–45.
51. Chaudhury, 'The rise and decline of Hugli', p. 14.
52. Campos, *History of the Portuguese in Bengal*, pp. 154–7.
53. Bernier, *Travels in the Mogul Empire*, p. 175.
54. Sarkar, *The history of Bengal*, p. 366.
55. Bernier, *Travels in the Mogul Empire*, p. 176.
56. Elliot and Dowson (eds), *The history of India*, vol. 7, p. 34.
57. Manrique, *Travels of Fray Sebastien Manrique*, vol. 2, p. 323.
58. Cabral, 'The fall of Hugli', vol. 2, p. 396.
59. Ibid., pp. 392–422. The description of the siege that follows is based on Cabral's account, unless otherwise indicated.
60. Sarkar, *The history of Bengal*, p. 326.
61. Cabral, 'The fall of Hugli', p. 419. The Padshahnama gives Mughal casualties at 1000 and suggests that 10,000 slaves were set free when the city was taken. See Elliot and Dowson (eds), *The history of India*, vol. 7, p. 35.
62. See the 'Note by Fr. L. Nessi, S.J.' in Manrique, *Travels of Fray Sebastien Manrique*, vol. 2, pp. 423–4.
63. Campos, *History of the Portuguese in Bengal*, p. 144.
64. Hosten, 'A week at the Bandel convent, Hugli', p. 40.
65. On the arrival of the Dutch and English at Hooghly, see Chaudhury, 'The rise and decline of Hugli', pp. 16–35.
66. Bowrey, *A geographical account*, p. 167.
67. Campos, *History of the Portuguese in Bengal*, p. 65; and on the Portuguese influence on the Bengali and other Indian languages, pp. 204–27.

2. MURSHIDABAD: THE KINGDOM OF THE NAWABS OF BENGAL

1. On Murshid Quli Khan's humble origins and career before arriving in Bengal, see Karim, *Murshid Quli Khan*, pp. 1–2; and Aurangabadi, *Ma'asir al–Umara*, pp. 719–21.
2. Chaudhury, 'The rise and decline of Hugli', on p. 33.
3. Darian, *The Ganges in myth and history*, p. 142.
4. See Richards, *The new Cambridge history of India*, pp. 58–78 for a detailed explanation.
5. Karim, *Murshid Quli Khan*, pp. 19–20.
6. Salim, *Riyazu-s-salatin*, p. 252.
7. O'Malley, *Murshidabad*, pp. 205–6.
8. Karim, *Murshid Quli Khan*, pp. 24–5.
9. Ibid., pp. 43–8; Salim, *Riyazu*, pp. 260, 281.
10. Salim, *Riyazu*, p. 271.
11. Ibid., p. 272.
12. See Richards, *The new Cambridge history of India*, pp. 79–93.
13. Karim, *Murshid Quli Khan*, pp. 220–2.
14. Salim, *Riyazu*, p. 260.
15. Ibid., p. 257.
16. Ibid., pp. 258, 283; Karim, *Murshid Quli Khan*, pp. 71–3.
17. On the court rituals, see Rahim, *Social and cultural history of Bengal*, pp. 144–6.
18. Karim, *Murshid Quli Khan*, pp. 237–8.
19. Salim, *Riyazu*, p. 282.
20. Ibid., p. 280.
21. Das, 'Religious buildings of Murshidabad'.
22. Karim, *Murshid Quli Khan*, p. 242.
23. Eaton, *The rise of Islam*, p. 50.
24. Karim, *Murshid Quli Khan*, p. 233.
25. The modern valorisation of Sitaram began with Bankim Chandra Chatterjee's eponymous novel about the ruler, published in 1886.
26. Salim, *Riyazu*, p. 259.
27. Karim, *Murshid Quli Khan*, pp. 88–92; Rahim, *Social and cultural history of Bengal*, pp. 203–5.
28. Karim, *Murshid Quli Khan*, p. 67; Salim, *Riyazu*, p. 252.
29. Salim, *Riyazu*, p. 283.
30. See Doogar, 'From merchant–banking to zamindari'.
31. Karim, *Murshid Quli Khan*, pp. 99–100.
32. Das, 'Religious buildings of Murshidabad', p. 69.
33. Rahim, *Social and cultural history of Bengal*, pp. 153–6.
34. Ibid., p. 137.
35. Hossein Khan, *Seir mutaqherin*, vol. 1, p. 374.

36. Salim, *Riyazu*, p. 288.
37. Ibid., p. 290.
38. Hossein Khan, *Seir mutaqherin*, vol. 1, p. 323.
39. Ibid., p. 280.
40. Salim, *Riyazu*, p. 291.
41. Datta, *Alivardi and his times*, pp. 9–16.
42. Ibid., pp. 16–19.
43. O'Malley, *Murshidabad*, p. 60.
44. On the coup, see Datta, *Alivardi and his times*, pp. 31–5; and Hossein Khan, *Seir mutaqherin*, vol. 1, pp. 330–4.
45. Salim, *Riyazu*, p. 317.
46. Ibid., p. 320.
47. Hossein Khan, *Seir Mutaqherin*, vol. 1, pp. 352–5.
48. For an overview, see Nadkarnia, *The rise and fall of the Maratha Empire*.
49. The wars between the Marathas and the forces of Alivardi Khan are described in detail in Datta, *Alivardi and his times*, pp. 56–143, from which the following details of the campaigns are taken, unless otherwise indicated.
50. Hossein Khan, *Seir mutaqherin*, vol. 1, pp. 379–88.
51. Salim, *Riyazu*, p. 341.
52. Hossein Khan, *Seir mutaqherin*, vol. 1, pp. 402–4.
53. The politicisation of the memory and representation of Shivaji in contemporary India is explored in chapter 19 of Khilnani, *Incarnations*.
54. Datta, *Alivardi and his times*, p. 177.
55. Hossein Khan, *Seir mutaqherin*, vol. 1, p. 421.
56. Ibid., p. 441.
57. Salim, *Riyazu*, p. 356; Hossein Khan, *Seir mutaqherin*, vol. 2, p. 40.
58. Datta, *Alivardi and his times*, p. 72.
59. Salim, *Riyazu*, p. 340.
60. Hossein Khan, *Seir mutaqherin*, vol. 2, pp. 118, 162.
61. Rahim, *Social and cultural history of Bengal*, pp. 284–7.
62. Skelton, 'Murshidabad painting'.
63. Losty, 'Murshidabad painting 1750–1820', p. 98.
64. Rahim, *Social and cultural history of Bengal*, p. 207.
65. Datta, *Alivardi and his times*, pp. 258–9; Das, *Murshidabad*, pp. 249–50.
66. Das, *Murshidabad*, pp. 65–6.
67. Eaton, *The rise of Islam*, pp. 77–82; Rahim, *Social and cultural history of Bengal*, pp. 348–51.
68. This was noted by, among others, the French traveller François Pyrard de Laval: 'Mahometans as well as Gentiles [Hindus] deem the water to be blessed, and to wash away all offences, just as we regard confession.' Pyrard de Laval, *The voyage of François Pyrard of Laval*, vol. 2, p. 336.

69. See Eaton, *The rise of Islam*, pp. 113–16, for a debunking of the conversion-by-the-sword thesis and a discussion of other much-cited theories of Islamisation. Eaton's study is hugely important to understanding the gradual spread of Islam in eastern Bengal and has had a major influence on explanations of the spread of religions more widely.

70. Eaton, *The rise of Islam*, pp. 117, 129–34.

71. Ibid., pp. 269–70.

72. Ibid., pp. 269–76. For a more general discussion of the problems inherent in the notion of religious conversion, see Viswanathan, *Outside the fold*.

73. See Eaton, *The rise of Islam*, pp. 194–303.

74. See chapter 6 on the impact of print technology on religious practices and beliefs.

75. The contributions and extensive collection of images in Das and Llewellyn–Jones (eds), *Murshidabad*, succeed well in evoking the capital at this moment.

76. Llewellyn–Jones, 'Introduction', p. 13.

77. For descriptions, see Rahim, *Social and cultural history of Bengal*, pp. 258–9; and Darian, *The Ganges in myth and history*, pp. 159–60.

78. O'Malley, *Murshidabad*, p. 207.

3. PLASSEY: THE ENGLISH EAST INDIA COMPANY'S ASCENT

1. A classic example is found in the writings of Thomas Babington Macaulay. See his essay, first published in 1840, on Lord Clive, British commander at Plassey, in Macaulay, *Critical and historical essays*, pp. 497–540.

2. On the early history of the English East India Company, see Keay, *The honourable company*; and Stern, *The Company-state*.

3. See his account in Foster (ed.), *The embassy of Sir Thomas Roe to India*.

4. Raychaudhuri, *Bengal under Akbar and Jahangir*, pp. 97–101.

5. Wilson, *The early annals of the English in Bengal*, vol. 1, pp. 1–21.

6. Ibid., p. 25.

7. Chaudhury, 'The rise and decline of Hugli', pp. 21–5.

8. Wilson, *The early annals of the English in Bengal*, vol. 1, p. 47.

9. Chaudhury, 'The rise and decline of Hugli', p. 56.

10. Wilson, *The early annals of the English in Bengal*, vol. 1, p. 34

11. See for example Ferguson, *Empire*.

12. Ahmed, *The stillbirth of capital*, p. 8.

13. Subrahmanyam, *Improvising empire*, pp. 117–25.

14. On the Dutch company in Asia, see Prakash, *The Dutch East India Company*.

15. Keay, *The honourable company*, p. 50.
16. Campos, *History of the Portuguese in Bengal*, pp. 154–7.
17. Karim, *Murshid Quli Khan*, p. 238.
18. Keay, *The honourable company*, p. 234.
19. Chatterjee, *Bengal in the reign of Aurangzeb*, pp. 120–3.
20. Ibid., p. 116.
21. Wilson, *The early annals of the English in Bengal*, vol. 1, p. 38.
22. Ibid., p. 89.
23. On the Mughal–Company war of 1686, see Keay, *The honourable company*, pp. 154–64; and Chatterjee, *Bengal in the reign of Aurangzeb*, pp. 144–51.
24. Wilson, *The early annals of the English in Bengal*, vol. 1, p. 161.
25. Firminger, *Historical introduction*, p. lxviii. This text contains a host of useful primary source materials on the British assumption of power in Bengal.
26. Wilson, *The early annals of the English in Bengal*, vol. 1, p. 66.
27. Karim, *Murshid Quli Khan*, p. 132.
28. Firminger, *Historical introduction*, p. lxxvii.
29. Karim, *Murshid Quli Khan*, pp. 168–73.
30. Datta, *Alivardi and his times*, pp. 156–8.
31. Ibid., p. 144.
32. Macaulay, *Critical and historical essays*, pp. 512–13.
33. Dutt, *The economic history of India*, pp. 18–19.
34. See Howell, *India tracts*, pp. 251–76. Howell, a Company servant, was one of the prisoners. His account of the episode was widely believed at the time but has subsequently been contested by historians. On the escalation of hostilities between Siraj and the English at this juncture, see Gupta, *Sirajuddaullah and the East India Company*, pp. 49–84.
35. Spear, *Master of Bengal*, p. 76.
36. Gopal, *How the British occupied Bengal*, p. 116.
37. Mukhopadhyay, *British residents*, p. 98.
38. Gopal, *How the British occupied Bengal*, p. 126.
39. Ibid., p. 147.
40. Ibid., p. 167.
41. Spear, *Master of Bengal*, pp. 73–86; Edwardes, *The Battle of Plassey*, pp. 128–31.
42. The battle is narrated in Edwardes, *The Battle of Plassey*, pp. 137–52, from which the following details are taken.
43. See for example Spear, *Master of Bengal*, p. 85.
44. Edwardes, *The Battle of Plassey*, p. 157.
45. Firminger, *Historical introduction*, p. clix.
46. Ibid., pp. xiv, clix.

47. See for example Storrs (ed.), *The fiscal-military state in eighteenth-century Europe*.
48. Ahmed, *The stillbirth of capital*, pp. 77–80.
49. Ibid., pp. 91–2.
50. Dutt, *The economic history of India*, p. 44; Firminger, *Historical introduction*, p. c.
51. Firminger, *Historical introduction*, p. cxiii.
52. Spear, *Master of Bengal*, p. 138.
53. Ibid., p. 146.
54. Firminger, *Historical introduction*, p. cliii.
55. Ibid., p. cliv.
56. Dutt, *The economic history of India*, p. 46. Dutt estimates the drain at £1.5 million per year. For a discussion of the longer term drain of resources from India to Britain during the colonial period, see Tharoor, *Inglorious empire*, pp. 16–23.
57. Gopal, *How the British occupied Bengal*, p. 304.
58. Spear, *Master of Bengal*, p. 113.
59. Gopal, *How the British occupied Bengal*, p. 281.
60. See the near-contemporary criticism of this society in Bolts, *Considerations on Indian affairs*, p. viii, discussed in further detail in chapter 4.
61. Gopal, *How the British occupied Bengal*, pp. 307–8.
62. Arnold, 'Hunger in the Garden of Plenty', p. 83.
63. Hunter, *The annals of rural Bengal*, vol. 1, p. 21.
64. Ibid., p. 26.
65. Arnold, 'Hunger in the Garden of Plenty', p. 84.
66. Mukhopadhyay, *British residents*, p. 394.
67. 'Account of the Late Dreadful Famine in India', pp. 205–6.
68. Firminger, *Historical introduction*, p. clxxvii.
69. Chaudhuri, *Cartier*, p. 172.
70. Firminger, *Historical introduction*, p. clxxxi.
71. Ibid., p. clxiii.
72. Hunter, *The annals of rural Bengal*, vol. 1, p. 24.
73. Ibid., p. 36.
74. Pearse, 'A Memoir of Colonel Thomas Deane Pearse of the Bengal Artillery', p. 318.
75. Firminger, *Historical introduction*, p. cxcix.
76. Ibid., p. clxiii.
77. Chaudhuri, *Cartier*, p. 62.
78. Arnold, 'Hunger in the Garden of Plenty', p. 82.
79. These questions were posed in a series of parliamentary enquiries into

the East India Company at Westminster after 1770. See also the late-eighteenth-century criticisms of the Company explored in chapter 4.
80. Arnold, 'Hunger in the Garden of Plenty', p. 97.

4. CHANDERNAGORE: THE FRENCH REVOLUTION IN BENGAL

1. On the events of the revolution at Chandernagore and Pondicherry, see Labernadie, *La révolution et les établissements français dans l'Inde*; and Sen, *The French in India*, pp. 426–93.
2. Ray, *The merchant and the state*, vol. 1, p. 282.
3. On the early French presence in Bengal and the foundation of Chandernagore, see ibid., pp. 282–320. A good French-language introduction to the Compagnie des Indes in its various iterations is Estienne, *Les compagnies des Indes*.
4. Malleson, *History of the French in India*, p. 40.
5. Ibid., p. 57.
6. Ray, *The merchant and the state*, vol. 2, pp. 611–16.
7. On Dupleix's career, see Clarin de La Rive, *Dupleix*.
8. Ray, *The merchant and the state*, vol. 2, pp. 805–937.
9. The course of the French–English wars in southern India has been frequently recounted. See for example Keay, *The honourable company*, pp. 271–95.
10. Hill, *Three Frenchmen in Bengal*, pp. 13–63.
11. Artz, *The Enlightenment in France*; Blom, *Wicked company*; and Israel, *Democratic enlightenment*.
12. Artz, *The Enlightenment in France*, pp. 50–8.
13. Montesquieu, *The spirit of laws*, p. 247.
14. Artz, *The Enlightenment in France*, pp. 58–65.
15. Ibid., pp. 66–70.
16. Voltaire, *Précis du siècle de Louis XV*, p. 232–42.
17. Voltaire, *Fragments on India*, pp. 2–3.
18. Ibid., p. 48.
19. Ibid., p. 49.
20. Ibid., p. 3.
21. On Bolts' career and writings, see Israel, *Democratic enlightenment*, pp. 590–3.
22. Bolts, *Considerations on Indian affairs*, p. viii.
23. Ibid., pp. 12, 120.
24. Dow, *The history of Hindostan*, p. lxxvii.
25. Marsh, *India in the French imagination*, pp. 124–31.
26. Ibid., p. 132.
27. On the text's distribution and influence, see Israel, *Democratic enlightenment*, pp. 420–1.

28. Marsh, *India in the French imagination*, p. 128.
29. Israel, *Democratic enlightenment*, pp. 413–25.
30. Ibid., p. 422.
31. Artz, *The Enlightenment in France*, pp. 99–101.
32. Raynal, *A philosophical and political history*, vol. 1, p. 477.
33. Ibid., p. 488.
34. Ibid.
35. Ibid., p. 518.
36. Ibid., pp. 521–2.
37. Ibid., p. 507.
38. Das, *Myths and realities of French imperialism in India*, pp. 28–9.
39. Marsh, *India in the French imagination*, pp. 130–1.
40. Raynal, *A philosophical and political history*, vol. 2, pp. 188–92.
41. Ibid., p. 509.
42. Sen, *The French in India*, p. 34.
43. Hill, *Three Frenchmen in Bengal*, p. 128.
44. Extract secret letter from Bengal dated 15 January 1773, The French in India Series, India Office Records, I/1/4.
45. Ray, 'A Note on Jean Baptiste Chevalier and Colonel de Montigny'; Deloche (ed.), *Les adventures de Jean–Baptiste Chevalier dans l'Inde orientale*.
46. Chevalier to W. Hastings and the Gentlemen of the Council at Calcutta, 9 December 1773, The French in India Series, India Office Records, I/1/4.
47. 'Echoes from Old Chandernagore', p. 377.
48. Extract secret letter from Bengal dated 21 November 1774, The French in India Series, India Office Records, I/1/4.
49. Sen, *The French in India*, p. 119; Chevalier, 'Plan of attack in India in case of an offensive war', p. 178.
50. Sen, *The French in India*, p. 119.
51. On Chevalier's diplomatic efforts, see Sen, *The French in India*, pp. 122–53; and Das, *Myths and realities of French imperialism in India*, pp. 228–42.
52. Chevalier, 'Project on India'.
53. See BatBedat, 'Au service des princes indiens'.
54. Sen, *The French in India*, p. 123.
55. Ibid., pp. 125–6.
56. Extract secret letter from Bengal dated 21 November 1774, The French in India Series, India Office Records, I/1/4.
57. Extract of General Letter to Bengal, 25 March 1770, The French in India Series, India Office Records, I/1/4.
58. Letter by Law de Lauriston, 9 February 1771, in Hatalkar (ed.), *French records*, vols 3–4, pp. 1–3, on p. 1.

59. J. B. Chevalier to Lord Terray, 6 January 1771, in ibid., pp. 182–207, on p. 202.
60. Hatalkar, *Relations between the French and the Marathas*, p. 176.
61. J. B. Chevalier to the Lord de Sartine, 15 December 1777, in Hatalkar (ed.), *French records*, vols 3–4, pp. 269–78, on p. 273.
62. Das, *Myths and realities of French imperialism in India*, p. 143.
63. Ibid., pp. 236–40.
64. J. B. Chevalier to the Lord de Sartine, 18 February 1778, in Hatalkar (ed.), *French records*, vols 3–4, pp. 278–80, on p. 278.
65. 'The Chandernagore Papers 1778–1783', vol. 4, p. 427.
66. On the conditions of the occupation, see 'The Chandernagore Papers 1778–1783', vol. 6.
67. Busteed, *Echoes from old Calcutta*, p. 231.
68. Israel, *Democratic enlightenment*, pp. 924–33.
69. Israel, *Revolutionary ideas*, p. 84.
70. Ibid., pp. 140, 265.
71. Sen, *The French in India*, pp. 455–7. Sen provides the most complete narrative of the events of the revolution at Chandernagore, on which the following description relies. See pp. 457–64.
72. Ibid., p. 457.
73. Ibid., p. 455.
74. Labernadie, *La révolution et les établissements français dans l'Inde*, pp. 279–90, on the Chandernagore constitution.
75. Pitts, *A turn to empire*, pp. 165–8.
76. Marsh, *India in the French imagination*, p. 84.

5. SERAMPORE: BAPTIST MISSIONARIES AND THE POWER OF PRINT

1. Aalund and Rastén, *Indo-Danish heritage*, p. 8. For a slightly later description of Serampore, see also Elberling, 'Description of Serampore'.
2. Aalund and Rastén, *Indo-Danish heritage*, p. 10.
3. Aalund and Rastén, *Indo-Danish heritage*, contains a wealth of detail on the Danish town, with images.
4. Khan, *William Carey*, p. 230.
5. Marshman, *The life and times*, vol. 1, p. 80.
6. Major existing studies of Carey's life and career on which this chapter draws include Marshman, *The life and times*; Khan, *William Carey*; Smith, *The life of William Carey*; and Pearce Carey, *William Carey*.
7. Carey, *An enquiry into the obligations of Christians*, p. 62.
8. Marshman, *The life and times*, vol. 1, p. 10.

9. Ibid., p. 52.

10. Smith, *The life of William Carey*, p. 62.

11. Marshman, *The life and times*, vol. 1, p. 37.

12. Grant, *Observations on the State of Society*, pp. 43, 113.

13. See Naïdenhoff, 'Les tentatives des missionnaires'.

14. Sherring, *The history of Protestant missions in India*, pp. 1–52.

15. 'The Serampore Form of Agreement', p. 134.

16. Carey, *An enquiry into the obligations of Christians*, p. 75.

17. 'The Serampore Form of Agreement', p. 130.

18. Carey, *An enquiry into the obligations of Christians*, p. 65.

19. 'The Serampore Form of Agreement', p. 136.

20. Smith, *The life of William Carey*, p. 119.

21. Ogborn, *Indian ink*, p. 217.

22. Khan, *William Carey*, pp. 197–8.

23. Shaw, *Printing in Calcutta to 1800*.

24. Ogborn, *Indian ink*, p. 208.

25. Smith, *The life of William Carey*, p. 238.

26. See Marshman, *The life and times*, vol. 1, p. 139, for a description of the baptism.

27. Ibid., p. 133.

28. See Kopf, *British orientalism*.

29. Dasgupta, *Awakening*, p. 53.

30. Carey, *Dialogues intended to facilitate the acquiring of the Bengalee language*.

31. De, *History of Bengali literature*, pp. 130–1.

32. Kopf, *British orientalism*, p. 134.

33. Marshman, *The life and times*, vol. 1, p. 191.

34. Kopf, *British orientalism*, p. 136.

35. 'The Serampore Form of Agreement', p. 133.

36. Ward, *A view of the history, literature and mythology of the Hindoos*, vol. 1, pp. 6, 12.

37. Ibid., p. 208.

38. Smith, *The life of William Carey*, p. 109.

39. Mukherjee, *Reform and regeneration*, pp. 245–50.

40. Enclosures in Governor-General's letter, 2 November 1807, relating to Missionaries, *Papers Relating to East India Affairs (Resident Europeans—Police—Missionaries—Weavers and Investments)*, HCPP, 1812–13 (142), p. 65.

41. Ibid., pp. 48–9.

42. Smith, *The life of William Carey*, p. 261.

43. Marshman, *The life and times*, vol. 1, p. 315.

44. Kopf, *British orientalism*, p. 136.

45. Marshman, *Advantages of Christianity*, p. 6.

46. *Brief Memoirs of Four Christian Hindoos*, p. iii.

47. Pearce Carey, *William Carey*, pp. 306–7.

48. Marshman, *The life and times*, vol. 1, p. 10.

49. Sherring, *The history of Protestant missions in India*, p. 78.

50. Smith, *The life of William Carey*, p. 165.

51. Marshman, *Hints relative to native schools*, p. 6.

52. Kopf, *British orientalism*, p. 156.

53. Marshman, *The life and times*, vol. 2, p. 157.

54. Smith, *The life of William Carey*, pp. 325, 384.

55. On this colonial educational debate, see Zastoupil and Moir (eds), *The great Indian education debate*; and Ivermee, *Secularism, Islam and education in India*, pp. 1–40, 60–5.

56. Laird, 'William Carey and the Education of India'.

57. Marshman, *The life and times*, vol. 2, p. 163.

58. Potts, *British Baptist missionaries in India*, p. 108.

59. On the development of these journals, see De, *History of Bengali literature*, pp. 230–8.

60. Peggs, *India's Cries to British humanity*, p. 5.

61. Ibid., p. 74.

62. Potts, *British Baptist missionaries in India*, p. 218.

63. Marshman, *The life and times*, vol. 2, p. 289.

64. Dasgupta, *Awakening*, p. 114.

65. Ibid., pp. 58–60.

66. Bayly, *Empire and information*, pp. 199–207.

67. On Rammohun Roy, see especially Collet, *The life and letters*; Mukherjee, *Reform and regeneration*; and Dasgupta, *Awakening*, pp. 99–144.

68. See his translations of the Vedanta and Upanishads in Nag and Burman (eds), *The English works of Raja Rammohun Roy*, part 2, pp. 1–72.

69. Mukherjee, *Reform and regeneration*, p. 129.

70. Dasgupta, *Awakening*, p. 118.

71. Kopf, *British orientalism*, pp. 205–6.

72. Dasgupta, *Awakening*, pp. 118–21.

73. Kopf, *British orientalism*, pp. 205–6.

74. Mukherjee, *Reform and regeneration*, pp. 181–7.

75. Roy, 'A Defence of Hindoo Theism', p. 91.

76. Collet, *The life and letters*, p. 71.

77. Mukherjee, *Reform and regeneration*, p. 180.

78. Roy, 'The Precepts of Jesus', p. 4.

79. Mukherjee, *Reform and regeneration*, p. 165.

80. Collet, *The life and letters*, p. 115.

81. Roy, 'An Appeal to the Christian Public', p. 65.
82. Mukherjee, *Reform and regeneration*, p. 167.
83. Roy, 'Second Appeal to the Christian Public'.
84. Collet, *The life and letters*, p. 124.
85. Roy, 'A Dialogue between a Missionary and three Chinese Converts'.
86. Dasgupta, *Awakening*, pp. 126–7.
87. See the trust deed of the Brahmo Samaj in Collet, *The life and letters*, pp. 468–77, on p. 471.
88. Ibid., p. 471.
89. On the wider Bengal Renaissance, see Dasgupta, *Awakening*.
90. Raja Rammohun Roy to a gentleman of Baltimore, 27 October 1822, in Nag and Burman (eds), *The English works of Raja Rammohun Roy*, part 4, pp. 85–6, on p. 86.
91. Marshman, *The life and times*, vol. 2, p. 473.
92. Elberling, 'Description of Serampore', p. 2.
93. Smith, *The life of William Carey*, p. 238.
94. Zastoupil, *Rammohun Roy and the making of Victorian Britain*, p. 118.
95. Smith, *The life of William Carey*, p. 417.
96. Ibid., p. 286.
97. Marshman, *The life and times*, vol. 2, pp. 415–16.
98. Zastoupil, *Rammohun Roy and the making of Victorian Britain*, p. 28.
99. As one scholar puts it, the Company government, 'far from quenching the missionary spirit ... had itself been infected by it.' Laird, 'William Carey and the Education of India', p. 103.
100. Natarajan, *A history of the press in India*, pp. 56–9; Bose and Moreno, *A hundred years of the Bengali press*, pp. 24–44.
101. Ogborn, *Indian ink*, pp. 267–9.
102. On the rise of the Young Bengal movement and the reaction to it, see Forbes, *Positivism in Bengal*; Salahuddin Ahmed, *Social ideas and social change in Bengal*, pp. 26–51; Bose, *Indian awakening and Bengal*, pp. 62–91; and Dasgupta, *Awakening*, pp. 164–99.
103. For example, controversies surrounding the publication of cartoons depicting the Prophet Muhammad in Europe and the banning of books in India such as Doniger's *The Hindus*, deemed offensive to Hindus.

6. CALCUTTA: THE UNFINISHED CONQUEST OF NATURE

1. *Imperial gazetteer of India*, vol. 1, p. 87.
2. Ibid., p. 393.
3. Roberts, *Scenes and characteristics of Hindostan*, vol. 1, p. 9. On the landmarks of the colonial city, see Dutta, *Calcutta*, pp. 58–83.

4. Goode, *Municipal Calcutta*, pp. 355–7.
5. *Imperial gazetteer of India*, vol. 1, p. 401.
6. Ibid., p. 354.
7. See Banerjee, *Calcutta and its hinterland*, for an overview of the city's nineteenth-century trade.
8. *Imperial gazetteer of India*, vol. 1, pp. 345, 416.
9. See chapter 3.
10. Rennell, *Memoir of a map of Hindoostan*.
11. M. Bhattacharya, *Charting the deep*, p. 59.
12. Roberts, *Scenes and characteristics of Hindostan*, vol. 1, p. 216.
13. Ibid.
14. Leonard, *Report on the river Hooghly*, pp. 4–5.
15. Ibid., pp. 13–17.
16. *Imperial gazetteer of India*, vol. 1, p. 219.
17. Ibid., p. 354.
18. Ibid., p. 408.
19. Roberts, *Scenes and characteristics of Hindostan*, vol. 1, p. 199.
20. Bernstein, *Steamboats on the Ganges*.
21. Robinson, *Account of some recent improvements in the system of navigating the Ganges*, p. 6.
22. Prinsep, *An account of steam vessels*, p. ii.
23. Ibid., pp. 1–10; Griffiths, *A history of the joint steamer companies*, pp. i-10.
24. Prinsep, *An account of steam vessels*, pp. 43–64.
25. Lalvani, *The making of India*, p. 93.
26. Account by Emma Roberts cited in Mahajan, *The Ganga trail*, p. 133.
27. von Orlich, *Travels in India*, vol. 2, p. 182. On Dwarkanath's life and career, see Kling, *Partner in empire*.
28. Kling, *Partner in empire*, pp. 78–99.
29. Ibid., pp. 122–7.
30. On Tagore's philosophy, see Mittra, *Memoir of Dwarkanath Tagore*, pp. 41, 123; and Kling, *Partner in empire*, p. 160.
31. Griffiths, *A history of the joint steamer companies*, p. 19.
32. Ibid., pp. 19–21.
33. Sinha, *Communication and colonialism in eastern India*, p. 192.
34. Henderson, 'On river steamers'.
35. Digney, *Journal of an experimental voyage up the Ganges*, pp. 1–2.
36. von Orlich, *Travels in India*, vol. 2, p. 210.
37. These arguments for the introduction of railways are neatly captured in the minute by Lord Dalhousie on the introduction of railways in India, 4 July 1850, in R. Srinivasan, *et al.* (eds), *Our Indian Railway*, pp. 23–39.

38. Letter from Messrs Kelsall and Ghosh to R. M. Stephenson, 14 September 1844, ibid., pp. 18–19.
39. Prinsep, *An account of steam vessels*, pp. i–ii.
40. Mittra, *Memoir of Dwarkanath Tagore*, pp. 86–103.
41. Stephenson, *Report on the practicability and advantages of the introduction of railways into British India*.
42. Bourne, *Railways in India*.
43. Andrew, *Railways in Bengal*, p. 16.
44. Westwood, *Railways of India*, p. 26.
45. See among others Kerr, *Building the railways of the Raj*; and Mukherjee, *The early history of the East Indian Railway*, pp. 112–40.
46. Huddleston, *History of the East India Railway*, p. 13.
47. Lalvani, *The making of India*, p. 168.
48. Mukherjee, *The early history of the East Indian Railway*, p. 116.
49. Westwood, *Railways of India*, pp. 17, 36.
50. Huddleston, *History of the East India Railway*, p. 25.
51. *Imperial gazetteer of India*, vol. 1, p. 207.
52. Kling, *Partner in empire*, pp. 139–43.
53. *Imperial gazetteer of India*, vol. 1, p. 227.
54. Huddleston, *History of the East India Railway*, pp. 88, 219.
55. Ibid., p. 68.
56. *Imperial gazetteer of India*, vol. 1, pp. 209, 242.
57. Ibid., pp. 383–4.
58. Beverley, *Report on the census of the town of Calcutta*, p. 39.
59. *Imperial gazetteer of India*, vol. 1, p. 394.
60. Ibid., p. 400.
61. See Goode, *Municipal Calcutta*, for a report on the success of these measures.
62. Ibid., pp. 407–9.
63. Ibid., pp. 19, 109.
64. Clark, *The drainage of Calcutta*.
65. Goode, *Municipal Calcutta*, p. 117.
66. Clark, *The drainage of Calcutta*, pp. 3–7.
67. Goode, *Municipal Calcutta*, p. 177.
68. Ibid., p. 182.
69. Ibid., p. 184.
70. Ibid., p. 366.
71. Huddleston, *History of the East India Railway*, p. 252.
72. Beverley, *Report on the census of the town of Calcutta*, p. 30.
73. One recent example is Lalvani, *The making of India*, which claims to chart the British 'build[ing] of a new nation' through investment in roads, railways, canals, bridges, ships, ports, and heavy industry. While

purportedly bringing 'balance and perspective' to debates on the legacies of British imperialism, the book uncritically recounts example after example of the 'success' of British enterprise. The 'untold story' that it professes to tell could almost have been written by one of the more patriotic, less discerning historians of British India during the colonial heyday.

74. Two important recent exceptions are Dewey, *Steamboats on the Indus*; and Sinha, *Communication and colonialism in eastern India*.
75. Black, *A memoir on the Indian surveys*, p. 121.
76. See Darian, *The Ganges in myth and history*, p. 155.
77. Gastrell and Blanford, *Report on the Calcutta cyclone*, p. 38.
78. Ibid., p. 144.
79. Ibid., p. 139.
80. *Imperial gazetteer of India*, vol. 1, pp. 69–73.
81. Goode, *Municipal Calcutta*, p. 201.
82. Kling, *Partner in empire*, pp. 166–7.
83. On the conflicting ideas of similarity and difference between coloniser and colonised in British imperial thought, see Metcalf, *Ideologies of the Raj*.
84. Kling, *Partner in empire*, pp. 243–5.
85. Ibid., p. 243.
86. Paranjape, *Making India*, p. 78.
87. Tagore, 'Religion in nature'.
88. 'The Meghadūta', in Tagore, *Selected poems*, pp. 50–2.
89. 'The Golden Boat', ibid., p. 53.
90. 'Snatched by the Gods', ibid., pp. 62–6.
91. Tagore, 'My understanding of Vedanta'; 'Brahmā, Visnu, Siva', in Tagore, *Selected poems*, pp. 45–7.
92. Sarkar, *The Swadeshi movement in Bengal*, p. 43.
93. Kling, *Partner in empire*, p. 246; Sarkar, *The Swadeshi movement in Bengal*, p. 93.
94. Sarkar, *The Swadeshi movement in Bengal*, pp. 112–13.

7. SAGAR ISLAND: THE HOOGHLY'S GLOBAL FUTURE

1. See the introduction on the story of the descent of the Ganges from heaven.
2. Eck, *India*, pp. 150–2.
3. Chatterjee, *Kapalakundala*, p. 16.
4. See the mid-nineteenth century estimate in Wilson, 'The Religious Festivals of the Hindus', p. 67.
5. Recent descriptions include Eck, *India*, pp. 150–2; Thomas, *To the mouths of the Ganges*, pp. 50–3; and Mallet, *River of life, river of death*, pp. 33–8.

6. Fenton, *The journal of Mrs Fenton*, p. 8.

7. Manrique, *Travels of Fray Sebastien Manrique*, vol. 1, pp. 74–5.

8. Cabral, 'The fall of Hugli', pp. 419–22.

9. Wilson, *The early annals of the English in Bengal*, vol. 1, p. 89.

10. See for example Ward, *A view of the history, literature and mythology of the Hindoos*, vol. 1, p. 212.

11. Marshman, *The life and times*, vol. 1, p. 158; Mukherjee, *Reform and regeneration*, pp. 210–17.

12. Graham, *Journal of residence in India*, p. 132.

13. For a discussion of Sagar Island in the nineteenth-century English colonial imagination, see Chattopadhyay, *Representing Calcutta*, pp. 21–8.

14. Graham, *Journal of residence in India*, p. 132.

15. Huggins, *Sketches in India*, p. 4.

16. *Correspondence relating to the settlement of Sagar Island*; Sarkar, *The Sundarbans*, pp. 83–6.

17. Huggins, *Sketches in India*, pp. 3–4.

18. *Imperial Gazetteer of India*, vol. 1, pp. 204, 356.

19. Sarkar, *The Sundarbans*, pp. 85–6.

20. Mallet, *River of life, river of death*, p. 221.

21. On migration across the Bay of Bengal during this period, see Amrith, *Crossing the Bay of Bengal*, pp. 101–80; and on the integration of Burma into colonial networks, Adas, *The Burma delta*.

22. Amrith, *Crossing the Bay of Bengal*, pp. 181–96.

23. Chatterjee, *Empire and nation*, p. 58.

24. Khan, *The Raj at war*.

25. Bhattacharya, *Charting the deep*, p. 138.

26. Mukherjee, *Hungry Bengal*, p. 131.

27. Bose, *His Majesty's opponent*; Fay, *The forgotten army*.

28. Iqbal, *The Bengal delta*, pp. 160–83.

29. Mukherjee, *Hungry Bengal*, pp. 63–5.

30. Ibid., pp. 131–8.

31. Amrith, *Crossing the Bay of Bengal*, p. 208.

32. See among other studies Hardy, *The Muslims of British India*, esp. pp. 168–97.

33. Das, *Communal riots in Bengal*; Chatterjee, *Struggle and strife in urban Bengal*.

34. Mukherjee, *Hungry Bengal*, p. 18.

35. Chatterji, *Bengal divided*, pp. 220–65.

36. *Report of the Bengal Boundary Commission*.

37. Talbot and Singh, *The Partition of India*, pp. 100–4. In the Punjab, by contrast, an estimated fifteen million people were displaced as a result of Partition and up to two million were killed.

38. Mallet, *River of life, river of death*, p. 219.

39. Parua, *The Ganga*, p. 96.

40. A detailed account of the construction project is found in Parua, *The Ganga*, pp. 97–106.

41. Nishat, 'Impact of Ganges water dispute on Bangladesh'.

42. Parua, *The Ganga*, pp. 300–1; Nishat, 'Impact of Ganges water dispute on Bangladesh', pp. 76–8; Dandekar, 'Lessons from Farakka as we plan more barrages on Ganga'.

43. Mallet, *River of life, river of death*, p. 222.

44. Amrith, *Crossing the Bay of Bengal*, pp. 251–8.

45. *Techno–Economic feasibility report for development of port at Sagar Island*. The report was produced for the Ministry of Shipping and Indian Ports Association. See also Government of India, Ministry of Shipping, 'Development of sea port at Sagar Island'.

46. Bear, *Navigating austerity*, p. 2.

47. Mallet, *River of life, river of death*, p. 208.

48. Bear, *Navigating austerity*, pp. 10–17.

49. Bear's *Navigating austerity* is an important anthropological contribution to our understanding of the impact of austerity on those living and working on the Hooghly today. See esp. pp. 31–51.

50. Bear, *Navigating austerity*, pp. 37–40,

51. Ibid., pp. 45–8.

52. Ibid., pp. 49–50.

53. Walker, 'Pollution worsens in the lower Ganga'.

54. Mallet, *River of life, river of death*, pp. 244–6.

55. Safi, 'Ganges and Yamuna rivers granted same legal rights as human beings'.

56. Walker, 'Pollution worsens in the lower Ganga'.

57. 'West Bengal government to make Sagar Island "no–plastic zone"'.

58. Mallet, *River of life, river of death*, p. 251.

59. Eck, *India*, pp. 183–8.

60. Sinha, 'Impacts of Ganga waterways plan on its ecology and the people'.

61. Amrith, *Crossing the Bay of Bengal*, p. 5.

62. Sarkar, 'Shrinking Sagar Island struggles to stay afloat'.

63. Amrith, *Crossing the Bay of Bengal*, p. 266.

64. Sarkar, 'Shrinking Sagar Island struggles to stay afloat'.

65. Vidal, 'Sea change'.

66. Sarkar, 'Shrinking Sagar Island struggles to stay afloat'.

67. Bear, *Navigating austerity*, pp. 208–10.

BIBLIOGRAPHY

Aalund, F., and S. Rastén, *Indo-Danish heritage buildings of Serampore* (Copenhagen: National Museum of Denmark, 2010).

'Account of the late dreadful famine in India', *Annual register, 1771* (London: 1775).

Adas, M., *The Burma delta: Economic development and social change on an Asian rice frontier, 1852–1941* (Wisconsin: University of Wisconsin, 2011).

Ahmed, S., *The stillbirth of capital: Enlightenment writing and colonial India* (Stanford: Stanford University Press, 2012).

Amrith, S., *Crossing the Bay of Bengal: The furies of nature and the fortunes of migrants* (Cambridge, MA: Harvard University Press, 2013).

Ancient India as described by Ptolemy (London: Thacker, Spink, & Co., 1885).

Andrew, W. P., *Railways in Bengal* (London: W. H. Allen & Co., 1853).

Arnold, D., 'Hunger in the garden of plenty: the Bengal famine of 1770', in A. Johns (ed.), *Dreadful visitations: Confronting natural catastrophe in the age of enlightenment* (London: Routledge, 1999), pp. 82–111.

Artz, F. B., *The Enlightenment in France* (Kent: Kent State University Press, 1968).

Aurangabadi, S. K., *Ma'asir al-Umara* (Patna: Janaki Prakashan, 1979).

Bagchi, K., *The Ganges delta* (Calcutta: University of Calcutta, 1944).

Banerjee, P., *Calcutta and its hinterland: A study in economic history of India* (Calcutta: Progressive Publishers, 1975).

BatBedat, J., 'Au service des princes indiens', in R. Vincent (ed.), *L'aventure des Français en Inde* (Pondicherry: Kailash, 2011), pp. 141–74.

Bayly, C. A., *Empire and information: Intelligence gathering and social communication in India, 1780–1870* (Cambridge: Cambridge University Press, 1996).

Bhattacharya, M., *Charting the deep: A history of the Indian Naval Hydrographic Department* (New Delhi: National Hydrographic Office, 2004).

Bear, L., *Navigating austerity: Currents of debt along a South Asian river* (Stanford, CA: Stanford University Press, 2015).

BIBLIOGRAPHY

Bernier, F., *Travels in the Mogul Empire, AD 1656–1668* (Westminster: Archibald Constable and Company, 1841).

Bernstein, H. T., *Steamboats on the Ganges: An exploration in the history of India's modernization through science and technology* (Bombay: Orient Longman, 1960).

Beverley, H., *Report on the census of the town of Calcutta taken on the 6th April 1876* (Calcutta: Bengal Secretariat Press, 1876).

Black, C. E. D., *A memoir on the Indian surveys, 1875–1890* (London: E. A. Arnold, 1891).

Blom, P., *Wicked company: Freethinkers and friendship in pre-revolutionary Paris* (London: Phoenix, 2012).

Bolts, W., *Considerations on Indian affairs; particularly respecting the present state of Bengal dependencies* (London: J. Almon, 1772).

Bose, N. S., *Indian awakening and Bengal* (Calcutta: Firma K. L. Mukhopadhyay, 1976).

Bose, P. N., and H. W. B. Moreno, *A hundred years of the Bengali press: Being a history of the Bengali newspapers from their inception to the present day* (Calcutta: H. W. B. Moreno, 1920).

Bose, S., *His Majesty's opponent: Subhas Chandra Bose and India's struggle against empire* (London: Penguin, 2013).

Bourne, J., *Railways in India* (London: J. Williams & Co., 1848).

Bowrey, T., *A geographical account of the countries round the Bay of Bengal, 1669 to 1679* (Cambridge: Hakluyt Society, 1905).

Brief memoirs of four Christian Hindoos, lately deceased (London: Gale and Fenner, 1816).

Busteed, H. E., *Echoes from old Calcutta: Being chiefly reminiscences of the days of Warren Hastings, Francis and Impey* (London: W. Thacker & Co., 1908).

Cabral, J., 'The fall of Hugli', in S. Manrique, *Travels of Fray Sebastien Manrique* (London: Hakluyt Society, 1927), vol. 2, pp. 392–422.

Campos, J. J. A., *History of the Portuguese in Bengal* (Calcutta: Butterworth, 1919).

Carey, W., *Dialogues intended to facilitate the acquiring of the Bengalee language* (Serampore: Mission Press, 1818).

———, *An enquiry into the obligations of Christians to use means for the conversion of the heathens* (London: Hodder and Stoughton, 1891).

'Chandernagore papers, The, 1778–1783', *Bengal past and present*, vol. 4 (1909), pp. 420–60.

'Chandernagore papers, The, 1778–1783', *Bengal past and present*, vol. 6 (1911), pp. 344–71.

Chatterjee, A., *Bengal in the reign of Aurangzeb 1658–1707* (Calcutta: Progressive Publishers, 1967).

Chatterjee, B. C., *Anandamath* (New Delhi: Frank Bros. & Co., 1998).

BIBLIOGRAPHY

————, *Kapalakundala* (New Delhi: Book Review Literary Trust, 2005).

Chatterjee, P., *Empire and nation: Selected essays* (New York: Columbia University Press, 2010).

Chatterjee, P. K., *Struggle and strife in urban Bengal, 1937–47: A study of Calcutta-based urban politics in Bengal* (Calcutta: Das Gupta & Co., 1991).

Chatterji, J., *Bengal divided: Hindu communalism and partition, 1932–1947* (Cambridge: Cambridge University Press, 2002).

Chattopadhyay, S., *Representing Calcutta: modernity, nationalism, and the colonial uncanny* (Abingdon: Routledge, 2005).

Chaudhuri, N. G., *Cartier: Governor of Bengal, 1769–1772* (Calcutta: K. L. Mukhopadhyay, 1970).

Chaudhury, S., 'The rise and decline of Hugli: A port in medieval Bengal', *Bengal past and present*, vol. 86 (1967), pp. 33–67.

Chevalier, J. B., 'Plan of attack in India in case of an offensive war', in V. G. Hatalkar (ed.), *French records (relating to the history of the Marathas)* (Bombay: Maharashtra State Board for Literature and Culture, 1980), vols 3–4, pp. 169–82.

————, 'Project on India', in V. G. Hatalkar (ed.), *French records (relating to the history of the Marathas)* (Bombay: Maharashtra State Board for Literature and Culture, 1980), vols 3–4, pp. 208–22.

Clarin de La Rive, A., *Dupleix: ou, les Français aux Indes orientales* (Lille: Brouwer & Cie, 1888).

Clark, W., *The drainage of Calcutta: A paper read at the Bengal Social Science Congress, held at the Town Hall, Calcutta, on the 2nd February 1871* (Calcutta: Thacker, Spink & Co., 1871).

Collet, S. D., *The life and letters of Raja Rammohun Roy* (Calcutta: Sadharan Brahmo Samaj, 1962).

Conrad, S., *What is Global History?* (Princeton, NJ: Princeton University Press, 2016).

Correspondence relating to the settlement of Sagar Island (Bengal: 1869).

Dandekar, P., 'Lessons from Farakka as we plan more barrages on Ganga', SANDRP (South Asia Network on Dams, Rivers and People), 25.11.2014, https://sandrp.wordpress.com/2014/11/25/lessons-from-farakka-as-we-plan-more-barrages-on-ganga/ (accessed 9.2.2018).

Darian, S. G., *The Ganges in myth and history* (Honolulu: University Press of Hawaii, 1978).

Das, D., *Murshidabad: A study of cultural diversity: from early eighteenth to early twentieth century* (Kolkata: Arpita Prakashani, 2008).

Das, N., 'Religious buildings of Murshidabad', in N. Das and R. Llewellyn-Jones (eds), *Murshidabad: Forgotten capital of Bengal* (Mumbai: Marg, 2013), pp. 54–71.

————, and R. Llewellyn-Jones (eds), *Murshidabad: Forgotten capital of Bengal* (Mumbai: Marg, 2013).

BIBLIOGRAPHY

Das, S., *Communal riots in Bengal, 1905–1947* (Oxford: Oxford University Press, 1991).

————, *Myths and realities of French imperialism in India, 1763–1783* (New York: Peter Lang, 1992).

Dasgupta, S., *Awakening: The story of the Bengal Renaissance* (Noida: Random House India, 2011).

Datta, K., *Alivardi and his times* (Calcutta: University of Calcutta, 1939).

De, S.K., *History of Bengali literature in the nineteenth century, 1800–1825* (Calcutta: University of Calcutta, 1919).

Deloche, J. (ed.), *Les adventures de Jean-Baptiste Chevalier dans l'Inde orientale* (Paris: École française d'Extrême-Orient, 1984).

Dewey, C., *Steamboats on the Indus: The limits of Western technological superiority in South Asia* (New Delhi: Oxford University Press, 2014).

Digney, J., *Journal of an experimental voyage up the Ganges, on board the Honorable Company's steamer "Megna"* (Calcutta: W. Risdale Military Ophan Press, 1846).

Doniger, W., *The Hindus: An alternative history* (Oxford: Oxford University Press, 2010).

Doogar, R., 'From merchant-banking to zamindari: Jains in 18th- and 19th-century Murshidabad', in N. Das and R. Llewellyn-Jones (eds), *Murshidabad: Forgotten capital of Bengal* (Mumbai: Marg, 2013), pp. 28–39.

Dow, A., *The history of Hindostan, from the death of Akbar to the complete settlement of the empire under Aurungzebe* (London: T. Becket, 1772).

Dutt, R., *The economic history of India under early British rule from the rise of the British power in 1757 to the ascension of Queen Victoria* (London: Kegan, Paul, Trench, Trübner & Co., 1906).

Dutta, K., *Calcutta: A cultural and literary history* (Oxford: Signal Books, 2003).

Eaton, R., *The rise of Islam and the Bengal frontier, 1204–1760* (California: University of California Press, 1996).

'Echoes from old Chandernagore', *Bengal past and present*, vol. 2 (1908), pp. 343–80.

Eck, D. L., *India: A sacred geography* (New York: Harmony Books, 2012).

Edwardes, M., *The Battle of Plassey and the conquest of Bengal* (London: B. T. Batsford, 1963).

Elberling, F. E., 'Description of Serampore, its population, revenues, and administration under the Danish government', 23 October 1845, Bengal Miscellaneous Public Documents, 1843–87, ISBE 108 (4).

Elliot, H. M., and J. Dowson (eds), *The history of India as told by its own historians: The Muhammadan period* (London: Trübner and Co., 1877).

Estienne, R. *Les compagnies des Indes* (Paris: Gallimard, 2013).

Fay, P. W., *The forgotten army: India's armed struggle for independence, 1942–1945* (Ann Arbor: University of Michigan Press, 1995).

BIBLIOGRAPHY

Federici, C., *The voyage and travaille into the East India* (Amsterdam: Da Capo Press, 1971).

Feldhaus, A., *Connected places: Region, pilgrimage, and geographical imagination in India* (Basingstoke: Palgrave Macmillan, 2003).

Fenton, E., *The journal of Mrs Fenton: A narrative of her life in India, the Isle of France (Mauritius) and Tasmania during the years 1826–1830* (London: Edward Arnold, 1901).

Ferguson, N., *Empire: How Britain made the modern world* (London: Penguin, 2004).

Firminger, K., *Historical introduction to the Bengal portion of "The Fifth Report"* (Calcutta: R. Cambray & Co., 1917).

Forbes, G. F., *Positivism in Bengal: A case study in the transmission of ideology* (Columbia: South Asia Books, 1975).

Foster, W. (ed.), *Early travels in India 1583–1619* (London: Oxford University Press, 1921).

———, *The embassy of Sir Thomas Roe to India 1615–19* (London: Hakluyt Society, 1927).

French in India series, The, India Office Records (British Library, London), n.d., I/1/4.

Gastrell, J. E., and H. F. Blanford, *Report on the Calcutta cyclone of 5th October 1864* (Calcutta: O. T. Cutter, Military Orphan Press, 1866).

Goode, S. W., *Municipal Calcutta: Its institutions in their origin and growth* (Calcutta: T. and A. Constable, 1916).

Gopal, R., *How the British occupied Bengal: A corrected account of the 1756–1765 events* (London: Asia Publishing House, 1963).

Government of India, Ministry of Shipping, 'Development of sea port at Sagar Island', 25.7.2016, http://pib.nic.in/newsite/PrintRelease. aspx?relid=147642 (accessed 9.2.2018).

Graham, M., *Journal of residence in India* (Edinburgh: Archibald Constable & Co., 1813).

Grant, C., *Observations on the state of society among the Asiatic subjects of Great Britain, particularly with respect to morals* (London: [1797]).

Griffiths, P., *A history of the joint steamer companies* (London: Inchcape & Co., 1979).

Gupta, B. K., *Sirajuddaullah and the East India Company, 1756–1757: Background to the foundation of British power in India* (Leiden: Brill, 1966).

Hardy, P., *The Muslims of British India* (Cambridge: Cambridge University Press, 1972).

Hatalkar, V. G., *Relations between the French and the Marathas (1668–1815)* (Bombay: Bombay University Press, 1958).

——— (ed.), *French records (relating to the history of the Marathas)* (Bombay: Maharashtra State Board for Literature and Culture, 1980).

BIBLIOGRAPHY

Henderson, A., 'On river steamers, their form, construction, and fittings, with reference to the necessity for improving the present means of shallow water navigation on the rivers of British India', *Report of the twentieth-eighth meeting of the British Association for the Advancement of Science* (London: John Murray, 1859), pp. 268–80.

Hill, S. C., *Three Frenchmen in Bengal, or the commercial ruin of the French settlements in 1757* (London: Longmans, Green, and Co., 1903).

Hossein Khan, S. G., *Seir mutaqherin; or view of modern times* (Calcutta: T. D. Chatterjee, n.d.).

Hosten, H., 'A week at the Bandel convent, Hugli', *Bengal past and present*, vol. 10 (1915), pp. 35–120.

Howell, J. P., *India tracts* (London: Becket & de Hondt, 1764).

Huddleston, G., *History of the East India Railway* (Calcutta: Thacker, Spink & Co., 1906).

Huggins, W., *Sketches in India, treating on subjects connected with the government, civil and military establishments; characters of the European, and customs of the native inhabitants* (London: John Letts, 1824).

Hunter, W. W., *The annals of rural Bengal* (London: Smith, Elder & Co., 1868).

Huyghen van Linschoten, J., *The voyage of John Huyghen van Linschoten to the East Indies* (London: Hakluyt Society, 1885).

Imperial gazetteer of India: Provincial series: Bengal (Calcutta: Superintendent of Government Printing, 1909).

Iqbal, I., *The Bengal delta: Ecology, state and social change, 1840–1943* (Basingstoke: Palgrave Macmillan, 2010).

Israel, J., *Democratic enlightenment: philosophy, revolution and human rights* (Oxford: Oxford University Press, 2013).

———, *Revolutionary ideas: An intellectual history of the French Revolution from The Rights of Man to Robespierre* (Princeton: Princeton University Press, 2014).

Ivermee, R., *Secularism, Islam and education in India, 1830–1910* (London: Pickering & Chatto, 2015).

Karim, A., *Murshid Quli Khan and his times* (Dacca: Asiatic Society of Pakistan, 1963).

Keay, J., *The honourable company: A history of the English East India Company* (London: HarperCollins, 1993).

———, *India: A history* (London: HarperCollins, 2001).

Kerr, I. J., *Building the railways of the Raj, 1850–1900* (Delhi: Oxford University Press, 1995).

Khan, M. S., *William Carey and the Serampore books (1800–1834)* (Copenhagen: Munksgaard, 1961).

Khan, Y., *The Raj at war: A people's history of India's Second World War* (London: Random House, 2015).

BIBLIOGRAPHY

Khilnani, S., *Incarnations: A history of India in 50 lives* (London: Penguin Books, 2017).

Kling, B. B., *Partner in empire: Dwarkanath Tagore and the age of enterprise in India* (Berkeley: University of California Press, 1976).

Kopf, D., *British orientalism and the Bengal Renaissance: The dynamics of Indian modernization, 1773–1835* (Berkeley: University of California Press, 1969).

Labernadie, M. V., *La révolution et les établissements français dans l'Inde, 1790–1793* (Paris: Librairie Ernst Leroux, 1930).

Lahiri, N., *Ashoka in ancient India* (Cambridge, Massachusetts: Harvard University Press, 2015).

Laird, M. A., 'William Carey and the education of India,' *Indian Journal of Theology*, X (July 1961), pp. 98–102.

Lalvani, K., *The making of India: The untold story of British enterprise* (London: Bloomsbury, 2016).

Latif, A., 'A description of north Bengal in 1609 A.D.', *Bengal past and present*, vol. 35 (1928), pp. 143–6.

Leonard, H., *Report on the river Hooghly* (London: George Edward Eyre, 1865).

Llewellyn-Jones, R., 'Introduction', in N. Das and R. Llewellyn-Jones (eds), *Murshidabad: Forgotten capital of Bengal* (Mumbai: Marg, 2013), pp. 10–17.

Losty, J. P., 'Murshidabad painting 1750–1820', in N. Das and R. Llewellyn-Jones (eds), *Murshidabad: Forgotten capital of Bengal* (Mumbai: Marg, 2013), pp. 82–105.

Macaulay, T. B., *Critical and historical essays contributed to the Edinburgh Review* (London: Longmans, Green and Co., 1883).

Mahajan, J., *The Ganga trail: Foreign accounts and sketches of the river scene* (New Delhi: Clarion Books, 1984).

Majumdar, R. C., *History of ancient Bengal* (Calcutta: G. Bharadwaj & Co., 1979).

Malleson, G. B., *History of the French in India: From the founding of Pondicherry in 1674 to the capture of that place in 1761* (Delhi: Gian, 1986).

Mallet, V., *River of life, river of death: The Ganges and India's future* (Oxford: Oxford University Press, 2017).

Manrique, S., *Travels of Fray Sebastien Manrique* (London: Hakluyt Society, 1927).

Marsh, K., *India in the French imagination: Peripheral voices, 1754–1815* (London: Pickering & Chatto, 2009).

Marshman, J., *Advantages of Christianity in promoting the establishment and prosperity of the British government in India* (London: Smith's, 1813).

———, *Hints relative to native schools, together with the outline of an institution for their extension and management* (Serampore: Mission Press, 1816).

Marshman, J. C., *The life and times of Carey, Marshman and Ward, embracing the history of the Serampore mission* (London: Longman, 1859).

BIBLIOGRAPHY

Metcalf, T. R., *Ideologies of the Raj* (Cambridge: Cambridge University Press, 1997).

Mittra, K. C., *Memoir of Dwarkanath Tagore* (Calcutta: Thacker, Spink & Co., 1870).

Monserrate, A., *The commentary of Father Monserrate S.J. on his journey to the court of Akbar* (London: Oxford University Press, 1922).

Montesquieu, *The spirit of laws* (Edinburgh: Ebenezer Wilson, 1762).

Mukerjee, R., *The changing face of Bengal: A study in riverine economy* (Calcutta: University of Calcutta, 1938).

Mukherjee, A., *Reform and regeneration in Bengal, 1774–1823* (Calcutta: Rabindra Bharati University, 1968).

Mukherjee, H., *The early history of the East Indian Railway, 1845–1879* (Calcutta: Firma KLM, 1994).

Mukherjee, J., *Hungry Bengal: War, famine and the end of empire* (London: Hurst & Company, 2015).

Mukhopadhyay, S. C., *British Residents at the darbar of Bengal nawabs at Murshidabad (1757–1772)* (Delhi: Gian, n.d.).

Nadkarnia, R. V., *The rise and fall of the Maratha Empire* (Bombay: Popular Prakashan, 1966).

Naïdenhoff, G., 'Les tentatives des missionnaires', in R. Vincent (ed.), *L'aventure des Français en Inde* (Pondicherry: Kailash, 2011), pp. 96–106.

Nag, K., and D. Burman (eds), *The English works of Raja Rammohun Roy* (Calcutta: Sadharan Brahmo Samaj, 1947–51).

Natarajan, S., *A history of the press in India* (Bombay: Asia Publishing House, 1962).

Nishat, A., 'Impact of Ganges water dispute on Bangladesh', in A. K. Biswas and T. Hasimoto (eds), *Asian international waters: From Ganges–Brahmaputra to Mekong* (Bombay: Oxford University Press, 1996), pp. 60–80.

Ogborn, M., *Indian ink: Script and print in the making of the English East India Company* (Chicago: University of Chicago Press, 2008).

O'Malley, L. S. S., *Murshidabad* (Calcutta: Bengal Secretariat Book Depot, 1914).

Osterhammel, J., and N. P. Petersson, *Globalization: A short history* (Princeton, NJ: Princeton University Press, 2005).

Papers relating to East India affairs (resident Europeans—police—missionaries—weavers and investments), House of Commons parliamentary papers, 1812–13, 142.

Paranjape, M. R., *Making India: Colonialism, national culture, and the afterlife of Indian English authority* (New York: Springer, 2013).

Parua, P. K., *The Ganga: Water use in the Indian subcontinent* (Dordrecht: Springer, 2010).

Pearce Carey, S., *William Carey D.D., Fellow of the Linnaean Society* (London: Hodder and Stoughton, 1923).

BIBLIOGRAPHY

Pearse, T. D., 'A memoir of Colonel Thomas Deane Pearse of the Bengal Artillery', *Bengal past and present*, vol. 11 (1908), pp. 305–23.

Peggs, J., *India's cries to British humanity, relative to the suttee, infanticide, British connexion with idolatry, ghaut murders and slavery in India* (London: Seely and Son, 1830).

Pitts, J., *A turn to empire: The rise of imperial liberalism in Britain and France* (Princeton: Princeton University Press, 2006).

Potts, E. D., *British Baptist missionaries in India, 1793–1837: The history of Serampore and its missions* (Cambridge: Cambridge University Press, 1967).

Prakash, O., *The Dutch East India Company and the economy of Bengal, 1630–1720* (Princeton: Princeton University Press, 1985).

Prinsep, G. A., *An account of steam vessels and of proceedings connected with steam navigation in British India* (Calcutta: Government Gazette, 1830).

Pyrard de Laval, F., *The voyage of François Pyrard of Laval to the East Indies, the Maldives, the Moluccas and Brazil* (London: Hakluyt Society, 1887).

Rahim, M. A., *Social and cultural history of Bengal* (Karachi: Pakistan Historical Society, 1963).

Ray, A., *The merchant and the state: The French in India, 1666–1739* (New Delhi: Munshiram Manoharlal, 2004).

Ray, C. C., 'A note on Jean Baptiste Chevalier and Colonel de Montigny', *Bengal past and present*, vol. 16 (1918), pp. 124–61.

Raychaudhuri, T., *Bengal under Akbar and Jahangir* (Delhi: Munshiram Manoharlal, 1969).

Raynal, G. T. F., *A philosophical and political history of the settlements and trade of the Europeans in the East and West Indies* (London: W. Baynes, 1813).

Rennell, J., *Memoir of a map of Hindoostan; or The Mogul Empire: with an introduction, illustrative of the geography and present division of that country: and a map of the countries situated between the head of the Indus, and the Caspian Sea* (London: 1788).

Report of the Bengal Boundary Commission (New Delhi: Government of India, 1947).

Richards, J. F., *The new Cambridge history of India 1.5: The Mughal Empire* (Cambridge: Cambridge University Press, 1993).

Roberts, E., *Scenes and characteristics of Hindostan, with sketches of Anglo-Indian society* (London: W. H. Allen & Co., 1837).

Robinson, A., *Account of some recent improvements in the system of navigating the Ganges by iron steam vessels* (London: John Weale, 1848).

Roy, R., 'A defence of Hindoo theism', in K. Nag and D. Burman (eds), *The English works of Raja Rammohun Roy* (Calcutta: Sadharan Brahmo Samaj, 1947–51), part 2, pp. 81–93.

———, 'A dialogue between a missionary and three Chinese converts', in K. Nag and D. Burman (eds), *The English works of Raja Rammohun Roy* (Calcutta: Sadharan Brahmo Samaj, 1947–51), part 4, pp. 75–80.

————, 'The precepts of Jesus, the guide to peace and happiness', in K. Nag and D. Burman (eds), *The English works of Raja Rammohun Roy* (Calcutta: Sadharan Brahmo Samaj, 1947–51), part 5, pp. 1–54.

————, 'An appeal to the Christian public in defence of "The precepts of Jesus"', in K. Nag and D. Burman (eds), *The English works of Raja Rammohun Roy* (Calcutta: Sadharan Brahmo Samaj, 1947–51), part 5, pp. 55–71.

————, 'Second appeal to the Christian public in defence of "The precepts of Jesus"', in K. Nag and D. Burman (eds), *The English works of Raja Rammohun Roy* (Calcutta: Sadharan Brahmo Samaj, 1947–51), part 6, pp. 1–97.

Safi, M., 'Ganges and Yamuna rivers granted same legal rights as human beings', *The Guardian*, 21.3.2017, https://www.theguardian.com/world/2017/mar/21/ganges-and-yamuna-rivers-granted-same-legal-rights-as-human-beings (accessed 9.2.2018).

Salahuddin Ahmed, A. F., *Social ideas and social change in Bengal, 1818–1835* (Leiden: E. J. Brill, 1965).

Salim, G. H., *Riyazu-s-salatin, a history of Bengal* (Calcutta: Baptist Mission Press, 1902).

Sarkar, J., *The history of Bengal: Muslim period 1200–1757* (Dacca: University of Dacca, 1943).

Sarkar, S., *The Swadeshi movement in Bengal 1903–1908* (Ranikhet: Permanent Black, 2014).

Sarkar, S., 'Shrinking Sagar Island struggles to stay afloat', thethirdpole.net, 8.3.2017, https://www.thethirdpole.net/2017/03/08/shrinking-sagar-island-struggles-to-stay-afloat/ (accessed 9.2.2018).

Sarkar, S. C., *The Sundarbans: Folk deities, monsters and mortals* (London: Routledge, 2017).

Sen, S. P., *The French in India 1763–1816* (New Delhi: Munshiram Manoharlal, 1971).

'Serampore Form of Agreement, The', *Baptist Quarterly*, 12 (1947), pp. 125–38.

Sharma, Y., 'Introduction', in Y. Sharma and J. L. Ferreira (eds), *Portuguese presence in India during the sixteenth and seventeenth centuries* (New Delhi: Viva Books, 2008), pp. xi–xvii.

Shaw, G., *Printing in Calcutta to 1800: A description and checklist of printing in late 18ᵗʰ-century Calcutta* (London: Bibliographical Society, 1981).

Sherring, M. A., *The history of Protestant missions in India* (London: Trübner & Co., 1875).

Sinha, D., 'Impacts of Ganga waterways plan on its ecology and the people', SANDRP (South Asia Network on Dams, Rivers and People), 11.8.2016, https://sandrp.wordpress.com/2016/08/11/impacts-of-ganga-water-ways-plan-on-its-ecology-and-the-people/ (accessed 9.2.2018).

BIBLIOGRAPHY

Sinha, N., *Communication and colonialism in eastern India: Bihar, 1760s–1880s* (London: Anthem Press, 2012).

Skelton, R., 'Murshidabad painting', *Marg*, vol. x, no. 1 (1956), pp. 10–22.

Smith, G., *The life of William Carey, D.D.* (London: John Murray, 1885).

Spear, P., *Master of Bengal: Clive and his India* (London: Thames & Hudson, 1975).

Srinivasan, R., *et al.* (eds), *Our Indian railway: Themes in India's railway history* (New Delhi: Foundation Books, 2006).

Stephenson, R. M., *Report on the practicability and advantages of the introduction of railways into British India* (London: Kelly & Co., 1845).

Stern, P. J., *The Company-state: Corporate sovereignty, and the early modern foundations of the British Empire in India* (Oxford: Oxford University Press, 2011).

Stewart, C., *The history of Bengal from the first Mohammedan invasion until the virtual conquest of that country by the English A.D. 1757* (London: Black, Parry and Co., 1813).

Storrs, D. (ed.), *The fiscal-military state in eighteenth-century Europe: Essays in honour of P.G.M. Dickson* (Farnham: Ashgate, 2009).

Subrahmanyam, S., *Improvising empire: Portuguese trade and settlement in the Bay of Bengal, 1500–1700* (Delhi: Oxford University Press, 1990).

———, 'Connected histories: notes towards a reconfiguration of early modern Eurasia', *Modern Asian studies*, vol. 31, no. 3 (1997), pp. 735–62.

———, *The Portuguese empire in Asia, 1500–1700: A political and economic history* (Chichester: Wiley-Blackwell, 2012).

Tagore, R., 'My understanding of Vedanta', in A. P. Sen (ed.), *Religion and Rabindranath Tagore: Select discourses, addresses and letters in translation* (New Delhi: Oxford University Press, 2014), pp. 186–7.

———, 'Religion in nature', in A. P. Sen (ed.), *Religion and Rabindranath Tagore: Select discourses, addresses and letters in translation* (New Delhi: Oxford University Press, 2014), p. 188.

———, *Selected poems* (London: Penguin, 2005).

Talbot, I., and G. Singh, *The partition of India* (Cambridge: Cambridge University Press, 2009).

Tavernier, J. B., *Les six voyages de Jean-Baptiste Tavernier* (Paris: 1679).

Techno-economic feasibility report for development of port at Sagar Island (Gurgaon: AECOM, 2016).

Tharoor, S., *Inglorious empire: What the British did to India* (London: Penguin, 2017).

'The Serampore Form of Agreement', *Baptist Quarterly*, 12 (1947), pp. 125–38.

Thomas, F. C., *To the mouths of the Ganges: An ecological and cultural journey* (Norwalk, CT: EastBridge, 2004).

Vidal, J., 'Sea change: the Bay of Bengal's vanishing islands', *The Guardian*,

29.1.13, https://www.theguardian.com/global-development/2013/jan/29/sea-change-bay-bengal-vanishing-islands (accessed 9.2.2018).

Viswanathan, G., *Outside the fold: Conversion, modernity and belief* (Princeton: Princeton University Press, 1998).

Voltaire, *Précis du siècle de Louis XV* (Paris: Mme Vve Dabo, 1824).

————, *Fragments on India* (Lahore: Contemporary India Publications, 1938).

von Orlich, L., *Travels in India, including Sinde and the Punjab* (London: Longman, Brown, Green, and Longmans, 1845).

Walker, B., 'Pollution worsens in the lower Ganga', thethirdpole.net, 19.8.2016, https://www.thethirdpole.net/2016/08/19/pollution-worsens-in-the-lower-ganga/ (accessed 9.2.2018).

Ward, W., *A view of the history, literature and mythology of the Hindoos* (Serampore: Mission Press, 1818).

Westwood, J. N., *Railways of India* (Newton Abbott: David & Charles, 1974).

'West Bengal government to make Sagar Island "no-plastic zone"', *Economic Times*, 27.12.2017, https://economictimes.indiatimes.com/news/politics-and-nation/west-bengal-government-to-make-sagar-island-no-plastic-zone/articleshow/62265781.cms (accessed 9.2.2018).

Wilson, C. R., *The early annals of the English in Bengal* (London: W. Thacker, 1895).

Wilson, H. H., 'The religious festivals of the Hindus', *Journal of the Royal Asiatic Society of Great Britain and Ireland*, vol. 9 (1847), pp. 60–110.

Zastoupil, L., *Rammohun Roy and the making of Victorian Britain* (New York: Palgrave Macmillan, 2010).

————, and M. Moir (eds), *The great Indian education debate: Documents relating to the Orientalist–Anglicist controversy, 1781–1843* (Richmond: Curzon, 1999).

INDEX

INDEX

INDEX

INDEX